Y0-CBG-678

LIVING ABROAD IN
BELIZE

VICTORIA DAY-WILSON

PRIME LIVING LOCATIONS IN BELIZE

THE CAYES

COROZAL

Majahual

Xcalak

Ambergris Cave

Barrier Reef

San Pedro

Cave Chapel

Cave Caulker

Northern Two Cayes

Lighthouse Reef

Turneffe Islands

Cave Bokel

Long Cave

Half Moon Cave

Belize City

Gales Point

Bahía de Chetumal

Chetumal

Consejo

Santa Elena

Sarteneja

Progresso

Corozal Town

COROZAL DISTRICT

Orange Walk Town

BELIZE

Shipyard

San Felipe

BELIZE DISTRICT

Burrell Boom

Bermudian Landing

BELMOPAN

Roaring Creek

Nicolas Bravo

Blue Creek Village

ORANGE WALK DISTRICT

Gallon Jug

Chan Chich

Bullet Tree

QUINTANA ROO

MEXICO

Xpujil

CAMPECHE

Uaxactún

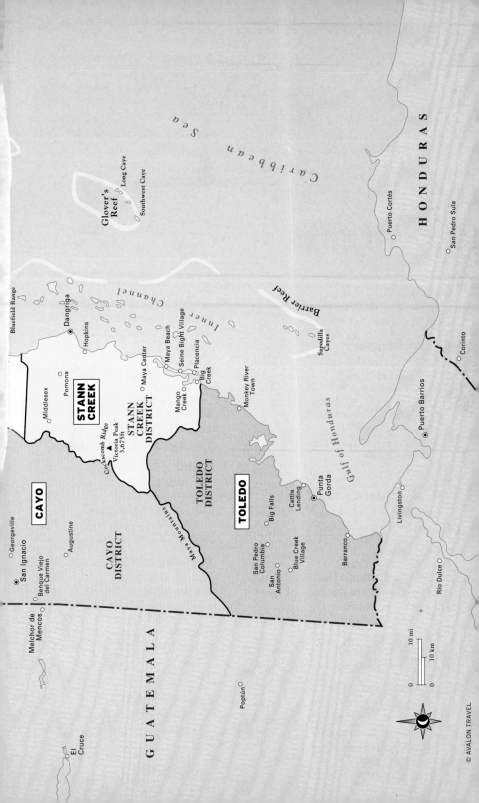

Contents

Life in Belize is generally spent outdoors, be it walking, canoeing, diving, swimming, fishing, snorkeling, riding, caving, white-water rafting, bird- and wildlife-viewing, or exploring ruins. When you run out of energy, collapse into your hammock – the one furniture item that appears on every Belizean veranda.

Imbued with a frontier spirit, Belize isn't for the faint of heart. Yet it is a place where the pace of life is slow and luxurious. Although crime exists and security measures are advisable, this generally does not affect expats who choose to make Belize their new home.

With a small population, burgeoning tourism, friendly people, beautiful fauna and flora, ancient history, and political stability, Belize is a unique place with a lot to offer. The quality of life is high, the cost of living is low, and the climate is temperate. This place is in touch with the rest of the world but still untouched enough to explore. Life is uncomplicated but always interesting. You may feel as though you've discovered paradise.

► WHAT I LOVE ABOUT BELIZE

- Waking up early in the morning with the mist over the jungle and toucans, woodpeckers, and exotic, long-tailed motmots knocking on my window with their beaks.

- The easy-going nature and friendliness of the people and their passion for their beautiful surroundings.

- The way bus drivers and their conductors help me with my shopping when I get off the bus, pick up little children and lift them off the bus with care, and assist the elderly.

- Looking in any direction and seeing the horizon, surrounded by nature, and feeling complete solitude, freedom, and space.

- Walking through the bustling Saturday market where exotic fruits are piled high and then, within minutes, canoeing home on rivers through a quiet jungle.

- Sipping ice-cold watermelon juice on a hot day.

- The variety and color of plants.

- Sitting under a waterfall after a long day.

- The local guides' passion and in-depth knowledge of their environment, and their commitment to protecting it.

- The way total strangers smile to greet me.

- Living life outdoors: snorkeling in the clear sea water, canoeing up a river deep into the jungle, and exploring hidden caves.

At Home in Belize

The Belize national motto, "Under the shade I flourish," captures the spirit of life in this small Central American paradise. From the thick jungles in Cayo to the white, palm-fringed beaches lapped by the waves of the turquoise Caribbean Sea, life in Belize thrives. It is a diverse country, from its landscape and wildlife to its people.

Belize is multiethnic and multicultural. Belizeans trace their heritage back to Mayan Indians, Europeans, Africans, and Caribs. Added to the mix are Americans, Chinese, and Arabs. Today's Belizeans, a diverse population of Mestizos, Creoles, Maya Indians, and Garifuna, speak English, the official language of Belize, as well as Spanish and Creole.

Colors dominate the landscape. Delicate sprays of orchids grow wild in the trees, scarlet bougainvillea tumbles over everything, and huge bushes are covered in large red hibiscus flowers. Thickly intertwined trees in a hundred shades of green and brown rise against the blue sky, and under them colorful markets feature myriad vegetables and fruit. From the tree branches, bright red, green, and blue macaws take flight.

Belize is steeped in adventure, history, and folklore. Overgrown Mayan ruins point to an ancient history only partially uncovered, while excavated temples rise proudly into the sky from their centuries-old foundations in jungle clearings. From howler monkeys to manatees to toucans and jaguars, Belize has an abundance of wildlife, thanks to careful conservation of the varied habitats across the small country.

WELCOME TO BELIZE

INTRODUCTION

Belize exudes an adventurous pioneering spirit while retaining a friendly, laid-back attitude that is rapidly vanishing in other parts of the world. It's also a stunning place: from the lush jungles and rivers of Cayo to the array of corals and fish around the Cayes. In many ways it really is like paradise. The people are nice, the climate is good, the cost of living is low, and there is an abundance of fresh fruit. It helps that the official language is English and that almost everyone speaks it. There aren't too many nasty diseases or poisonous reptiles. It's close to the U.S. and is a great base for traveling to the Caribbean and Central and South America. It really is a break from the rat race. The quality of life is high in Belize, and the warmth of the people matches the country's tropical climate, which rarely drops below 70°F.

The slower pace of life in Belize can be both charming and frustrating. Services may not be as efficient as in the U.S., and while there are some excellent laborers, some can be unpredictable, not turning up at the agreed-upon time. Things like spare parts for cars can be a challenge to get a hold of or take a

© VICTORIA DAY-WILSON

long time to obtain. Due to the bureaucracy involved, obtaining residency and citizenship can seem like an endless process. You might arrive at a set time for an appointment at the Department of Immigration, and after waiting in a long, hot queue, be told to come back at another time. In Belize, a healthy dose of patience is a requirement.

Belize also offers some challenges in the form of fungus, mold, and insects. Fungus is a problem due to the high humidity. It can grow on your clothes and in your shoes. Leather products are particularly susceptible. Fungus will also eat your CDs. Food should be stored in plastic containers so it doesn't get damp or moldy. Kitchens should have open shelves or cupboards to maintain easy airflow and to make it easy to clear away insects. You're likely to have more maintenance issues than you're used to. If your home is made of wood, you'll have an ongoing battle with termites and borer beetles.

Life in Belize can be unpredictable. Every so often the electricity or water will be cut without prior warning or information about when it will be turned back on. Contacting the power or water companies rarely makes a difference. The mobile phone system can be erratic, with error messages and texts bouncing back even when you appear to have good reception. Compared to the U.S., Belize has a smaller selection of food and general products, and there are sometimes brief shortages of foodstuffs like flour and sugar.

There is no question that living in Belize is not for everyone, but if you think you have what it takes to thrive here, it can be an amazing journey. Many of those who succeed here are self-sufficient, have a variety of interests, and are adaptable and resourceful. Living here will be a life-changing experience and to make it you'll need to relax your expectations and go with the flow.

When your wake-up call is a pair of brilliant red-headed woodpeckers tapping away at the papaya tree outside your house, or when you sit quietly overlooking the river, sipping coffee, and a huge owl flies down to perch next to you for a few magical moments, perhaps it won't be so hard. You might even find that it's the home you've been searching for all along.

IS BELIZE RIGHT FOR YOU?

Making a move to a new country is no small thing. Before you move, evaluate what's important to you in your future home. Think about the environment you'd like to live in—jungle, seaside, riverside, or something more urban? Ask yourself: Do you need easy access to an active social life? Can you build houses and fix things or do you prefer to have things done for you? Do you want electricity available at the flick of a switch and water at the turn of a tap? If you live remotely, can you keep yourself busy with work or interests? It's important to be self-sufficient in Belize no matter where you live. Are you looking for an investment property, vacation home, or full-time home? Think about whether you are ready to say goodbye to creature comforts and the availability of a variety of goods. Can you adapt to a culture that doesn't place a high value on punctuality and efficiency? If you have medical requirements, can they be catered for in Belize? If you have children, will you be happy with education in Belize? If you are married or in a relationship, how will the move affect your partner? The change of scene and adjustment can put a relationship to the test.

No matter what you choose, living in Belize means you have to go without some items you may be used to in your daily life back home, and you'll perhaps live a less luxurious lifestyle. Ask yourself if you are prepared for that. While there are certainly some drawbacks to living in a developing nation, there are many benefits to life in Belize, like less regulation, a slower pace of life, a good climate, and the ability to forge your own way in a new life among new neighbors.

The Lay of the Land

Belize is bordered by Mexico to the north, Guatemala to the west and south, and the Caribbean to the east. The capital city is Belmopan, in Cayo District. The original capital was Belize City before it was devastated by Hurricane Hattie in 1961. The coast of Belize runs the entire length of the country along a 300-mile long barrier reef, the largest in the Western hemisphere and second only globally to Australia's barrier reef. Three of the four atolls in the Western Hemisphere lie off the coast of Belize. There are over 400 islands, known as cayes (pronounced "keys" and also called *cayo* by Spanish speakers), many of them just mounds of sand, coral, and mangroves.

Inland, Belize starts with swampy savannah and ends up in lush tropical jungle combined with large tracts of agricultural land mainly planted with citrus. There are large lagoons scattered along the coastline and in the north of the country. There are a few large urban areas and many villages. Most areas are habitable; some just take a bit more work than others depending on how remote they are, whether the land needs clearing, availability of utilities, and property access. Most of the northern area of Belize is fairly flat, but as you go farther south the Maya Mountains run along the border between Cayo,

Toledo, and Stann Creek Districts. The rugged jungle-covered mountains are home to wild animals, waterfalls, rivers, and a vast network of caves, as well as some ancient Maya ruins. The highest peak in Belize is Doyles Delight at 3,688 feet, followed by Victoria Peak at 3,675 feet.

COUNTRY DIVISIONS

Belize is divided into six districts: along the coastline from north to south are Corozal (pronounced Cor-Roh-ZAHL), Belize, Stann Creek, and Toledo Districts; Cayo and Orange Walk Districts lie inland. Belize's largest islands, Ambergris Caye and Caye Caulker are part of Belize District, although Ambergris Caye is closest to the coast of Corozal.

Corozal

Belize's northernmost district, Corozal lies between Mexico and the Caribbean. The landscape is flat, swampy savannah with large tracts of agricultural land. Originally a private estate, Corozal Town is the district's capital and was founded in 1848 by refugees escaping the War of the Castes in Mexico. The refugees brought sugar cane with them, which gave birth to the sugar industry that became the district's economic mainstay. Corozal Town is situated on an ancient Maya trading place called Santa Rita, between the New River and the Rio Hondo. It is located along Corozal Bay and is the northernmost town in Belize. It lies 9 miles from the Mexican border, where there is an official

© VICTORIA DAY-WILSON

A pier jutts into the sea in Consejo, Corozal.

SYMBOLS OF BELIZE

After becoming independent, Belize established and exhibited its identity through the selection and use of national symbols. The Belizean flag is made up of three main colors: red, white, and blue, which symbolize the country's two political parties. Red and white are the colors of the United Democratic Party (UDP) and blue and white represent the People's United Party (PUP). The white circle in the middle of the flag has a coat of arms divided into three sections. The bottom section represents a ship sailing, a saw and axe are on the top right, and the top left has a paddle and a mallet. Two woodcutters, one with a paddle and the other with an axe, stand on either side of the shield. A mahogany tree rises high behind the shield. These images were chosen as symbols of the mahogany industry that was at the heart of Belize's economy during the 18th and 19th centuries. Below the coat of arms are the Latin words *Sub umbra floreo* – under the shade of the tree I flourish. Around the coat of arms is a wreath of 50 leaves symbolizing the PUP, which formed in 1950.

The national flower is the black orchid, a small green and yellow flower with a purple base that grows in damp areas and blooms year round.

The national bird is the keel-billed toucan, a colorful bird with a black and yellow chest, and a large green, blue, red, and orange bill.

The national tree is the mahogany tree, which can grow up to 100 feet. Today it is still used for lumber and furniture.

The largest animal in the Americas, the tapir, is the national animal. Known locally as the mountain cow, it is related to the horse and rhinoceros, and is a dusty brown color. The tapir is a vegetarian, weighs up to 600 pounds, and is protected under the Wildlife Act of Belize.

© VICTORIA DAY-WILSON

The town clock in Punta Gorda features a tapir, Belize's national animal.

border crossing at Santa Elena, 85 miles north of Belize City. The popular island of Ambergris Caye is a brief 15-minute flight away.

Orange Walk

Belize's second largest district, Orange Walk, lies between Belize and Corozal Districts in the north of the country along the Guatemalan and Mexican borders. Orange Walk Town, the district capital, is 54 miles up the Northern

Highway from Belize City. Two rivers run through the district, the Rio Hondo, which also forms part of the border with Mexico, and the New River. Belize's largest body of water, the New River Lagoon, is also in Orange Walk. Although the district's main earner is agriculture, it is becoming a popular tourist destination due to its birdlife—there are more than 400 recorded species—and Mayan temples.

Cayo

The largest of Belize's districts, Cayo, lies inland in the western part of the country along the border of Guatemala. Home to Belize's capital, Belmopan, most of the district is covered in rainforest, waterfalls, caves, and pine trees. Mayan ruins rise out of the jungle, which is also home to a rich variety of wildlife. More than 60 percent of Cayo District is protected as a wildlife sanctuary, national park, or forest reserve. The Mopan and Macal Rivers snake through the jungle and connect to form the Belize River.

Belize District

In the center of the country, bordered by the Caribbean to the east, Belize District is crisscrossed by several rivers, including the Northern River, Sibun River, Manatee River, and the longest in the country, the Belize River. Originally, the ancient Maya and subsequent settlers lived along these rivers and plied their trade on them. It was the first area to be settled by Europeans. Their presence is still evident in many place names, as each estate often bordered on a river,

© VICTORIA DAY-WILSON

the Courthouse and boats in Belize City

thus becoming known as Lord's Bank (as in riverbank), Flowers Bank, and Isabella's Bank. The names stuck and now belong to small communities and villages. The district includes various offshore islands, including Ambergris Caye, Caye Caulker (also known as Caye Corker), St. George's Caye, Caye Chapel, English Caye, and Goff's Caye. The landscape is mainly flat with large areas of mangrove swamp and marshland near the water that give way to pine savannah and tropical bush inland. There are four beautiful lagoons in the district, two to the south and two to the north.

The Northern and Western Highways cross through Belize District, which is home to the country's largest city, Belize City. The city lies below sea level, and historians say that it is built on a foundation of loose corals, logwood chips, and rum bottles. The city is divided in two—North Side and South Side—by Haulover Creek, where the Belize River runs into the Caribbean.

Stann Creek

A beautiful drive from Belmopan down Belize's most scenic road, the Hummingbird Highway, leads into Stann Creek District through the rugged Maya Mountains, lush broadleaf tropical jungles, Maya ruins, and the Cockscomb Basin. Stann Creek lies 90 miles from Belize City by land and 36 miles by sea. The Hummingbird Highway and the Southern Highway, which continues into Toledo District, cut through the Stann Creek District. The district lies between Cayo District and the Caribbean, below Belize District and above Toledo District. Stann Creek is Belize's second largest district and is home to

© LORENZO FORBES

houses on the beach in Placencia, Stann Creek

the country's two highest peaks, Doyle's Delight at 3,688 feet and Victoria Peak at 3,675 feet. Closer to the sea, the land becomes flat and dry with more savannah and pine trees.

Toledo

The least-visited region in Belize, Toledo is the southernmost district in the country, the most sparsely populated, and the least developed. Although virtually untouched, the area is rising in popularity with tourists. With the highest recorded rainfall in Belize, the interior is covered by large tracts of true broadleaf rainforest, rivers, waterfalls, and intricate cave systems that taper off into pine ridge savannahs and mangrove-surrounded coastal lagoons. Off the coast lie beautiful islands. A small town on the shores of the Caribbean, Punta Gorda, locally known as PG, is the capital of the district and its commercial center. It lies about 200 miles by road from Belize City and is the last real town in Belize. Punta Gorda provides a gateway to Honduras and Guatemala via its small port.

The Cayes

There are over 400 islands off the coast of Belize within 50 miles of the mainland. There are four known atolls in the Western Hemisphere; three of them are located in Belize: Glover's Reef, Turneffe Islands, and Lighthouse Reef. Typically the remains of a sinking volcano, an atoll is an island of coral that encircles a lagoon. The 185-mile long Belize Barrier Reef is the largest coral reef system in the Western Hemisphere and the second largest in the world.

© LORENZO FORBES

a boat off the Cayes

The islands can range from small coral or sand spits to mangrove islands to larger cayes, such as the popular Ambergris Caye (pronounced am-BURR-griss), Caye Caulker, St. George's Caye, Caye Chapel, English Caye, South Water Caye, Tobacco Caye, Ranguana Caye, Coco Plum Caye, and Goff's Caye. Ambergris Caye and Caye Caulker are considered two of the country's primary tourism areas and are also popular with expats.

Belize's biggest island, Ambergris Caye is 25 miles long and over 4 miles wide. Northern Ambergris Caye is separated from the southernmost tip of Mexico's Yucatán Peninsula by a small channel. It is believed that that Maya had a major trading center here around A.D. 200, and they dug up the channel to create a coastal trading route.

The main town on the island, San Pedro, is only about a mile long and a few blocks wide. Some streets are still covered in sand and there are few cars; the main mode of transport is by foot or golf cart. San Pedro can be accessed by a 20-minute flight or by boat from Belize City.

The second largest of Belize's islands, Caye Caulker lies 21 miles northeast of Belize City and 11 miles south of Ambergris Caye. The island is a half-mile wide and less than five miles long. It is the second most populated Belizean Caye with 1,300 full-time residents. Flights and boats are available from Belize City and San Pedro. Once on the island, the main mode of transportation is by foot and bicycle, though golf carts are on the rise. In 1961, Hurricane Hattie divided the north and south ends of the island. Caye Caulker Village lies on the south side and is made up of three main streets.

CLIMATE

Belize has a sub-tropical climate with a wet and a dry season. Weather patterns are somewhat erratic, but generally it's hot and humid, roughly similar to southern Florida. The average year-round temperature is 79°F. The coolest month is January and the hottest is May. The rainy season usually lasts from May to December, and the dry season from January to April. In March–October temperatures can reach 88°F; temperatures drop to 66°F during November–February. It can get cold enough at higher altitudes during the rainy season to warrant the use of a duvet or heavy blanket.

Although Belize is generally a warm place, don't expect to stay dry. Even if it's often sunny during the rainy season, there are some spectacular storms with rumbling thunder and flashes of lightning across the sky, and when it rains it is as if the heavens have opened. Sometimes it can rain for days, and while you may still be walking around in shorts, everything gets wet and muddy and nothing dries—not a good time to do your laundry (unless you have a tumble dryer). The rainy

HURRICANES THAT MADE HISTORY

- **2007: Hurricane Dean.** Corozal was affected the worst by Dean, which hit as a Category 5 hurricane 25 miles north of the Belize/Mexico border. There were no major injuries, but the government estimated the damage to Belize's papaya industry at $30 million and to the sugar industry at $3.6 million.

- **2001: Hurricane Iris.** In early October, Iris devastated the Placencia Peninsula and Toledo with winds of up to 145 mph. It took the lives of 21 people.

- **2000: Hurricane Keith.** Hitting the Belizean Cayes, Keith brought a lot of rain to Ambergris Caye and Caye Caulker for three days. Hurricane Keith was designated a Category 4 hurricane with wind gusts of up to 155 mph. However, it was its slow-moving speed that made Keith such a problem, especially to the Cayes, where Keith caused $150 million in damage. As Keith moved to Belize's mainland, it quickly diminished into a tropical storm.

- **1998: Hurricane Mitch.** Although Mitch made landfall in Honduras and not Belize, this hurricane caused severe damage to various areas within the country. Mitch was a catastrophic hurricane with winds up to 180 mph.

- **1961: Hurricane Hattie.** Tracked directly into Belize City, Hattie's eye had winds of 115 mph with gusts estimated at 200 mph. The eye passed between Belize City and Dangriga, causing 307 deaths in Belize City alone. It was this hurricane that resulted in George Price and the People's United Party (PUP) relocating their capital city from Belize City to the safer location of Belmopan.

- **1955: Hurricane Janet.** The eye of Janet packed winds of up to 135 mph and made landfall on a small Mexican village north of San Pedro Town. In Corozal Town, the eye reached winds of up to 170 mph. There were devastating winds and massive flooding in the northern districts, 16 deaths, and 20,000 people left homeless. In San Pedro, the houses on back streets were damaged, the beach homes and lots were reduced to large mounds of sand, and the width of the beach increased by many feet.

- **1931: Unnamed hurricane.** In early September, this hurricane swept through Belize City and the Northern Cayes at 110 mph. There were an estimated 2,500–3,000 deaths.

season is interspersed with dry and sunny days when everything dries up again. Most people begin their day early when it is still cool and crisp and you can get the majority of your chores out of the way before the heat really sets in. March is the driest month and October the wettest. Rainfall varies across the country, with the highest levels in the south in Toledo and Stann Creek, and the lowest in the north in Corozal and Orange Walk. Annual rainfall figures range between 50 and 70 inches. Seawater temperatures vary between 75°F and 84°F.

For Belize's climate, a light, rainproof jacket comes in handy, as do light, loose, casual, and comfortable clothing. When it's hot, an overhead or standing electric fan will take the edge off, as well as intermittent, light, cool breezes. A quick dip in the river, sea, or a pool, will cool you down and refresh you, but watch out for the river current, which is strong in places.

Hurricanes

The hurricane season in the Caribbean runs June 1–November 30. Historically, Belize hurricanes usually occur in October and November. The National Emergency Management Organization (NEMO, www.nemo.org.bz/preparedness.php) in Belize has a thorough emergency plan ready to be enacted in the event of a hurricane, and it provides information on emergency shelters and helpful district organizations. Belizeans always know when it is hurricane season from the echoes of neighbors hammering wooden shutters over their windows. NEMO has also devised a warning system using flags to indicate the imminence of a hurricane threat.

Flora and Fauna

Thanks to a serious approach to conservation, ecotourism, and sustainable development, Belize has an abundance of beautiful fauna and flora ranging from thick jungle to savannah. Sixty percent of the country remains forested, creating an ecosystem for 145 known species of mammals, 139 reptiles and amphibians, over 500 bird species, and over 5,000 plant species. Over 45 globally threatened species rely on this critical habitat and at least 18 species can be found nowhere else on earth.

FLORA

Unlike many other Central and South American countries, Belize is unusual because it protects 60 percent of its tropical forests. Almost half of Belize's primary forest is still standing. It has an abundance and variety of trees, with over 700 species recorded, and 4,000 different varieties of flowering plants, including 250 types of orchid.

There are national parks, reserves, and sanctuaries all over Belize. You are never far from one; take some time to travel around and explore them. Wander around your garden, swap cuttings with friends, and stand back and observe plants, how they grow, and if they flower—you will often be happily surprised by a dazzling display.

© VICTORIA DAY-WILSON

red ginger flower

Medicinal Plants

Belize has an ancient history of plant medicine. Many common plants have medicinal properties that are in use today. Copal, potato skin, and aloe vera are commonly used to ease discomfort and heal wounds, among other things. The copal tree was a sacred tree of the ancient Maya. A powder is made from the bark to apply to wounds, sores, and skin infections. The bark is also used as a tea to treat intestinal parasites and stomach cramps. Aloe vera can be used for general skin complaints too, including sunburn, and has scar-preventing properties. It is also a laxative. A similar looking plant, the snake plant, helps delay the spread of snake venom. It's also used to treat minor rashes and skin sores. The poisonwood tree can cause a severe reaction if you just brush against it. Fortunately, right next to it grows the gumbo-limbo, also known as tourist tree (because it's red and peeling!), which counteracts the poison from the poisonwood tree. Gumbo-limbo tree leaves are used to make tea to treat backaches, urinary tract infections, colds, flu, and fevers.

Breadfruit tree leaves can be used to lower high blood pressure; they are also bound on the forehead to ease a headache. Wild pineapple leaves mashed up with salt make a good poultice for bruises, sprains, and fractures. Cohune palm oil is popular for skin, hair, and healing dry, chapped skin. The boiled leaves of the trumpet tree can be used for heart ailments, high blood pressure, and liver and kidney problems. If you run out of your favorite moisturizer, try papaya— it keeps the skin soft and is the best thing to apply if you've trodden on a sea urchin. The resin of bush papaya can also be used to treat ringworm.

Sorrell is a very efficient detoxifier and decongestant; it flushes out your system—just be sure to take it in small doses. After drinking too much of it at a party without realizing what it was (it's delicious and refreshing), my friend was in some discomfort for about 24 hours, but felt like a million dollars afterwards.

The allspice tree is used for intestinal problems and will help if you have

Belize Belly. If you place some bay cedar bark in your shoe, it helps treat foot fungus. Hot lips—so named due to its red lip–shaped flower with a yellow center—is crushed and boiled to help expel the placenta after birth and is also used as a general painkiller for ear aches, coughs, headaches, sprains, and bruises.

Cocolmeca is boiled in water and drunk by men to stimulate their sexual performance. Boiling the stalk and leaf of the butterfly tree can be used to bathe wounds. Conventional medicines with plant-based properties include willow bark in aspirin; cinchona tree in quinine (anti-malarials); dioscorea in steroids, cortisone, and the birth control pill; the opium poppy in codeine and morphine; valerian root in valium; yeast molds in penicillin; and belladonna in atropine.

Fruit Trees

Common fruit trees of Belize include cashew, coconut, custard apple (or sugar apple), guava, mango, papaya, banana, pineapple, and mammee. Fruit and vegetables tend to be seasonal. Have a look in the local market and you'll find an interesting variety. Banana, mango, papaya, avocado, and watermelon are popular. Don't miss out on the beautiful star fruit and the delicious and very nutritious, reddish-purple, pitaya fruit, which comes from a cactus. Most people grow some citrus, papaya, mango, and avocado trees on their land. Get advice about the poisonwood tree (in the cashew tree family) as it looks quite common: You don't want to accidently brush against one and get the resulting painful rash. It is best to know where they are if you live on a property with trees.

FAUNA

As you settle in your home and the resident animals get used to your presence and realize you are not trying to harm them, you will start to see more of them. Birds tend to vary from month to month, but you will start to recognize common varieties. It's beautiful to watch as the sun catches the iridescent, frantically-flapping wings of hummingbirds as they feast on the nectar in the bright red or orange heliconias.

There is an abundance of lizards and iguanas in all shapes, sizes, and colors. Some look quite prehistoric, others have intricate patterns that virtually camouflage them; others still can be bright emerald green. My favorite lizard is quite big and lives in a hollow tree just below the house, I play hide and seek with him. He pretends not to see me while gripping in the hollow upside down and tucking his head in.

© VICTORIA DAY-WILSON

hummingbird on heliconia

Though they're not always easy to spot, keep an eye out for pretty, brightly-colored little frogs. There is a colorful array of butterflies and moths, brightly patterned caterpillars, and a variety of spiders. There are also many ants and beetles. Keep an eye on them to make sure they aren't eating your house!

It's best to buy special anti-insect yellow light bulbs for your home because if you use normal light bulbs, your house will be full of all sorts of flying creatures of the night. Though some are beautiful, such as moths and beetles. If your house is open, come evening, the mosquitoes will join you. Lighting an anti-mosquito coil usually keeps them at bay.

There are a variety of different ants. The leaf cutters, known locally as "wee wee ants" strip plants. Fire ants are aptly named because, although not dangerous, their bite burns, even after you've picked them off. It feels a bit like a mild jellyfish sting, nothing serious, just uncomfortable at the time. You'll rapidly learn to look out for them and not stand in a nest!

Mammals

While Belize does have an abundance of wildlife, many animals—particularly the bigger ones—are shy, well camouflaged, and nocturnal. I love the fact that whenever I go for a walk, I never know what I may see: a bird I haven't seen before; a huge iguana scuttling away like a naughty child; colorful lizards; beautiful butterflies and moths; the odd (harmless) snake; and caterpillars in a rainbow of colors. Occasionally I see what the locals call rabbits, happily hopping around—except they look more like overgrown guinea pigs since they lack big ears and a round tail.

Eventually your eye will become attuned to the landscape, and even though it's still hard to spot a lot of wildlife, you'll learn to pick out quite a few. You'll become familiar with the spots where some of them live. It's useful to keep a book on Belizean birds and reptiles. I'm always dashing off to dip into it. We had a family of jaguarundis on our property, but I never saw them, and

BELIZE ZOO

If you want to see the big cats, go to the Belize Zoo. It is possibly the best zoo in Central America. None of the animals were captured; they were given as gifts from other zoos, orphaned, born in the zoo, or rehabilitated. The zoo started in 1983 as a result of the making of a wildlife film, *Path of the Rain God,* after which a variety of semi-tame animals could no longer fend for themselves in the wild. They are not kept in cages, but in enclosures spread over 29 acres of tropical savannah just off Mile 29 on the Western Highway. The enclosures are adapted to the original habitat of each animal. There are over 125 animals, birds, and reptiles, all native to Belize.

Visiting the zoo is a truly inspiring experience and the handlers are a friendly, helpful, knowledgeable, and dedicated bunch who are passionate about what they do. The enclosures are so well designed that sometimes it is hard to spot the animals. The personnel can help and gently coax the animals out so that you will have a chance to admire the animals up close without disturbing them and to get some nice photos!

an ocelot at the Belize Zoo

© VICTORIA DAY-WILSON

a neighbor was told that there's a jaguar on her land. In the evening, you are likely to encounter harmless bats. Unfortunately, many of the animals have become more reclusive due to hunting and poaching by the local population and human development.

There are several reserves and sanctuaries to look for jaguars and tapirs. You aren't always guaranteed to see one, but it's an interesting adventure all the same.

Belize is home to the only designated jaguar preserve in the world, the Cockscomb Basin Wildlife Sanctuary in Stann Creek District. The jaguar was one of the most revered animals by the ancient Maya. There are four other cat species in Belize: ocelot, puma, jaguarundi, and margay.

The Community Baboon Sanctuary lies on the border of Orange Walk District and Belize District. It was established in 1985 by primate biologist Rob Horwich together with the local community. The sanctuary protects one of the few healthy black howler monkey populations left in Central America.

Baird's tapir is listed as an endangered species and has almost disappeared from Central America and Mexico. But a sizeable population of Baird's tapir exists in Belize. Manatees are also protected in Belize, which is said to have the largest population of them outside of the United States. Other mammals in Belize include the river otter, rough-toothed dolphin, Atlantic bottle-nosed dolphin, Brainville's spotted dolphin, peccary, hickatee, deer, armadillo, and gibnutt (a relative of the guinea pig). It is illegal to keep or hunt wild animals in Belize. If you encounter one, call the Belize Zoo.

Reptiles

You are sharing your home with many weird and wonderful creatures, so use your common sense, pay attention, and be aware of your surroundings. If you are out walking at night, use a flashlight. When rifling through a pile of old materials such as wood or leaves, keep an eye out for snakes. There are also small scorpions around, so watch where you walk and check inside your shoes.

There are eight species of sea turtle in the world, three of which are known to nest in Belize. The green, loggerhead, and hawksbill turtles have all been declared endangered. You can swim with them in Shark Ray Alley, along with nurse sharks and enormous stingrays. It is an exhilarating experience! Their nesting season is June 1–August 31.

There are several species of snake. Many are harmless to humans and you will rarely see them. The poisonous ones are the Central American coral snake, eyelash viper, fer-de-lance (also known as the as the yellow-jaw Tommy Goff and one to watch out for because it is aggressive), hognose viper, jumping viper, Mexican moccasin (or Mexican cantil), and the neotropical rattlesnake. For coral snakes there is a little limerick that helps identify the dangerous varieties: *Red on black, OK Jack; red on yellow, deadly fellow.* This indicates the visual difference between the venomous Western and Eastern coral snakes and the non-venomous milk snake and king snake.

It's wise to keep an eye open for snakes and to familiarize yourself with the poisonous varieties. The majority of snakes are harmless and will slither away long before you get a chance to see them. Many of the snakes (which you will most likely remain unaware of) are useful because they keep down the rodent population and maintain an ecological balance by eating birds, frogs, and lizards; and some even eat venomous snakes. They're all part of the circle of life and it's best not to upset the balance. Some have striking patterns and colors, and they come in all sizes.

Other reptiles include the green iguana, or "bamboo-chicken," and the black or land iguana, locally called a "wish-willy."

There are two crocodile species in Belize: the American crocodile, which occurs mainly in coastal areas, and Morelet's crocodile, which is found in the Community Baboon Sanctuary. The Creole name for both is "alligator." Morelet's is endangered and there are only an estimated 10,000–20,000 wild American crocodiles left worldwide, making them as rare as polar bears. Belize is their last main stronghold but human-crocodile conflicts are increasingly becoming a problem due to development and illegal feeding of crocodiles. The American Crocodile Education Sanctuary (ACES) is a non-profit organization dedicated to the conservation of the crocodiles. It also captures crocodiles in built-up areas such as Ambergris Caye and relocates them to sanctuaries.

Social Climate

MULTICULTURALISM

Belize's history has led to a unique, multicultural population where each culture depends on the other in ways rarely seen in other parts of the world. No particular group has been totally self-sufficient. In the days of the early settlements, the different groups of people came together in order to defend against attempted invasions, such as the Battle of St. George's Caye.

Mestizos, people of Spanish and Maya descent, make up almost half the population of Belize. A quarter of the population is made up of Creoles, who have European and African ancestry. There are also three tribes of Maya Indians and

carving of a Maya god

© VICTORIA DAY-WILSON

a population of the Garifuna people, who have Carib Indian and African heritage.

There are about 46,000 foreigners who have made Belize their home, including Americans, Canadians, Europeans, Chinese, Jamaicans, Central Americans, and others. According to the Statistical Institute of Belize's (SIB) 2010 Housing and Population census, there are 27,000 Central Americans, primarily from Guatemala as well as El Salvador and Honduras, in Belize. There are East Indian, Filipino, Chinese, Lebanese communities, and traditional and progressive Mennonite groups.

Don't be surprised or insulted by phrases and terms used to describe ethnic groups that would be considered politically incorrect in the West: white people are commonly known as "gringos" or "white man"; people with Chinese heritage are known as "China man"; and black people of African descent are generally referred to as "black man."

One of the best examples of multiculturalism in Belize can be found in the music played on local buses. It's never the same. It varies between Western pop, Spanish music, reggae, hip hop, punta rock, brukdown, marimba, and everything in between.

SOCIAL INTERACTIONS

Generally speaking, people tend to socialize within their own distinct group, but there is a lot of exposure to and interaction among the different groups. For example, when you shop, you'll wander from a fruit stall, often run by a Mestizo, to the butcher, who can be Belizean or in my case Zimbabwean, to the baker, mine is a French bakery run by a German, and the general supermarket, usually run by Chinese. You'll get to know the different stores and chat with the stall owners.

While there is some intermarriage and there are friendships outside of one's group (mostly among those with higher education levels), this is not the rule. These barriers of separation are somewhat broken down by the younger generations of Belizeans who attend school together, where socializing is not limited to nationality or race.

There is a busy, social expat scene here, but whether you engage in it depends on you. There are also various opportunities to get to know people through the market and volunteer work.

SOCIAL VALUES

In general, Belizeans value respecting others, being polite, and treating others as you would like to be treated. People here take time to speak to each other.

Children and the elderly are respected and looked after. On local buses, the ticket collectors will always help lift small children off buses, offer a hand to the elderly, or help carry shopping bags.

ATTITUDE TOWARD FOREIGNERS

How Belizeans react to foreigners in their midst depends on the individual Belizean and on the foreigner. If you are polite, considerate, and willing to listen and learn about local customs and ways of approaching problems, you will be accepted and treated fairly. On the other hand, if you arrive with an attitude that, because you come from a developed nation, you think you know how to do things better than Belizeans, you may encounter resentment and coolness. Friendliness goes a long way; introduce yourself, and people will most likely chat and share experiences. You will encounter smiles and waves to greet you, even from total strangers. Ask advice, and interesting conversations ensue; everyone has a story to tell.

Upon first encounters, some Belizeans may be hesitant to accept foreigners as friends or as part of an extended family. The economic divide between the majority of the local population and foreigners from North America and Europe cannot be denied and informs many interactions between foreigners and some Belizeans. Many Belizeans aspire to move to the United States, but immigration laws and financial barriers make it difficult or impossible. And although Belizeans take great pride in their home country, many are poor by Western standards and may not understand why an American would want to move here. Additionally, there is an assumption that if someone has the money to move here, they must be wealthy. With this assumption comes the idea that foreigners should be lending a (financial) helping hand to people here. Sometimes you may find a gringo price (more expensive) and a Belizean price (a lot cheaper) for the same item or service. The reality is that foreigners generally do have more money than most Belizeans, so it's wise pay a price that is fair to both parties.

There is also a problem with theft in Belize. The unemployment rate is 23 percent, and in 2010 the average Belizean's salary was BZ$850 per month. Many Belizeans live a hand-to-mouth existence in simple wooden structures without luxuries such as electricity and vehicles. Therefore, stealing from those who have more becomes an appealing option for some.

In general, Belizeans are welcoming to foreigners, and both locals and expats view their encounters as an opportunity to learn from one another and forge new relationships.

HISTORY, GOVERNMENT, AND ECONOMY

For a little country only slightly smaller than Massachusetts, with a population just over 300,000, Belize packs a big punch in terms of variety and diversity. Originally made up of several Mayan city-states, dating back to 2,500 B.C., Belize has a rich history and cultural heritage. This chapter endeavors to provide a general guideline and overview with approximate dates.

Belize gained its independence from the British in 1981 and remains part of the British Commonwealth. Its government is democratic and based on the British parliamentary system.

The country's economy traditionally relied on forestry, and on mahogany production in particular. Today tourism makes up the largest portion of Belize's foreign income at US$400 million a year. It also accounts for a third of the country's employment.

© VICTORIA DAY-WILSON

History

Belize is best known for its history of the ancient Maya and it has over 900 historic locations. Many are still unexcavated and rise as jungle-covered hills when you ride through the plains and forests. The Mayan civilization lasted six times longer than the Roman Empire, had a population of around 400,000, and on any given day, the rivers that are now virtually empty were packed with more than 4,000 canoes. Of course Belize did not have borders then and was not the country as we know it now, but archaeologists have unearthed a lot of discoveries in various locations across the country, giving us a clearer idea of its original history and earliest inhabitants. However, experts agree that there are chronological and geographical gaps; extensive research is ongoing into the Maya civilization because they suspect it to be more developed than we currently know.

The earliest evidence of habitation in Belize dates back to the Paleo-Indians around 11,500–8000 B.C. They led a nomadic life and hunted big animals. A few primitive artifacts and animal remains—such as rudimentary bone, wood, and stone instruments—were found in the Belize, Orange Walk, and Corozal Districts. There isn't a lot of information on the Archaic period (circa 8000–900 B.C.), but it is thought that the local population relied more on plants to eat and used ceramic tools. During the Late Archaic period (3400–1000 B.C.) there seem to have been periods where there were temporary settlements and plants replaced meat as the main source of food. Ceramic tools were found from this period. The people lived along lagoons, river valleys, and in swamps, as well as on higher land.

The first recorded European presence was in the 15th century. Pirates, buccaneers, and loggers abounded as the Spanish and British fought for supremacy, which the British finally gained in 1840 when the country became known as British Honduras. In 1973 the country's name was changed to Belize and it became independent in 1981.

As Belize is an independent joint realm state of the British Commonwealth, Queen Elizabeth II is the head of state. Following national elections in 2008, the United Democratic Party (UDP) took over power from the People's United Party (PUP) with Dean Barrow as Prime Minister. The UDP remained in power after the 2012 elections. Belize has a parliamentary democracy with a prime minister, elected house, appointed senate, and Supreme Court. The legal system is based on English Common law and all official matters are conducted in English.

THE MAYA CIVILIZATION

The ancient Maya civilization spread over what is now Belize, Honduras, Guatemala, El Salvador, and Mexico (the entire region is also known as Mundo Maya) from around 2500 B.C. to around A.D. 900, after which it mysteriously deteriorated. There are various hypotheses on why this happened, ranging from war to disease to climate change, or perhaps a combination of all three. Maya civilization lasted through several periods (Early Preclassic 2500–800 B.C.; Middle Preclassic 800–400 B.C.; Late Preclassic 400 B.C.–A.D. 250) until it reached its height during the Classic period (A.D. 250–900). Settlements from the Late Preclassic period can be found at the Cuello ruins and Colha in Orange Walk, and from around 2000 B.C. in Santa Rita in Corozal.

Small agricultural communities were established, land was cleared, and crops like corn and beans were planted. Early inhabitants made oval platforms with thatched houses on top and created red, simple ceramics known as Swasey pottery. A social, political, and economic hierarchy formed with chiefdoms passed down through families. During the Late Preclassic period, trade of jewelry, pottery, tools, and food increased with other civilizations, like the Olmecs. This fuelled further growth and spurred the Maya to build settlements at strategic locations on trading routes, such as Cerros close to the mouth of the New River on Corozal Bay, and Lamanai farther inland on the river.

During the Classic period (A.D. 250–900) the Maya civilization grew and flourished. Major Mayan settlements were built at Altun Ha in Belize District; at Xunantunich and Caracol in Cayo, close to the Guatemalan border; and at

© VICTORIA DAY-WILSON

ancient Maya art on Xunantunich

ANCIENT MAYA BELIEFS AND RITUALS

The Maya placed great significance on the network of caves that lies under Central America, as they believed that was the direction they passed after death on their way to the place of rest. The nine layers of the Maya "hell" were guarded by the Lords of the Night. Deep caves were thought to connect with the underground, which was believed to be connected with the earth and then 13 layers of heaven by the roots and branches of the ceiba tree. This tree is sacred to the Maya and is still not cut down today, and is also the national symbol of Guatemala.

The ancient Maya believed in reincarnation and left food out for their ancestors, believing that they would be haunted otherwise. Corn, beans, avocadoes, jutes (snails from the river), and anato seeds were left in a pot. This ritual could take up to three days. The pot was then "killed" by drilling a hole in it or smashing it to release the spirits; it is probable that the holes were drilled with obsidian blades. The same place was never used twice for the ceremony, as it was believed that would offend the ancestors. The practice continues today on November 1 and 2 in a ceremony called Día de los Muertos, Spanish for Day of the Dead. People place their ancestor's favorite things on their graves. A table of food is prepared with candles and food for the ancestors. Ashes are laid down surrounding the table. The following morning footprints are visible in the ashes (probably from animals who came in the night and took the food); the Maya believe that their ancestors return in animal form.

Bloodletting was also popular as a way to communicate with ancestors in a practice called the image of the vision serpent. The Maya would ingest plants with hallucinogenic qualities such as magic mushrooms,

© VICTORIA DAY-WILSON

Mayan ceremonial pots in the Actun Tunichil Muknal Cave

water lilies, and peyotes and enter a cave. Their torch light reflected on the rock formations and created shadows, which they believed represented their ancestors. Once inside the cave, tongues, nipples, and penises would be cut to release blood, which would then be dripped onto paper made from the bark fibers of the ficus tree and pasted with lime. The paper would be burned and from out of the smoke the ancestor would appear from the mouth of a serpent.

Bats are considered bad luck by the Maya as according to legend they are believed to be the messengers of death. The gods in the underworld sent bats to summon the Hero Twins to a ball game. Myth has it that the hero twins angered the gods while playing the ball game and were therefore killed. One twin head was put in a calabash tree, which came alive as a reminder, and people were warned not to go near the tree. One day a curious princess walked past the tree and the skull spat on her and she became pregnant, giving birth to a new pair of smarter hero twins. The gods wanted to test how smart the twins were and gave them a cigarette that they were told to keep alight all night. The twins outsmarted the gods by tying a scarlet macaw tail to the end of a stick. This gave the impression of a scarlet and blue flame. When the gods tried to lure the twins down to Xibalba to create a garden, the twins enlisted the help of cutter leaf ants. The twins got the cutter leaf ants to bring them flowers, which they presented to the gods to appease them.

To the Maya, our world is the third version of the earth. The first was populated by beings created from mud, these were of no use, so the gods killed them with a huge flood. The second were beings made from sticks, the gods were unhappy with these too and sent a huge fire to kill them; some escaped by climbing trees and evolved into monkeys. The monkeys were symbols of respect as were turtles, since they were considered to be the land floating on the sea.

Why the Maya ventured so far into jet black caves with only torches for light along treacherous routes is much debated by archaeologists. Some theories suggest that the Maya were desperate about something, as their religious and spiritual ceremonies became more complex and were carried farther into the depths of the caves.

A common theory on the demise of the ancient Maya civilization centers around climactic change and, as a result, their dissatisfaction with the Maya rulers. In A.D. 50-600 the rains were regular and bloodletting and animal sacrifices were carried out to predict the rains. Around A.D. 600 the climate changed and the rains did not come as predicted. As a result, the Maya people turned against their rulers, believing they were responsible for angering the gods; the Maya communities moved to the highlands and human sacrifice began. Archaeologists found that sacrifices were made specifically to Chak, the rain god. Around this time, children were taken for sacrifices by a short green monster called Tata Duende. Thus, the Maya lived in fear of Tata Duende. The explanation is fairly simple, however: Dwarves often assisted shamans. But to this day, some parents still use the threat of Tata Duende to discipline their children.

Lubaantun in Toledo. Trade was very active all along Belize's coastline and was so important that the Maya dug a canal to create access for their canoes at the southern end of the Yucatán Peninsula, thus creating the island of Ambergris Caye. The Mayans expanded on the concept of city states, supporting agriculture, administration, politics, trade, culture, religion, and architecture. A social hierarchy of rulers, traders, and farmers developed. Wars were fought between city states to expand territory and power. Research is giving us a clearer idea of the lives of the Maya, which were astonishingly advanced. They used glyphic writing to record events on slabs of stone called stela and books were made using bark. They used math and invented the concept of zero, a millennium before Western civilization cottoned on to the idea. Their strong interest in astronomy led to the creation of several calendars, one of which is very close to ours with 365 days. Interestingly, they calculated that the Maya era began on August 11, 3114 B.C., and ends on December 21, 2012. Their priests had important roles in the community and were keen astronomers.

The Maya had dogs, turkeys, and bees, and hunted deer and peccaries with darts, and wild birds with blow guns; they set snares for armadillos and practiced several kinds of fishing. Every household had its own kitchen garden where vegetables and fruit trees, like papaya, avocado, custard apple, sapodilla, and the breadnut tree, were grown. Merchants traded on land and sea with salt, cotton, cocoa, fish, honey, feathers, shells, and precious stones. Farmers grew corn, beans, squash, cocoa, chili peppers, and cotton. The Maya crafted clay pots, created clothing dye, and learned to weave; they used stone to construct buildings and sculptures. They crafted jewelry and ornaments from gold, silver, copper, bronze, and jade. Their cities had temples, palaces, plazas, ball courts, and public areas. Research carried out at Caracol shows that the Maya used the concept of city planning, connecting a network of markets through causeways, administrative sections, and residential areas. Consideration was given to health, and water control for agricultural use and human consumption. Caracol was established by A.D. 250–550 and had a population of 115,000 under dynastic rule. Caracol waged war against Tikal in Guatemala and Navanjo, and became dominant in the area. After such prosperous civilizations, it took about a century for the Maya communities to decline. Nobody knows exactly why, but trade ties diminished, conflict increased, alliances broke down, the population declined, construction virtually ground to a halt, record-keeping lessened, and cities collapsed and were abandoned. Although what we know of the ancient Maya civilization declined, the Maya continued to live in Belize, had various settlements, and fought off the Spanish in the 1600s. Three different Maya tribes are spread across Belize today.

WESTERN COLONIAL RIVALRY: PIRATES AND LOGGING

By A.D. 1500 Belize's population was estimated to be around 200,000 and there were many established Maya communities. The first known Europeans to come to Belize were shipwrecked Spanish sailors in 1511. Some of the sailors were sacrificed or used as slaves. One of the shipwrecked sailors, Gonzalo Guerrero, fell in love with the daughter of a Maya chief. He converted to the Maya way of life and went on to become a military advisor for the Maya against the Spanish. He was the first known European to make Belize his home and his children were the first known Mestizos in Belize.

During this time, the Spanish were trying to colonize Central and South America and claimed sovereignty over the whole area, with the exception of areas in South America that had been given to the Portuguese. Initially the Spanish showed no interest in Belize, claiming it was too swampy and had too many mosquitoes. They eventually crossed over from Mexico into Belize and tried to gain a foothold in the country. But the Maya fought back. In 1618 two Spanish priests pushed farther inland to Tipú on the Macal River in the Cayo District. They punished the Maya for worshipping idols, the Maya burned down a church, and by 1638 a full-scale Maya rebellion ensued. The Spanish continued to send missions into the area to try to convert the local populace to Catholicism and struggles between the Maya and Spanish continued until 1707 when the population at Tipú was forcibly evicted to an area near modern-day Flores. A Spanish mission was established at Lamanai in 1750, but the church was burned down. As a result, the Spanish abandoned Western Belize as they couldn't settle without a labor force.

The first recorded European settlements were in 1638 at the mouth of the Belize River. In 1655, after the British captured Jamaica from Spain, British sailors and soldiers started coming to Belize. They settled along the coast and became buccaneers (or pirates) attacking Spanish ships. Many of the buccaneers voluntarily gave up plundering Spanish ships and in 1670 the Treaty of Madrid put an end to the piracy (in theory) and encouraged the settlers to turn their attention to logwood, but piracy continued through the 1700s. However, cutting logwood, which was exported back to England and used as a clothing dye, became a thriving industry and the logwood cutters became known as Baymen. At this same time, Britain competed with France and the Netherlands to gain a foothold in the Caribbean, and government-sanctioned pirates—referred to as privateers—plundered the Spanish treasure-filled galleons. The British never fully recognized the Baymen as subjects and more or less left them to their own devices. But Spain disputed their right to the territory

frequent skirmishes ...nish and the British over the right of the British to settle in the area and cut logwood. As a result, several treaties were drawn up between Spain and Britain in an attempt to outlaw the Baymen from logging, even though Britain profited from the trade. The Spanish attacked the settlement several times and forced the British to leave in 1717, 1730, 1754, and 1779. In the 1763 Treaty of Paris the Spanish gave the British permission to get involved with the logwood industry. This was reaffirmed in 1783 in the Treaty of Versailles, and in 1786 the Convention of London extended a logwood concession.

© VICTORIA DAY-WILSON

The former colonial administration offices and courts in Belize City are now known as the Courthouse.

In the 1760s the logwood trade declined and the export of mahogany for furniture-making took over. Settlers moved farther inland in search of mahogany and made contact with the Maya. Records show that although the British didn't try to colonize or convert the Maya, they used them as slave labor or traded them in Jamaica. By this time the Maya population had dwindled so much and suffered from diseases that they caught from the Europeans that they put up little resistance. War continued between the British and the Spanish until the governor of Jamaica agreed to send troops to help the Baymen at their request. In 1765 Admiral Burnaby visited Belize from Jamaica and found the Baymen in such a state of disorder that he introduced Burnaby's Code, a set of laws that gave authority to magistrates and a jury to uphold some order and regulation. The Baymen adhered to the code to a certain degree but raids on Spanish ships continued and resulted in reprisals from the Spanish. On September 15, 1779, the Spanish captured St. George's Caye, home to many settlers, and shipped 140 prisoners and 250 slaves to Havana. The final showdown came in 1796 when war broke out between Britain and Spain. The Spanish in Mexico assembled 32 war ships and 2,000 troops determined to drive the British out of Belize. On September 3, 1798, they attacked St. George's Caye. The battle lasted seven days. Though the Spanish had strong forces, they were no match for the Baymen who had better knowledge of the coastal waters and were supported by an armed sloop (HMS *Merlin*), released and armed slaves, and a few companies of troops from Jamaica. On September 10, 1798, Lieutenant-Colonel Barrow led the British to victory and the Spanish retreated, never trying to control Belize again. To this day, September 10 is a national holiday in Belize.

SLAVERY AND THE GARIFUNA

The British woodcutters needed additional labor but couldn't find enough locally so they used slaves. The earliest record of black slaves in Belize was reported by a Spanish missionary in 1724. Slaves often came through markets in Jamaica, but some were brought directly from Africa or the United States. Most of the slaves originated from present-day Nigeria in West Africa, and farther south from Congo and Angola. When the logwood trade died out and mahogany took over, settlers and slaves trekked inland to find the trees. After 1770, 80 percent of all male slaves aged 10 years or older logged mahogany. In 1790, Belize's settlement population was 2,900, of which 2,100 were slaves. Slaves frequently escaped, and though some did fight alongside their owners at the Battle of St. George's Caye, others ran away. Many ended up in Maroon settlements in Gales Point, a Creole village that still exists today on a narrow peninsula on the southern point of Southern Lagoon in Belize District. There were several records of slave revolts between 1745 and 1820, something the minority of white settlers feared almost as much as a Spanish attack.

The nature of slavery in the logging industry differed from that in the sugar plantations. Due to the nature of the work, slaves and their masters had to rely on each other quite a bit. The logging gangs often worked in small groups, sometimes with their masters, deep in the forests. Slaves were armed in order to protect themselves from the Maya and to hunt food. They cut and transported the wood, which was very heavy and had to be tied together as rafts and floated down the rivers, often during the rainy season.

Manumission—the act of a slave buying freedom or being given freedom in a will or simply as a gift—was more common in Belize than in the Caribbean islands. However, slaves were still harshly treated. Owners were allowed to give 39 lashes of the whip or imprison their slaves, and were even compensated if their slave was hanged for rebellion. The settlers were finally recognized as British subjects and the Abolition Act of 1807 made it illegal for British subjects to continue with the slave trade (but it didn't stop them from transporting slaves from one British colony to another). As Belize was not a colony, slaves could not be transported there from Jamaica. The Abolition

Act of 1833 ended slavery throughout the British Empire and a special clause was added to include Belize.

The Garifuna

In 1635 two Spanish slave ships carrying slaves from Nigeria to the Spanish colonies were shipwrecked near the island of San Vicente. The African slaves initially clashed with the inhabitants of the island, Arawak Indians (also known as Caribes), but they eventually settled and the result was a black Caribbean population known as the Garifuna. By 1750 the Garifuna population had grown and become prosperous. French colonists arrived on the island, shortly followed by the British in 1763. The Garifuna refused to give up their land and a 32-year conflict ensued with the French siding with the Garifuna against the British. In 1775 the British decided to take over the entire island and the French finally surrendered in 1796, although the Garifuna and Arawaks continued to fight but also eventually gave up. In 1796 the British deported 5,000 Garifuna to a nearby island called Balliceaux and then onto to the island of Roatán in 1797, one of the Bay Islands off Honduras; only 2,500 Garifuna survived.

A few years later the Spanish took control of the island and used the Garifuna to supplement their labor force. The Garifuna turned out to be good soldiers and were sent to other areas along the coast. In 1802, 150 Garifuna arrived on the coast of Stann Creek as woodcutters. They got to know the coast well and became excellent smugglers, evading the Spanish who forbade trade with the British. The Garifuna population grew and prospered in Stann Creek. When European settlers arrived there in 1823, Methodist missionaries attempted to convert them to Christianity and failed. In 1832, hundreds of Garifuna led by Alejo Benji migrated to Belize. This is known as Garifuna Settlement Day and is still celebrated annually on November 19. During WWII the Garifuna joined the crews of British and American merchant ships.

INDEPENDENCE AND THE GUATEMALA DISPUTE

Aside from Burnaby's Code of laws introduced in 1765, the first steps by the British to accept Belize as a territory and to put some type of administration in place were imposed in 1786 by a superintendent named Captain Despard. Despard struggled with the settlement, which didn't want "interference" from London. The powers of the superintendent grew, and in 1854 an elected Legislative Assembly was formed which established the start of a democratic colonial parliament. The assembly formerly requested recognition as a British colony and on May 12, 1862, Belize became known as the colony of British

Honduras. In 1871 it was recognized as a crown colony in line with colonial policy throughout the West Indies, controlled by a governor appointed by the Colonial Office. In 1901 Belize's population was 37,500.

WWI brought on dissent and unrest in British Honduras. Belizean troops volunteered for the British West Indian Regiment but when they arrived for battle they were told they were not allowed to fight and were relegated to labor battalions in Mesopotamia due to the color of their skin. When they returned from the war in 1919 bitterness led to violence and many Belizeans joined in looting and rioting. The unrest was due to a combination of race riots, poor working conditions, lack of employment, and lack of adequate support for the unemployed. This marked the beginning of the independence movement.

In 1934, following the hardship of the depression of the 1930s, poor labor conditions, and mismanagement by the British, Antonio Soberanis founded the Labourers and Unemployed Association (LUA) to protest the conditions of the working class countrywide. The British government intervened by banning marches and increasing their own power to deal with civil disturbance. WWII boosted Belize's forestry industry and Belizeans were able to work abroad. But conditions when they returned weren't much better than after WWI. Political parties formed, including the People's United Party (PUP) in 1950, which is a Christian Democratic party, and the National Party (NP) in 1951. The parties and the General Workers Union (GWU) pushed for an amendment to the constitution to allow all literate adults over the age of 21 to vote. An election was called in 1954 and about 20,801 electors voted, representing 70.5 percent of the total electorate. A coalition of PUP, led by George Price, and the GWU walked away with eight out of nine seats, with one additional representative from the National Party. In 1964 Belize gained self-government. In 1973 the United Democratic Party (UDP) was formed. The party is a center-left social democratic party. The PUP and UDP are the main parties in Belize today.

Due to a dispute with Guatemala over a treaty signed with Britain in 1859 independence was delayed as Guatemala did not recognize Belize as a self-governing territory, but rather as the 23rd state of Guatemala and referred to it in Spanish

© VICTORIA DAY-WILSON

the seal on Belize's flag

HISTORICAL TIMELINE FOR BELIZE

- 11,500-8000 B.C. – Earliest evidence of habitation in Belize dates back to the Paleo-Indians.
- 8000-900 B.C. – Archaic period.
- 3114 B.C. – According to a Mayan calendar, August 11 was the beginning of their civilization.
- 3400-1,000 B.C. – Late Archaic period.
- 2500 B.C. – First signs of ancient Maya.
- 2500-800 B.C. – Early Preclassic period; the Maya begin building trade centers and living in communities.
- 800-400 B.C. – Middle Preclassic period.
- 400 B.C.-A.D. 250 – Late Preclassic period.
- A.D. 250-550 – Caracol is established.
- A.D. 250-600 – Early Classic period; the build up to the height of Maya civilization.
- A.D. 600-900 – Late Classic period; the height and gradual downfall of the Maya civilization.
- A.D. 900-1200 – Early Postclassic period.
- 1511 – The first known Europeans to come to Belize are Spanish shipwrecked sailors.
- 1618 – Two Spanish priests push farther inland to Tipú on the Macal River in the Cayo District.
- 1635 – Two Spanish slave ships carrying slaves from Nigeria to the Spanish colonies are shipwrecked near the island of San Vicente.

- 1638 – Full-scale Maya rebellion flares up against the Spanish.
- 1638 – The first recorded European settlements at the mouth of the Belize River.
- 1655 – British sailors and soldiers start coming to Belize after the British capture of Jamaica from Spain.
- 1670 – The Treaty of Madrid puts an end to the British piracy of Spanish ships (in theory).
- 1707 – The Spanish forcibly evict the Maya population at Tipú to an area near modern-day Flores.
- 1717, 1730, 1754, and 1779 – The Spanish attack the British settlement several times and force the British to leave.
- 1724 – The earliest record of black slaves in Belize was reported by a Spanish missionary.
- 1750 – A Spanish mission is established at Lamanai, but the church was burned down.
- 1760s – The logwood trade declines and the export of mahogany for furniture-making takes over.
- 1763 – The Treaty of Paris is drawn up, in which the Spanish gave the British permission to get involved with the logwood industry.
- 1763 – French colonists arrive on San Vicente, shortly followed by the British.
- 1765 – Burnaby's Code is enacted.
- 1775 – The British decide to take over San Vicente from the French.
- 1779 – The Spanish capture St. George's Caye, home to many

settlers, and ship 140 prisoners and 250 slaves to Havana.

- 1783 – Treaty of Versailles reaffirms the 1763 Treaty of Paris.

- 1786 – The Convention of London extends a logwood concession to the Baymen.

- 1796 – War breaks out between Britain and Spain.

- 1796 – The French finally surrender San Vicente to the British, although the Garifuna and Arawaks continue to fight but also eventually give up.

- 1796 – The British deport 5,000 Garifuna to a nearby island called Balliceaux.

- 1797 – The British move the remaining Garifuna to the island of Roatán, one of the Bay islands off Honduras, but only 2,500 survive.

- 1798 – The battle of St. George's Caye is fought between the British and the Spanish. The British win and September 10 later becomes a national holiday in Belize.

- 1802 (some say 1832) – 150 Garifuna arrive on the coast of Stann Creek.

- 1807 – The Abolition Act passes, which makes it illegal for British subjects to continue with the slave trade and the settlers are recognized as British subjects.

- 1823 – Methodist missionaries arrive in Stann Creek and attempt (and fail) to convert the Garifuna to Christianity.

- 1832 – Hundreds of Garifuna, led by Alejo Benji, migrate to Belize. This is known as Garifuna Settle-

ment Day and is still celebrated annually on November 19.

- 1833 – The Abolition Act is enacted to end slavery throughout the British Empire and a special clause is added to include Belize.

- 1847 – The Caste Wars of Yucatán begin, following a riot by Maya troops.

- 1848 – Mexico sends troops to put down the rebellion, and thousands of Maya and Mestizo refugees flee to Belize.

- 1854 – An elected Legislative Assembly is formed which establishes the start of a democratic colonial parliament.

- 1859 – Belize and Guatemala sign a treaty over Belize. In Article 7, Britain agrees to build a road from Guatemala City to the Atlantic Coast; when this is achieved, Guatemala will drop its claim to Belize.

- 1862 – On May 12 the Belize settlement becomes known as the colony of British Honduras.

- 1871 – Belize is recognized as a crown colony in line with colonial policy throughout the West Indies, controlled by a governor appointed by the Colonial Office.

- 1919 – Race riots ensue after Belizean troops are mistreated by the British in WWI.

- 1926 – On March 9 Baron Bliss dies. He was British and bequeathed US$2 million to the people of Belize. Baron Bliss Day becomes a national holiday.

- 1934 – The Labourers and Unemployed Association (LUA) is founded by Antonio Soberanis

(continued on next page)

HISTORICAL TIMELINE FOR BELIZE (continued)

to protest the conditions of the working class countrywide.

- 1950 – The People's United Party (PUP) is formed.

- 1951 – The National Party (NP) is formed.

- 1951 – The constitution is amended to allow all literate adults over the age of 21 to vote.

- 1948 – Guatemala makes the first of many threats over four decades to invade Belize and recover its land.

- 1954 – Belize's first election takes place and the PUP, led by George Price, wins.

- 1958 – The first 500 Mennonites arrive in Belize.

- 1964 – Belize gains self-government.

- 1972 – Guatemala threatens invasion and Britain beefs up reinforcements in Belize.

- 1973 – United Democratic Party (UDP) is founded.

- 1973 – British Honduras changes its name to Belize.

- 1977 – Guatemala again threatens invasion and Britain again beefs up reinforcements in Belize.

- 1978 – The voting age is lowered from 21 to 18 years of age.

- 1981 – Belize gains independence on September 21. This becomes a national holiday.

- 1981–1993 – Dame Minita Gordon is governor-general.

- 1984 – UDP wins the first election in post-independent Belize with Manuel Esquivel as prime minister.

- 1989–1993 – PUP, led by George Price, regains power.

- 1990 – Guatemala agrees to recognize Belize's borders after the two countries set up a joint commission to settle the dispute.

- 1993–present – Sir Colville Young is governor-general.

- 1993–1998 – UDP is back in power, led again by Manuel Esquivel.

- 1998–2008 – PUP is back in power, led by Said Musa.

- 2002 – A disagreement over the borders of territorial waters leads to further negotiations between Guatemala and Belize.

- 2008–present – UDP is in power with Dean Barrow as prime minister.

- 2011 – Belizean government announces in March that 23 miles of road will be constructed between Toledo and the Guatemalan border at a cost of $48 million.

- 2011 – Death of George Price on September 19.

- 2012 – End of Maya civilization predicted by ancient Maya calendar for December 21.

- 2012 – Parliamentary elections were held in Belize.

as *Belice*. In the treaty the British recognized Belize and her borders as they are today but the Guatemalans disputed this view unless Article 7 was implemented. In Article 7 Britain agreed to build a road from Guatemala City to the Atlantic Coast, when this was achieved, Guatemala would drop its claim on Belize. A route was surveyed but the British considered the road too expensive to be built. (Ironically, the Belizean government announced in March, 2011, that 23 miles of road will be constructed between Toledo and the Guatemalan border at a cost of $48 million, funded by the Kuwait Fund for the Arab Economic Development and AFID (OPEC Fund for the International Development), the Central American Bank for the Economic Integration (CABEI), and the Government of Belize. There are local concerns that while this may bring economic opportunity to Toledo, there may also be a cultural impact on the Mopan Maya who live in the area: Road access from Guatemala may affect safety by attracting criminal elements from across the border.)

In 1948 Guatemala made the first of many threats over four decades to invade Belize and recover the land. The British responded by deploying its military. In 1972 and 1977 Guatemala threatened invasion and Britain beefed up reinforcements in Belize. Finally, partially due to international opinion, Belize gained independence on September 21, 1981, and is a member of the British Commonwealth. In 1990 Guatemala agreed to recognize Belize's borders after the two countries set up a joint commission to settle the dispute. A disagreement over the borders of territorial waters led to further negotiations in 2002. Although both countries are willing to negotiate, relations are still tense between Guatemala and Belize.

Government

After Belize became independent, the Queen of England remained as the titular head of state, but the governor-general was replaced by a Belizean citizen. To date these have been Dame Minita Gordon (1981–1993) and Sir Colville Young (November 1993–present). The governor-general is recommended by the prime minister. The government is democratic and is based on the British parliamentary system with a few adaptations. There are three branches of government: the legislature, made up of members from the Senate and House of Representatives, whose members are elected every five years in a general election; the executive; and the judiciary. Laws are introduced in the House of Representatives, which currently has 29 members, and the Senate, which has 13 members. The main function of the Senate is to review and pass bills introduced

headquarters for the United Democratic Party in Belize City

by the House of Representatives, authorize the ratification of treaties, handle foreign affairs such as establishing foreign military bases, and appoint ambassadors and judges. The executive branch consists of the governor-general, the prime minister, and the cabinet. There are also other government agencies, such as the public service and local government bodies. The prime minister decides the composition of the cabinet. The judiciary branch is in charge of the legal system and its execution. There is a Supreme Court and a Court of Appeal.

The highest court in Belize is the Privy Council in London, but there are proposals in place to replace that with a Caribbean Court of Justice. Local governance is broken down into a city council for Belize District and town boards for the other five districts. Village councils govern villages, and the alcalde system is in place in some Maya villages.

In 1978, the voting age was lowered from 21 to 18 years of age. Belize's government seems to rotate between United Democratic Party (UDP) and People's United Party (PUP) in power. On December 14, 1984, UDP won the first

House of Parliament in Belmopan

election in post-independent Belize with Manuel Esquivel as prime minister. In 1989–1993, PUP regained power and was led by George Price. In the 1993–1998 term, UDP was back in control, led again by Manuel Esquivel; in 1998–2008, PUP was in power, this time led by Said Musa. From 2008 to now, the UDP has been in power with Dean Barrow as prime minister. Voter figures in 2008 were high with 116,194 voters, a turnout of 74.49 percent of all registered voters. The last parliamentary elections took place in 2012. Belize or British Commonwealth citizens who are domiciled or have resided in the country for at least one year immediately before polling day, 18 years or older, are eligible to vote.

Economy

Traditionally, Belize relied on forestry as its main industry, and recently there's been a resurgence of forestry with the growth of tropical hardwoods. Out of Belize's US$2.5 billion GDP, tourism is its largest foreign income earner at US$400 million a year. Tourism also accounts for a third of the country's employment. Agriculture and fisheries are Belize's second biggest source of income; fish, shrimp, and lobster are exported along with citrus, sugar, and bananas. Research and diversification is ongoing in order to increase Belize's agricultural sector as only about 15 percent of the country's 38 percent of land viable for agriculture is in use. Other export products include clothing, molasses, wood, and crude oil. Main export partners are America, Mexico, the United Kingdom, the European Union, Central America, and the Caribbean Community (CARICOM) member states. Food processing and construction industries contribute towards the GDP. There is undoubtedly an income from drugs as Belize is a very convenient transit location, but figures for this are obviously unavailable.

The Belize dollar has been pegged at 2 to 1 to the U.S. dollar since 1976. Annual growth is around 3 percent and inflation about 4 percent. External debt lies at about US$2 billion. Belize receives aid mainly from the United States and the European Union. In 2010, unemployment stood at 23 percent (30,000 people), average monthly incomes were $900, and the public sector accounted for about 15 percent of the working population. About 185 U.S. companies have operations in Belize, including MCI, Duke Energy International, Archer Daniels Midland, Texaco, and Esso. There is a lack of strong industry in Belize, possibly due to expensive labor and strict labor laws, the high cost of energy, and a small domestic market. Goods such as food, consumer goods, machinery and transportation equipment, chemicals, pharmaceuticals, tobacco, mineral fuels, and lubricants are imported. Belize continues to rely heavily on foreign trade; when global economic slowdowns affect America and Europe, Belize suffers. In 1990, Belize passed the International Business Companies Act, targeting offshore investors. In 10 years, over 15,000 companies have registered.

PEOPLE AND CULTURE

Belize is a melting pot of cultures, religions, languages, and ethnicities. Those who make up the majority of the population include Creoles of mixed African and European heritage, Mestizos of mixed Indian and European heritage, Maya, Garifuna of African and Caribbean Indian heritage, East Indians, Chinese, Mennonites, Lebanese, North and Latin Americans, and Europeans. The result is a friendly, accommodating people who live mostly in harmony. Belize's unique blend of people and cultures is related to its history; many people ended up here by accident or through persecution elsewhere. It is one of the many charms of Belize that such a diverse group can live together in relative peace while still practicing their own religions, engaging with their own traditional cultures, and speaking different languages. English is the official language, but Spanish, Creole, Garifuna, and Mayan dialects are also spoken.

Ethnicity and Class

MESTIZOS

There are 11 main ethnic groups in Belize and about 6 percent of the overall population is of mixed ethnicity. The largest group, which makes up almost half of Belize's population, is the Mestizo group, also referred to as Spanish or Latinos. Mestizos are people of mixed Spanish and Central American Indian heritage. Their first language is usually Spanish, though most also speak English. Mestizos were first recognized in Belize sometime after 1511, when Spanish sailors shipwrecked on the coast of Belize mixed with the locals. Although, there must have been many Mestizos in Central America prior to this, due to the Spanish colonization of the region. The first recorded Mestizos in Belize were children of Gonzalo Guerrero, one of the sailors who survived the wreck and fell in love with the daughter of a Maya chief.

There was a large influx of Mestizo refugees from Mexico during the Caste Wars of the Yucatán in 1848. Today, the majority of Mestizos live in Cayo, followed by Orange Walk, Corozal, and Belize Districts; they live mainly on the Cayes. There was another influx of about 40,000 Mestizos to Belize in the 1980s as people escaped conflict and repression in El Salvador, Guatemala, and Honduras. Most have integrated into Belize culture and learned to speak Creole, although not all speak English. Many Mestizos have Belizean citizenship, as do their children, and have become part of the country's multicultural fabric. Underlying tensions developed in recent times, however, as many of the latest Central American immigrants to Belize are willing to work for low pay, and other Belizeans feel they are losing work opportunities to them.

A Mestizo girl dances.

CREOLES

The Creoles are the second largest group in Belize, with a population of about 63,000 according to the 2010 census. Most Creoles are descendants of the first African slaves, who arrived in Belize around 1720 to help in the logging industry. The majority live in Belize District, with smaller populations in Cayo, and a few thousand spread around other districts. They speak English and Creole, a type of Pidgin English.

MAYA

The Maya number about 30,000 and are spread across three tribes, the Kekchi, Mopan, and Yucatec. According to the 2010 census, the Maya make up 10 percent of Belize's population. There are 17,000 Kekchi Maya in Belize, 10,500 Mopan, and just over 2,000 Yucatec.

People surround a bicycle cart selling fruit and drinks.

Some Mayans living in Belize may be descendants of the original ancient Maya Indians in Belize, while others migrated here from elsewhere in Central America. The Kekchi came from Guatemala and El Salvador to work in cacao plantations in Toledo, where they are concentrated. They continue to migrate to Belize in small numbers. The Yucatec live mainly in Cayo, though they originally settled in northern Belize as many were escaping the Caste Wars. The majority of the Mopan live in Stann Creek and Toledo.

Each tribe speaks a different dialect, but the Mayan languages are decreasing as Spanish and English become more commonly spoken. The Maya in Toledo have won land rights from the government; this has become a contentious issue as some of the land is in areas where there are logging and oil interests.

GARIFUNA

The Garifuna (pronounced gah-RIF-oo-na) make up about 4.6 percent of Belize's population. They are descendants of African slaves who were shipwrecked in 1635 near the island of San Vicente among the island's native Arawak Indians (also called Caribes). The ships were carrying slaves from Nigeria to the Spanish colonies in South America.

On November 19, 1802, the Spanish sent 150 Garifuna to be woodcutters in Stann Creek. To this day, the date is celebrated as Garifuna Settlement Day. There are 14,000 Garifuna in Belize today and about 600,000 spread across

© VICTORIA DAY-WILSON

the Caribbean Coast in Honduras, Guatemala, Nicaragua, St. Vincent, and the Grenadines, and in cities such as New York, Los Angeles, New Orleans, and London. The largest Garifuna population in Central America is in Belize. Outside of Belize, the largest population is concentrated in New York, followed by Los Angeles.

The Garifuna have held onto their traditional beliefs, language, and customs. Their language is more similar to the indigenous Arawak Indian than their original African dialect, but their traditional music and dancing has a distinct African beat and feel to it. Their religion is a combination of ancestor worship with shamanism and Catholicism.

MENNONITES

The Mennonites are German-speaking Europeans who arrived in Belize in 1958 and number about 11,000. They are mainly settled in Corozal, Orange Walk, and Cayo. They wanted to administer their own communities, not pay tax, and not get called up for military service, so they left their home countries to come to Belize. They had a long arduous trip from the Netherlands to Switzerland, Prussia, Russia, Canada, Mexico, and finally agreed to a mutually beneficial pact with the Belizean government and have settled and flourished here. They have several communities spread around the country and

are divided into two groups: traditional Mennonites, *Altkolonier,* who wear dark overalls and straw hats, don't use modern technology, ride in carts pulled by horses, and farm; and progressive Mennonites, *Kleine Germeinde,* who have a modern dress sense, are actively involved in trade such as running hardware stores, and use electricity and vehicles. Both groups keep to themselves and live in their own communities, but you will see them around town or on the roads. In Cayo, the Mennonite settlement of Spanish Lookout is the place to go for large stores that sell hardware, a variety of foods, and other practical items.

© VICTORIA DAY-WILSON

a progressive Mennonite father and his sons   The progressive Mennonites are also involved in businesses such as information technology and communications. Their first language is German, but some speak English.

ASIAN POPULATIONS

East Indians originally came to Belize in the mid-1800s as indentured laborers. There are more than 6,000 living in Belize today. They are scattered across the country with concentrations in Belize District, Corozal, and Toledo.

There's a sizeable Chinese community who originally arrived in the 19th century as laborers on sugar plantations. Cantonese and Taiwanese populations followed in the 1980s. Many Asians in Belize run restaurants and grocery stores for their livelihood.

OTHER ETHNIC GROUPS

Other ethnicities include the Lebanese, who are small in number but a sizeable force in the economy of the country; Hindus; and Filipinos. There are a few thousand described as Blacks/Africans and Whites/Caucasians. In the 2010 census there are no exact figures for the foreign-born population, of which Central Americans are the majority. North Americans number just under 4,000, but in terms of expats in general, they are mainly Americans, a sizeable and increasing Canadian population, Brits, and Europeans. A few expats arrived in the 1940s–1970s. They have a wealth of experience and interesting anecdotes. Most of them don't really think of themselves as expats,

© VICTORIA DAY-WILSON

Rastafarian decorated car

many have held Belizean citizenship a while, and some have intermarried with Belizeans. The more traditional expats arrived in the last 20 years or less, and return quite frequently to visit their countries of origin.

ECONOMIC CLASS STRUCTURE

Belizean social structure is mainly determined by political and economic power, rather than by ethnic grouping. Though there is a correlation between power and ethnic groups, this has more to do with how some ethnic groups traditionally clustered in small, tight-knit communities that functioned as economic driving forces in Belize.

The majority of Belize's political and economic power lies with the minority groups of light-skinned Creoles, East Indians, Chinese, Lebanese, Palestinian, and to a large extent, the Mennonites, and with the Mestizos, the largest group in the country. History plays a role in this socio-economic stratification. The lighter-skinned Creoles are descendants of the 19th century Creole elite. The Creole and Mestizo commercial-business and professional families originally gained power politically and economically toward the end of the 19th century. Lebanese and Palestinian merchant families immigrated to Belize in the beginning of the 20th century, followed by the Chinese and Indian groups. The Mennonites arrived in the 1950s and started from scratch; they worked hard and established efficient farms and construction and agricultural retail businesses. Most of the Belizean elite live or have a residence in Belize City, and are tied together by religion; they send their children to the same religious schools. Most attend university in the United States, Britain, or the Caribbean. Intermarriage has held communities together.

Economically, North Americans and Europeans rank higher in the economic strata simply because most of them are better off financially. At one point, around 90 percent of private land, including prime agricultural areas and tourist operations, was owned by foreigners, mainly from North America. However, this does not make them part of the social elite. Economic interests held by Belize's elite tend to be in the retail trade, commercial and financial enterprises, local manufacturing, the state system, and, to a lesser degree, export agriculture. Foreign companies play a large role in exporting agricultural produce from Belize.

The Belizean middle class is growing and is more ethnically diverse than the upper class and yet it is unified through its pursuit of improved education, cultural respectability, and upward social mobility. It is made up of a combination of poor relatives of the elite, members of the working class, and self-made professionals who reached a higher level of education and economic success.

The group is made up of businesspeople, lawyers, accountants, medical professionals, teachers, civil servants and other government workers, skilled manual workers, and office workers. The Belizean middle class tends to work hard; sometimes people make enormous sacrifices so that their children can enjoy a higher level of education than they were able to attain for themselves.

The Garifuna, Maya, Mestizo farm workers, and darker-skinned Creoles fall into the lower economic classes. They have lower levels of education, often just reaching an elementary level, or none at all. Access to good education, even at the elementary school level, is difficult in rural areas. Central American refugees, who work for less pay and often do the jobs Belizeans won't, such as unskilled agricultural labor, are also part of the lower classes. The majority of this group is unemployed or work as unskilled laborers in transient employment and have poor living conditions. The Maya and the Garifuna operate in tribal societies and often have the highest levels of poverty. There has been a breakdown in the family unit that is more prevalent among these groups, with many households run by single parents, often women. The lack of employment opportunities for the lower classes has led to an increase in crime, as many people become involved in the drug trade, which in turn fuels gang warfare.

Customs and Etiquette

ADDRESSING OTHERS BY NAME

Belize is not a first-name culture. It is more formal and traditional than the United States is in this regard, but things are slowly changing. As a general rule, don't ask people their first names; refer to them by their titles and surnames. You will find that you will be addressed using your title and then either your first name or surname. For example, you may be addressed as Miss Emma or Mr. Smith.

GENDER ROLES

Gender roles in Belize are fairly stereotypical and traditional. Several NGOs and international bodies are working to improve women's rights in Belizean society. Currently, Belize has no strong political, economic, social, or religious representation by women, although that is slowly improving. Belize is on a par with Saudi Arabia, Qatar, and Brunei in last position on the Gender Gap Index for political empowerment for women according to the Global Gender Gap Report 2010. However, in daily life outward appearances are different, with quite a few women running their own businesses and often raising families on their own. This is more common among the Garifuna and Creole communities than the Maya and Mestizos. The other exception to the rule is that in rural communities women and men are often equal as healers and shamans.

Marriage and Family

Although many women in Belize are religious, and value is placed on marriage, Belizean women often have children at quite a young age and not necessarily within a marriage. Some do go on to marry or remain in common-law unions and have more children. Others never do marry and, as a result, extended families, siblings, and friends frequently pitch in and help raise the children. Requirements for divorce are quite strict, yet single-parent families are fairly common and socially accepted.

Particularly in poorer families, women are often economically dependent on men. Women will often stay home to look after and raise the children and maintain the household while men earn money for the family. While a chauvinistic culture exists, men take part in raising children and display tenderness toward kids not often seen in North America and Europe. Outwardly, women don't seem to be downtrodden.

There are some Belizeans, mostly over the age of 30, who feel that respect and manners have become worse among the younger generation and that there has been a loss of values and decline in morals. The feeling is that this is par-

© VICTORIA DAY-WILSON

Sisters enjoy the afternoon together.

tially due to children being spoiled, a lack of adequate discipline, and people having children too young—barely having grown up themselves.

Education and the Workplace

According to the 2010 census, boys outnumbered girls in elementary education in Belize, but girls outnumbered boys in high school education, and there was a ratio of two girls to one boy at the university level. One Belizean explained this by saying that boys can always go out and find manual labor, which is harder for girls, so if resources are limited, girls may be sent on to higher education in the hopes that they can qualify and at least find work in an office. However, women recorded twice the unemployment rate of men, with as much as three times recorded in Toledo District. On the whole, men earn more than women. In 2010 the average monthly income for a man was $922 compared with $822 for a woman.

DRESS

Belizean women are generally proud of their appearance and are often well groomed, and their children usually look neat and tidy. The expat clothing culture is very casual and informal. Light cotton and linen are recommended. For women who do not wish to attract attention in public, it is sensible to wear loose-fitting clothing and knee-length skirts or shorts.

MALE-FEMALE SOCIAL INTERACTIONS

Single women on their own may get approached or hit on. Be firm and polite and move on; this is usually effective and does not cause insult to the pursuer. Cat-calling is common and is targeted at both Belizean women and expats. Use your best judgment and move on without giving attention to the caller.

Though rapidly becoming a rarity in the West, chivalry is still part of the culture in Belize. Small gestures, like men offering to carry things and hold doors open for women, are common.

While there are many Belizean male guides who are used to taking female tourists caving, canoeing, or riding, for some reason Belizean men on the whole are often surprised that a gringa would contemplate doing such activities, do them well, and perhaps even do them on her own. It may be less common for local women to take an interest in exploring the outdoors.

GAY AND LESBIAN CULTURE

With a combination of strict laws against same-sex relationships, the power of the church, and a machismo society, there isn't much of a gay scene in Belize.

While there are those who at minimum disagree with homosexuality, Belize overall is a fairly tolerant place. It is highly unlikely that Belizeans will display overtly negative behaviors or attitudes about homosexuality. Belizeans do not openly discuss or display homosexuality. But public displays of affection are rare even among heterosexual couples here.

There are same-sex expat couples who moved here to start a new life, but they are mostly very discreet. One couple told me they were fairly sure their laborers, neighbors, and Belizean acquaintances were aware of their sexual orientation but no one had ever referred to it and they had never been treated poorly.

SENSE OF TIME

Belizeans have a laid back, relaxed culture, which means that punctuality is not a high priority. Don't be surprised if people turn up late, or in some cases don't turn up at all—there is no hurry in Belize. Stay calm and be polite if you are kept waiting.

MONEY

There isn't a culture of haggling or bargaining in Belize. You may politely ask if a stated price is the final price, and generally you will be told that it is. Leave it there and don't bargain further. Always double-check prices as sometimes you will be quoted a gringo price—often a lot higher than the real price simply because you are an expat and therefore it is assumed you have the money to pay. Some people leave tips; it isn't done by everyone but it's a nice gesture if you feel you received excellent service. A sufficient tip is 5–10 percent.

PHOTOGRAPHY

If you are taking photos, always ask first as a sign of general courtesy. Be aware that the Mennonites and the Maya are particularly sensitive to having their photo taken. Don't be surprised or upset if they say no. Others will quite happily allow their photos to be taken, and if they see you taking pictures will encourage you to take photos of them.

Culture

FOOD

Belize's food culture draws on the country's diverse heritage. Mainstream cuisine utilizes American, British, Mexican, and Caribbean flavors. Staples in various forms include rice and beans; Mexican food like tamales, tacos, burritos, enchiladas, empanadas, *garnaches,* or frittatas; and Belize's famous chili sauces, placed on every table.

Gibnut (a type of deer), iguana (also known as bamboo chicken), armadillo, and turtle are considered delicacies but are illegal to hunt. Slices of fruit in small bags are sold on every street corner. Smoke rises with tantalizing aromas from BBQ pork and chicken on the streets, usually served in a Styrofoam box with some coleslaw and a tortilla. Conch, lobster, crab, shrimp, and fish are also popular, along with a variety of soups; ceviche appears on most menus. A lot of food is fried in fat or oil. Delicious little meat or vegetable pies are served everywhere, along with small lobster or conch fritters. More Western foods such as burgers and slices of pizza are also available.

There are several good Belizean beers, including Belikin ale and stout, and Lighthouse. Cheap local rum is popular, as are sodas and various fruit drinks. To satisfy the Belizeans' sweet tooth, an assortment of cakes are sold and bread can be rather sweet.

Prevalent ingredients and vegetables used in cooking are coconuts, lime, honey, chilies, garlic, tomatoes, onions, black beans, plantain, yams, sweet

© VICTORIA DAY-WILSON

A menu painted on a building lists local dishes.

CELEBRATIONS FOR THE BATTLE OF ST. GEORGE'S CAYE IN CAYO

September is a festive time in Belize with many celebrations surrounding the **Battle of St. George's Caye on September 10** and **Independence Day on September 21.** Across the country there are beauty pageants, parades, children's talent shows, karaoke competitions, motorcades, marching bands, fireworks, track and field meets, parties, and a torch run. On September 9 in San Ignacio and Santa Elena there are sirens and a motorcade parade, followed by marching bands, and musical entertainment with fireworks at midnight.

On the day of commemoration for the victory at the Battle of St. George's Caye, September 10, Cayo is decorated with bunting in red, white, and blue, and Belizeans flags everywhere flutter in the breeze. People line the streets and gather in front of the Administration Building where a podium is ready for speeches and the crowning of the Queen of the West. The mood is festive, people are happy, and anticipation for the afternoon and evening celebrations hangs in the air. At 2 P.M. the Belize Defence Force (BDF) goes through a few drills, followed by a speech by the town mayor reflecting on the battle and Belize's past and future. Foreigners are welcome to take part in the festivities and thanked for joining in the event. The local band plays, fronted by eight dancing girls. They have Belizean flags painted on their faces and flags tucked into their instruments. The outgoing Queen of the West crowns the incoming Queen, who makes a brief speech and the procession heads off down all the main streets of San Ignacio and Santa Elena.

The whole town vibrates with the music from the Belizean band, followed by a Guatemalan band, a float with the beauty queens, a float with

potatoes, kidney beans, cabbage, carrots, chocho (a type of squash), calaloo (a type of spinach), sour sop, cabbage, cassava, string beans, and avocadoes. Bananas, papaya, mangoes, watermelon, citrus fruits, star fruit, and pitaya (a delicious succulent purple fruit with small black seeds) are common fruit you will see in most markets.

ARTS AND ENTERTAINMENT

Belizeans love drama, song, and dance, and they celebrate their public holidays—many derived from their history—with great spirit and enthusiasm. They also love to party and celebrations can last until dawn. Celebrations are worth attending and are great fun.

Visual Art and Crafts

There are many wood carvers in Belize, who mainly produce animals and bowls. Ceramics, engravings on slate, and basket and cloth weaving are also

© VICTORIA DAY-WILSON

Trumpet players march in the Independence Day parade in San Ignacio.

It's a real family event attended by all ages. The children dance alongside the parade, their parents join in, and the elderly smile indulgently, swinging their hips to the beat. The atmosphere is festive and light-hearted; it's really an amazing experience.

After three hours of marching, dancing, and playing music while walking through the streets in the hot sun, the mood is no less jubilant. The parade culminates with the crossing on the low bridge into San Ignacio over the Macal River, up the hill, and into the Macal River Park, where food and drink stands are waiting and a large tent with a live band hums with people. The bands keep playing, bursting into an impromptu jam session. Everyone takes to the floor: Children dance with their parents and grandparents; young couples enjoy themselves, while others look on, never still, always swaying to the beat of the music. Don't miss it!

loudspeakers playing more music, and a police escort. The whole event is extremely well organized.

common. Bright threads are stitched in a variety of patterns and designs onto a black background and used as tablecloths or turned into bags and pouches. These are mainly sold to tourists.

There is a flourishing art scene in Belize. The artists often draw inspiration from their surroundings, depicting locals or local scenes in bright colorful strokes. Some well-known artists include Lola Delgado, Pen Cayetano, Carolyn Carr, Eluterio Carillo, Benjamin Nicholas, Terryl Godoy, The Garcia Sisters, George Gabb, Eduardo Alamilla, Walter Castillo, Nelson Young, Orlando Garrida, and Mike Gvarra.

Music

Belizeans love music and they like to play it loudly. There is a long history of music in Belize with contributing influences from multiple ethnic groups. You will hear a wide variety of music from reggae, Spanish ballads, hip hop, Western pop, marimba, calypso, soca, punta, brukdown, and steel drumming.

© VICTORIA DAY-WILSON

Girls dance at the front of the band in the Battle of St. George's Caye celebrations.

Brukdown was originally developed by Creoles working in logging camps during the 18th and 19th centuries. Its main instruments include an accordion, banjo, harmonica, and a percussion instrument (whatever comes to hand, for example, using a stick to rattle the teeth in the jawbone of an animal). Wilfred Peters Boom and Chime Band are best known for brukdown music.

Punta rock originated in Dangriga in the 1970s; it draws on Garifuna music, combining Creole rhythms and heavy African percussion, and is sung in Creole or Garifuna. Andy Palacio and the Punta Rebels are probably the most well known punta rock group. A satire on the tourist business, *Bikini Panti* was a big hit of Palacio's in 1988. Punta rock has since been expanded on and mixed with other styles such as R&B, jazz, and pop to create punta pop. If you like reggae or calypso music, you'll probably like punta rock, but be prepared for vigorous hip shaking and gyrating!

Mestizo music draws on both traditional Maya music that uses log drums, rattles, and shells, and Spanish classical music. Marimba music is also popular in Mestizo communities in Belize.

Sports and Recreation

While Belizean sports aren't highly recognized at the international level, Belizeans are passionate about sports and have struggled with a lack of finance and facilities. Soccer has the biggest following in Belize, followed by basketball. It's worth going to a Belizean soccer match just to experience the atmosphere, the highs and lows, the euphoria, the praise shouted at players when the home team does well, and the abuse (which could make you blush!) heaped on them when they make a mistake. It's not personal; the fans just get caught up in the heat of the moment.

Cycling is popular and, if you are up early driving, you will often see teams of cyclists racing along in training for the many national races held on national holidays. Canoeing is a part of life and also an annual challenge in the form of La Ruta Maya Belize River Challenge, a four-day canoe race across 80 miles of river on Baron Bliss Day in March. Along the coast, water sports are popular and cater to Belizeans as well as to the tourist market for economic necessity.

There are three golf courses in Belize; as the number reflects, it's not a major sport here. You will see quite a few horses around. Traditionally there was not really a horse event circuit in Belize, although there is horse racing in Burrell Boom on national holidays. A few expat establishments, primarily in Cayo, are changing the horse-racing scene; for instance, there's a major race in Cayo called the Triple Crown Endurance Race, run by Light Rein Farm and Belize Equestrian Academy.

RELIGION

There are 16 different religions in Belize. Roman Catholicism is the largest by far, though its following is decreasing slightly. Other popular denominations are Seventh Day Adventists, Baptists, Anglicans, and Pentecostals. Interestingly, the largest group after the Catholics in the 2010 census is the people who said they didn't belong to any religion. That number had doubled since the last census.

Religion is a force to be reckoned with in Belize and has a large following. Christian churches of various denominations work in partnership with the government to run the state schools. Church groups often do a lot of good community work. Unfortunately there are some church groups that prey on the poor and vulnerable by providing a community service and then requiring a mandatory contribution to the church. It is reputed to be a common fraud.

The Garifuna have their own religion, as do some of the Maya. The Mennonites—although Christian—follow their own church. There are pockets of other religions in Belize, such as Hinduism, Islam, and the Baha'i faith.

PLANNING YOUR FACT-FINDING TRIP

If you are considering a move to Belize, the best thing is to visit first to get a sense of the place and find out if it feels right for you. Of course it would be a crying shame to travel all this way and not follow the tourist trail and see at least a few sights, but remember this isn't really a vacation; it's the first step towards a potentially life-changing decision. One of the many attractions of Belize is that it's a small country; you can get around most of it quite easily. Another benefit is that there are quite a few transportation options depending on how much time you have. There is a good road network to get around key locations, and you can rent a car. One of the best ways to see the country is by car. But if you're in a hurry, there are plenty of flights around most of the country and the view is spectacular.

If you have flexible dates, have a look at the different festivals, celebrations, and events and try to plan your trip so that you have the opportunity to experience at least one festival. It's fun and gives a great feel for national pride, the culture, and the people. September is quite a busy month for national

© VICTORIA DAY-WILSON

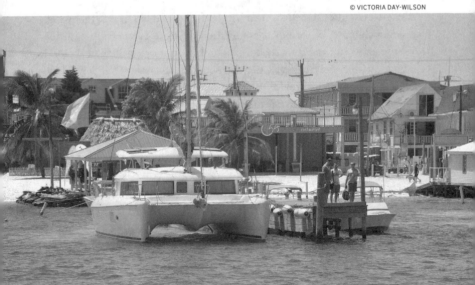

celebrations with both Independence Day and the celebration of the Battle of St. George's Caye. Many tourist facilities are run by expats—people similar to you; people who once came out to Belize wondering if this was a country they could move to and what they would do here. They are a great resource.

When planning your trip it's important to think about your priorities. For example, if you have children, you will need to spend time looking at schools. If you're looking at private schools, this will require a focus on Belmopan, San Pedro, and the surrounding areas. If you have a medical condition (and even if you don't), it's worth spending time looking around medical facilities. Having a look in other public facilities, such as post offices, communications companies, markets, and shops is also important (goods and prices vary considerably).

There are suggested itineraries in this chapter that are meant to serve as guidelines for your fact-finding trip. You should adapt them to suit your timeframe and places of interest. If you know which part of Belize you are interested in, spend your time there. However, if you have the time, it can be helpful to see parts of Belize you haven't considered. Several expats moved to one part of the country and then months or years later, found somewhere else more to their liking. Whereas it does take time to get to know a place, most of us can fairly quickly get a feeling for whether we want to stay somewhere or not. Go with your gut and listen to your intuition. At the same time, keep an open mind. Be open to new things; you may surprise yourself!

Preparing to Leave

An important part of preparing for a fact-finding trip is doing as much research as you can over the Internet and by reading books on the subject. Make sure you buy a decent map and familiarize yourself with the territory, towns, and roads. You need to research the country and different geographical areas to help you decide where to focus; you should have a look at a variety of property listings from different real estate agents. The Belize Forum (www.belizeforum.com/belize) and Ambergris Caye Forum (http://ambergriscaye.com/forum) can provide helpful information.

The other thing to consider is your budget. Work out a budget and then double that. Fact-finding, buying property, moving to a new country, and turning a property into your dream home is an expensive endeavor, and you will end up spending more than you budgeted for. If possible, try to keep your home in the U.S. and budget for renting in various parts of Belize for a minimum of six months to a year. It's the best way to really find out if Belize is right for you.

DOCUMENTS

A passport valid for at least six months is required to enter Belize. It's a good idea to have a few photocopies of your passport in case anything happens to it. When you sign into a hotel you will be asked to write down your passport number; this is normal procedure. North Americans do not need visas. You will be issued a 30-day tourist visa, which you must renew on or before the date stamped in your passport if you stay beyond 30 days. You can do this at a cost of $50 at any Department of Immigration in the main towns and cities. Parents or adults traveling with children who are not their biological children will be required to show documented evidence that they have responsibility for the child/children. Accepted documents include notarized letters from the parent(s), custody or adoption papers, and even death certificates in situations where one or both parents are deceased. There is a departure tax of US$40, which must be paid in U.S. currency.

IMMUNIZATIONS AND MEDICATIONS

It is recommended to receive vaccines for hepatitis A and B, typhoid, rabies, measles, mumps, and rubella (MMR) if you didn't get them as a child, and tetanus/diphtheria. Vaccinations and medication such as chloroquine pills for malaria and dengue fever are optional. The exception to this is that you must have a yellow fever vaccination if you are coming from a part of the world where yellow fever is a problem, like Africa or South America. If you have traveled to those areas, bring your vaccination certificate as proof. If you are planning on getting vaccinations, see your doctor 4–6 weeks before you travel. You can also check the Centers for Disease Control (CDC) website and the U.S. Department for State, or the Foreign Commonwealth office (FCO) if traveling from the United Kingdom. It is sensible to heed the advice, however some people don't take medication or have any vaccinations.

There are many precautions you can take against malaria without taking medication: use insect repellent—Deet usually does the job; use a mosquito net (make sure it's tucked into your mattress); wear long sleeves and pants; burn a coil; or—if you have the choice—stay in accommodations with a strong breeze. Most places also have mosquito netting covering windows and doors. In Toledo, there are Maya-based non-pharmaceutical repellents made by Western doctors, which are citronella-based, as well as copal cream for insect bites.

PACKING LIST

Belize is very laid-back and informal, so leave your suits and ball gowns behind! High heels are not really useful either. Loose, comfortable, casual clothes are best, and flip-flops or sandals. I recommend linen and thin cotton clothes. Of course, what you pack depends on where you are going. You probably won't use as much as you think! Your packing list will vary depending on the season (dry or wet) and the destination (by the sea and/or inland in jungles). The following list covers most areas.

CLOTHING AND ACCESSORIES

- A few T-shirts/blouses
- A few vests
- Hat
- Hiking boots and socks
- Hiking pants
- A knee-length skirt
- Light-weight, rain-proof jacket
- Light-weight slacks or jeans
- Light-weight sweater
- Sarong
- A long-sleeve shirt
- Shorts
- A sundress or two
- Swimwear
- Sunglasses
- Waterproof, sturdy sandals

SUNDRIES

- Alarm clock
- Anti-itch cream

- Antiseptic cream or gel
- Band-aids
- Binoculars
- Camera and battery charger
- Converter plug (if traveling from Europe)
- Favorite remedies for common problems
- Field country guides and maps
- Flashlight
- Insect repellent
- Phone charger
- Prescription medication
- Silica gel packets and ziplock bags
- Small, light-weight bag to carry things on a day trip
- Sunscreen and lip balm

OPTIONAL

- Laptop
- Mask, fins, snorkel, diving gear (these can be rented)
- Umbrella

WHAT TO PACK

If you take prescription medication, make sure you have enough with you to cover your stay and an extra supply. Other useful items include sunscreen, hat, sunglasses, after-sun cream for sunburn, anti-itching cream or gel for when you've been bitten, over-the-counter anti-diarrheal medication, pain killers, Band-aids, and antiseptic and antibiotic wipes or cream for cuts, as well as anything you normally take to treat existing conditions. While most of these items are available in shops in Belize, it's advisable to bring them from home. If you have any favorite cosmetics or brands, bring them with you, as the selection in Belize isn't very big.

TIME ZONE, ELECTRICITY, AND CURRENCY EXCHANGE

Belize is on Central Standard Time (CST), which is six hours behind Greenwich Mean Time (GMT).

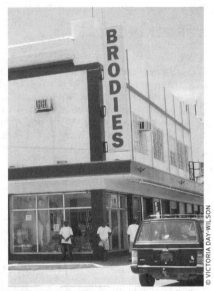
Brodies is a big department store in Belize City and Belmopan.

© VICTORIA DAY-WILSON

Belize does not observe Daylight Savings Time (DST) but Mexico does, so during the summer Belize is an hour earlier than Mexico, something worth bearing in mind if you are traveling through Mexico.

The main electrical supply is 110 volts AC with American-style two or three-pin sockets. Europeans will need to bring a plug adapter and possibly a transformer.

The U.S. dollar is pegged at 2:1 against the Belizean dollar and both currencies are used. You will find that sometimes you are given a combination of change in both currencies, and this is acceptable.

Arriving in Belize

AIRPORTS AND AIRLINES

Belize's international airport is Philip S. W. Goldson International Airport, located about 30 minutes outside Belize City in Ladyville. You can rent a car at the airport or take a taxi for the next leg of your journey, or you can fly. Domestic airlines, Tropic Air and Maya Island Air, offer regular flights to San Pedro and Caye Caulker from Belize City. Another option is to fly into Cancún, which is a popular choice because it is cheaper. You can charter flights from

Cancún to Belize City and the Cayes. Alternatively, you can catch a Mexican bus run by the ADO company which takes five hours to Chetumal, and from there you can either catch a taxi or a bus, which will stop at the border, and then at Corozal or just continue to Belize City where you can change buses for the direction you need. The Mexican buses and bus terminals are very clean and tidy, and the buses have such good air-conditioning that it gets cold on the bus—bring a sweater!

If you're coming from Europe or America the main feeder cities for Belize are in the United States and include Houston, Miami, and occasionally Charlotte and Atlanta. There are also flights from Toronto, Vancouver, and Montreal. Prices tend to go up during the high season (December–April). For travelers from Europe you need to fly through the United States and occasionally Canada, sometimes with a 24–48-hour stopover. If you fly into Mexico you will be given a green slip of paper called a Multiple Immigration Form (MIF). Look after it, as you will need to show it when you fly out of Mexico. Europeans will need an Electronic System for Travel Authorisation (ESTA) visa if you are traveling through the United States, and a machine-readable passport is essential. The ESTA can be obtained online or from an American embassy. Make sure there is enough time between connections because in the United States you will have to check out of immigration, collect your bags, and check back in again. This can be very time-consuming, particularly in Miami.

The main airlines which fly into Belize are American Airlines, Continental, Delta, US Airways, and El Salvador–based TACA. There are no direct flights to Belize from Europe, and flights are currently very expensive because the American airlines have a monopoly. There is talk of expanding the landing strip at Philip S. W. Goldson International Airport. An airport was built on the Placencia Peninsula, which will in theory be able to accommodate international flights—though when both runways will be complete is still undetermined. However, should they be completed, and if the Belizean government signs mutual agreements with other airlines, then there should be more flights to Belize, some may be direct, and the prices may come down a bit.

You can travel overland from the United States through Mexico (currently not recommended because of the drug cartel-related violence). The trip can take 3–4 days. You need a credit card to pay a bond to prove you won't sell your car (or any goods) in Mexico and additional insurance for your drive through the country. When crossing the Belizean border you may run into customs charges. U.S., Canadian, EU, South African, Australian, and New Zealand driving licenses are valid in Belize, but it's best to bring an international license. After six months in the country you should get a Belizean license.

WHEN TO GO

The most popular time to go to Belize is during the high season, which is roughly the same time as the dry season. Belize is hot and humid most of the year; there is little change in temperature. Prices for flights and accommodations go up during the high season. Peak times are around mid-December–January and Easter.

The rainy season is not a bad time to go, as prices are lower. Even though you will experience some magnificent rainstorms, there are many dry, sunny days too. The days can be very humid, which can be exhausting. The least rainfall is in the north of the country, increasing the farther south you go. During low season you will avoid crowds of tourists and save money, but roads may be hard to access, as are some caves. The sea and river water may become a bit murky as opposed to clear turquoise or just clear, respectively. There are more mosquitoes during the wet season. If you're thinking about moving to Belize it's best to experience the throng of tourists as well as the mosquitoes and rain. Try to stay there long enough that you spend time during both times of year or come back at a different time.

CURRENCY

Although Belize is cheap in comparison to North America, it is the most expensive country in Central America. You are bound to spend more than you anticipated. There is a 9 percent tax on hotel rooms, sometimes included in the price, as well as a separate 10 percent General Sales Tax (GST). To enter most national parks and reserves and some Mayan ruins you will need to pay a small fee.

If you're flying into Mexico, take some pesos with you. There are ATMs, but it's easier if you have cash in hand for expenses like taxis and accommodations. The ATMs will charge a handling fee if you draw money on your credit card. If you're flying into Belize make sure you have small denominations of U.S. dollars, as people often don't have change for larger notes.

It's easy to draw money from ATMs in most towns but, again, you will be charged a fee. If you're traveling off the beaten path make sure you have enough cash with you, as there may be no ATMs or credit card facilities. Major credit cards are accepted in most of the larger areas. To avoid surprises, check if prices are quoted in U.S. dollars or Belizean dollars.

FACT-FINDING CHECKLIST

The following are some points to consider when checking out Belize as your potential new home.

- Where in Belize would you like to live? This can be determined by simple preferences: Are you a sea person or do you prefer the jungle?

- Do you enjoy creature comforts? Do you need to live centrally or could you "rough it" off the grid?

- Are you gregarious? Do you have an active social life? If so, you may not want to be in a remote area or somewhere that is hard to access.

- Are you a practical hands-on type of person? Can you fix things and build things?

- What are your interests and hobbies? It helps to be self-sufficient and to have things to do that keep you engaged. This may also affect where you choose to live. For example, if you are a keen angler or diver, choose a place near the coast.

- Do you take prescription medication? Is it available and affordable in Belize?

- Are you happy with the medical facilities in Belize?

- If you have children, what do you think of the schools?

- If you are an animal lover, do you have pets that you'd like to take with you to Belize and would your pet adapt to Belize? A very thick coat, for example, might be uncomfortable for a pet here due to the heat and humidity. Alternatively, you can adopt a pet from the Humane Society; visit one of their branches in Belize.

- Shop in an average Belizean supermarket, check the prices, and the products. The selection is somewhat limited – can you live with that?

- Experience the roads, traffic, and Belizean driving. There are no four-lane highways and few traffic lights. Belizean driving is not the same as North American driving and can be a bit hair-raising.

- Do you spend much time in shopping malls, food courts, and cinemas? You won't find these in Belize. Can you live without them? Alternatively, could you live close to them? For example, if you live in Corozal near the border with Mexico you will have access to all of the above in Chetumal.

- If you're interested in volunteer work, take the opportunity to look into some of the options available.

- Take time to speak to Belizeans, try local food, read local newspapers, go to the market, ride a bus, and go to a festival or celebration to get a feel for the local culture.

CUSTOMS

This is pretty straightforward in Belize: Don't bring drugs, weapons, or ammunition with you. Although there is a level of drug trafficking and transiting in Belize, there is no tolerance if you are caught with drugs. You will be jailed and fined. Large amounts of money attract negative attention and will require explanations. On arriving in Belize, plant or animal products may be taken from you, and you may be taxed on packaged items that look new.

SECURITY

Petty theft is a problem in Belize. Don't leave valuables lying around or flash money about. Check the locks on your hotel door, and keep an eye on your bags. If you have valuables you are concerned about, you lock them up in a safe (most high-end resorts have safes).

In general it's considered safe for women to travel alone in Belize. Use common sense when out alone, and stick to well-lit areas at night.

COMMUNICATION

Public phones are prevalent, as are Internet cafés. Speed and reliability does vary though. If you are dialing a Belizean number from the United States, start with 011 and then 501, the country code for Belize. Once in Belize you only need to dial the seven-digit number.

If you want to get a Belizean phone number, you can buy a sim card from Smart or Belize Telecommunications Limited (BTL), the two main phone providers in the country. The BTL cards are called Digicell. In some areas service works well, in others service is unreliable. Urban areas are generally fine. But if you're outside of town you may have problems with reception, or even if you have good reception you will have difficulty making and receiving calls, and texts will sometimes bounce back. BTL tried to block Skype, so calling BTL numbers from Skype doesn't work very well either. Both phone providers have a variety of promotions. Once a month Digicell has an offer called "double-up." They will double any credit you pay up to $50, which they will triple. You will receive a text message when it's double-up time (usually mid-month).

TRANSPORTATION

Bear in mind that this isn't just a vacation. Don't only go to tourist haunts and expat joints. Get out and travel around; get familiar with Belize. If you are looking at property you will probably be going off the beaten track quite a lot,

© VICTORIA DAY-WILSON

San Pedro airport

so it's best to rent a four-wheel drive. Driving allows you to see the landscape and get a better feel for the country. There is fairly good, regular bus service in Belize, but it only travels down main highways and roads, and is slow. There are lots of flights all over Belize run by Tropic Air and Maya Island Air. This is a faster way to get around if you're short on time.

Sample Itineraries

ONE WEEK IN CAYO

This isn't a realistic period to do jungle and beach exploring. If you only have one week, it's best to focus on one area and then come back and check out another area. It takes more than a few days to get a feel for a place and explore. It also takes time and patience to look at properties. In-depth research will be very useful and save you time. Make sure you know the area well. Try to have a fairly clear idea of what you're looking for. Knowing what your budget is should help narrow down this process. Take into account that getting to know a place will be more tiring with the high temperatures and humidity. Explore the area on foot, speak to locals and expats, have a look at different shops, banks, health facilities, and restaurants, and read local newspapers. Take a trip on a local bus, try some Belizean food, and look at the prices and selection of items in shops. Most local store, bar, restaurant, and hotel owners are helpful and can offer a wealth of information. With the short timeframe, flying to your destination is best. But do try to drive around a bit to get a feel

driving into Santa Elena on the Western Highway

for the landscape, the roads, and the traffic. Different people will have different priorities; you should adjust this itinerary accordingly. For example, if you have children, make sure to check out the schools.

Day 1: Arrive in Belize City and rent a car at the airport. Ideally you will have prearranged this so the car is waiting for you. Drive up the Western Highway to San Ignacio. Check into your hotel.

Day 2: Meet up with a realtor (ideally you will have prearranged a few meetings before arrival in Belize). Check out the area between San Ignacio and Bullet Tree Village, and then go along the road to Benque at the border.

Day 3: Explore the road from San Ignacio to San Antonio, passing Cristo Rey.

Day 4: Drive down the Western Highway and up to the Pine Ridge (optional, as this area is very remote and there aren't many freehold properties available since most of it is part of a Forest Reserve). Or you could use this day to explore

Agricultural vehicles are common on the roads.

Placencia or spend a day wandering through the supermarkets, hospitals, banks, the market, shops, restaurants, and bars in San Ignacio.

Day 5: Travel down the Western Highway to Belmopan.

Day 6: Get up early and drive down the Hummingbird Highway. Continue to Placencia if you have the time.

Day 7: Return to Belize City to fly out.

TWO WEEKS

This itinerary covers quite a lot of Belize with the exception of Cayo and Toledo. It's a bit of a whirlwind tour, but will give you a feel for the coastal areas. Alternatively, if you have a clearer idea of which area you are interested in, this would be a good period to rent and to try and get a feel for the local community, and have a look around properties at a slightly slower pace. Details can become blurred when you look at too much too fast, so it is better to focus if you can.

Day 1: Arrive in Belize City. Fly to San Pedro on Ambergris Caye. Check into a hotel or condo. Stay somewhere central if you don't have much time. The Ambergris Caye website (http://ambergriscaye.com) is an excellent resource for this. Settle in and rent a golf cart. Find a realtor (ideally you would have set this up via email).

Day 2: Have a look around properties in San Pedro. Get your bearings. Look at grocery stores, bars, hospitals, banks, and restaurants. Buy a local paper.

Day 3: Explore properties on the northern part of the island.

Day 4: Explore the southern part of the island.

Day 5: Fly to Corozal. Meet with a realtor. Familiarize yourself with Corozal Town.

Day 6: Drive out to Consejo and have a look around.

Day 7: Travel to Progresso Lagoon and explore.

Day 8: Fly to Caye Caulker via San Pedro. Spend the rest of the day familiarizing yourself with the island.

Day 9: Travel to the southern tip of the island and to the north (if you want to see it—it is still very undeveloped).

Day 10: Fly to Dangriga; rent a car. Check out the basic amenities in Dangriga and head for Hopkins.

Day 11: Explore the Sittee River area.

Day 12: Drive to Riversdale at the tip of the Placencia Peninsula and continue down to Placencia Village.

Day 13: Have a look at Placencia Village and the Peninsula.

Day 14: Fly to Belize City and head home.

© VICTORIA DAY-WILSON

boats moored on the Sittee River

ONE MONTH

If you can get away for a month, this is the ideal amount of time to spend fact-finding. Again, if you know which area you're interested in, this gives you the opportunity to spend a chunk of time here. Alternatively, you could split your time up between two different places, for example, Cayo and the Cayes, or Corozal and Placencia. This itinerary also gives you two days of flexibility if you want to stay somewhere a little longer.

Day 1: Arrive in Belize City. Rent a car and drive to Corozal Town.

Day 2: Meet with a realtor. Familiarize yourself with Corozal Town.

Day 3: Drive to Consejo and have a look around.

Day 4: Travel to Progresso Lagoon and have a look there.

Day 5: You could pop over the border to see what the shopping is like in Chetumal, as this is one of the reasons people choose to live in Corozal, or you could take it easy and revisit a place you really liked.

Day 6: Take your time in the Corozal area.

Day 7: Fly or take a water taxi to San Pedro. Get your bearings. Look at grocery stores, bars, hospitals, banks, and restaurants. Buy a local paper.

Day 8: Have a look around properties in San Pedro.

Day 9: Explore properties on the northern part of the island.

Day 10: Explore the southern part of the island.

Day 11: Take a water taxi to Caye Caulker. Spend the rest of the day familiarizing yourself with the island.

Day 12: Travel to the southern tip of the island and to the north (if you want to see it—it is still very undeveloped).

Day 13: Take a water taxi to Belize City. Take some time to wander around Belize City and look at major shops and attractions. Spend some time at the Belize Zoo. Drive up the Western Highway to San Ignacio.

Day 14: Meet with a realtor (ideally you will have prearranged a few meetings before arrival in Belize). Check out the area between San Ignacio and Bullet Tree Village, and then go along the road to Benque at the border.

Day 15: Explore the road from San Ignacio to San Antonio, passing Cristo Rey.

Day 16: Drive down the Western Highway and up to the Pine Ridge (optional, as this area is very remote and there aren't many freehold properties available since most of it is part of a Forest Reserve). Or, you could spend a day exploring supermarkets, hospitals, banks, the market, shops, restaurants, and bars in San Ignacio and head up to Spanish Lookout to have a look around their stores. It's the main place people head for hardware supplies.

Day 17: Travel down the Western Highway to Belmopan. Have a look at properties along the road and in Belmopan. Visit the shops in Belmopan, as some are larger and have more variety than in San Ignacio.

Day 18: Get up early and drive down the Hummingbird Highway to Dangriga. Check out basic amenities in Dangriga and head for Hopkins.

Day 19: Explore Hopkins.

Day 20: Have a look around the Sittee River area.

© VICTORIA DAY-WILSON

a supermarket in Placencia

Day 21: Have a look around False Sittee Point.

Day 22: Drive to Riversdale at the tip of the Placencia Peninsula and continue down to Placencia Village.

Day 23: Explore Placencia Village.

Day 24: Visit properties and developments on the Placencia Peninsula.

Days 25-29: Leave these days to look into personal priorities (such as schools), spend longer in an area you really liked, go back to see a property or two, enjoy some of Belize's sights, or rest.

Day 30: Fly to Belize City and home.

Practicalities

There tends to be a quick turnover of resorts and restaurants in Belize so before you go out, take some time to look at accommodations and places to eat on the Internet. There is a lot of variety and it saves time to make a short list of places you think suit you. You will find prices vary between high season and low season. You can also check sites like Trip Advisor for supplemental information—I take those sites with a pinch of salt because views are not impartial, but they give you a rough guideline. It's tempting to stay in beautiful beach and jungle resorts if you have the budget. But it's far more practical to stay centrally located in towns in each area so that it's easy to drive to outlying areas to look at properties and quick to shop, eat, or wander around town. It also gives you a better feel for real life in that area.

CHOOSING YOUR ACCOMMODATIONS

Your choice of accommodation will depend on your budget, length of stay, and how you are spending your time. If you are rushing around the country for a week, then a hotel may be more practical since it provides regular meals. If you do stay in a hotel, try to eat out at least a few times. There are a variety of hotels for different budgets, but they are all usually more expensive than B&Bs or guesthouses. Budget B&Bs and guesthouses, although very basic (for example, often lacking hot water, which you don't need most of the year anyway, and sometimes with shared bathrooms), are usually clean. They don't supply meals and very rarely have cooking facilities; this means you end up eating out all the time, which can add up. In the end, it's probably worth it to pay a bit more for a place that at least includes breakfast.

Renting is by far the best option: It gives you more freedom and space, and is the closest to actually living in your area. Finding rentals is tricky, as they are often word of mouth. A few websites are included here and if you speak with a realtor, they may be able to advise you as well. Make sure to interact with the local population, go shopping, and do some basic cooking (you can eat out some nights if you're tired).

FOOD AND DRINK

Water is generally clean with the exception of Caye Caulker. However, in order to avoid any problems, it's best to buy bottled water. Try some local food. This may involve buying BBQ chicken off the side of the road or meat pies from a vendor—don't worry, it is delicious and you are unlikely to get ill. If you are renting and doing your own food shopping, buy local brands; don't buy the expensive imported ones that you may recognize from home—that's when Belize becomes expensive. Try local brands, many are good, and find your favorite. There are no fast food outlets in Belize; you have to go to Chetumal for that. The closest you will get to fast food is buying food from local vendors on the street. With the exception of a few high-end restaurants and some exclusive hotel dining options, restaurants in Belize follow the culture: They are probably more basic than you may be used to and less fancy, with simple décor.

COROZAL
Accommodations

Almond Tree Hotel Resort (425 Bayshore Dr., South End, Corozal, tel. 628-9224 or 628-9224 [Intl], info@almondtreeresort.com, www.almondtreeresort.com, US$85–300) is a beautiful, upscale place with very helpful owners.

Tony's Inn (South End, Corozal Town, tel. 422-2055 or 800/447-2931, tonys@btl.net, www.tonysinn.com, US$75–105 high season, US$65–95 low season) is a nice, friendly, and popular place to stay. The restaurant, Y Not Grill, is very good.

Copa Banana Guesthouse (409 Bay Shore Dr., South End, Corozal Town, tel. 422-0284, relax@copabanana.bz, www.copabanana.bz, US$55/day or US$350/week) is a good, budget option with a shared kitchen. There is also an option to rent an apartment. The owners run a real estate business.

Las Palmas Hotel (123 5th Ave., Corozal Town, tel. 422-0196 or 602-5186, info@laspalmashotelbelize.com, www.laspalmashotelbelize.com, US$45–75) is conveniently located in the center of town and has reasonable prices. The hotel also has an option to rent out an accommodation for a minimum of a month.

Mirador Hotel (4th Ave. and 1st St. South, Corozal Town, tel. 422-0189, info@mirador.bz, http://mirador.bz, US$30–90), owned by a local business couple, is in the center of Corozal Town.

Dining

Corozo Blue's Restaurant Bar (South End, on the bay, tel. 422-0090, corozoblues@yahoo.com) is a new restaurant, which opened in 2011 at the south end of town on the bay. It serves breakfast, lunch, and dinner. The restaurant has a brick pizza oven and the food and service are good.

Patty's Bistro (4th Ave., Corozal Town, tel. 402-3796) serves good, affordable combinations of Belizean, Mexican, and American food.

Purple Toucan (52 4th Ave., Corozal Town, tel. 603-0266) is a place where expats meet up for lunch, usually on the second Tuesday of the month. Is serves good Mexican food, which can be quite spicy.

Scotty's Bar and Grill (17 G St. North, Corozal Town, tel. 422-0005) offers delicious hamburgers and pizza, as well as sandwiches, beer, and drinks. Scotty's Bar sometimes has live music and darts competitions.

In the heart of Consejo village, **Millenium Restaurant** (Consejo Village center, no phone) serves excellent food. There is a variety of seafood and the proprietor is very friendly.

CAYO

Cayo District is big with most properties outside of town and off the beaten path. Therefore, it is best to stay somewhere central, like in San Ignacio or Santa Elena (just across the river; the two are more like one town separated by the Macal River). If you do move to the area, this is where you will do most of your regular errands, so you may as well get to know the town while you have the chance. If you are not renting a car at the airport you can take a taxi or a bus to San Ignacio. Alternatively, some hotel packages offer airport pickup, as do PACZ tours and other operators in the area.

Accommodations

For rentals, have a look at www.redroofpropertymanagement.com/property.

San Ignacio Hotel (18 Buena Vista St., San Ignacio, tel. 824-2125 or 824-2034, reservations@sanignaciobelize.com, www.sanignaciobelize.com, US$150–300 high season, US$135–300 low season) lies on one of the hills in San Ignacio with a beautiful view of the valley. It's a 5–10-minute walk into the heart of town. It's the most fashionable hotel in San Ignacio and offers all the trappings of a high-end hotel. Local expats will go here occasionally as a special treat.

© VICTORIA DAY-WILSON

Burns Avenue in San Ignacio, Cayo District

The Aguada (Aguada St., Santa Elena, tel. 804-3609, aguada@btl.net, www.aguadahotel.com, US$40–65 for a double) is a clean hotel with modern amenities; it's more mid-range compared to the San Ignacio. You will need to take a taxi or use a car to get into central San Ignacio from here.

Casa Blanca Guest House (10 Burns Ave., San Ignacio, tel. 824-2080, casablanca@btl.net, bettyguerra01@yahoo.com, www.casablancaguesthouse.com, US$20–50), in central San Ignacio, won Belize's "Best Small Hotel" award. It's a convenient place to be right in the middle of things.

Martha's Guest House (10 West St., San Ignacio, tel. 804-3647, marthasguesthouse@gmail.com, www.marthasbelize.com, US$60–80), in the center of San Ignacio, will give you a real feel for the town, as it's easy to wander around town from here. Martha's has a reputation of being a home away from home.

Cahal Pech Village (Cahal Pech Rd., San Ignacio, tel. 824-3740, info@cahalpech.com, cahalpechresort@gmail.com, www.cahalpech.com/, US$79–119) lies farther up the hills in San Ignacio, in an area called Cahal Pech, but is still in the town.

Dining

Serendib (27 Burns Ave., tel. 824-2302), in the center of town on one of the busiest streets, is a good place to get a meal and either watch the streetlife from the front or relax in the garden in the back.

Pops (West St., tel. 824-3366), across from Martha's, is also in the center of town. This is a good place to try some Belizean cooking.

© VICTORIA DAY-WILSON

The market in San Ignacio (Cayo District) on Saturdays is popular.

Mr. Greedy's Pizzeria (34 Burns Ave., tel. 804-4688), in the middle of town, serves the best watermelon juice (very refreshing on a hot day!) and has good pizza. Expats, tourists, and local guides hang out here and keep the place busy. There is also free wireless service.

Hode's Place Bar & Grill (Savannah Rd.), a popular hangout with expats, is near the Macal River, just a bit farther on from the market. It is bigger than it looks and has a pleasant garden and a play area for children.

Corkers Wine Bar & Restaurant (top floor, Hibiscus Plaza, Belmopan, tel. 822-0400 or 633-5323, info@corkersbelize.com, www.corkersbelize.com) is a lovely, centrally-located, breezy, open place to stop for a meal or a drink in Belmopan.

Wolf's Burger Restaurant (near Blackman Eddy Village btwn. Mile 56 and 57 on the Western Highway, tel. 605-4640, www.belize24.de) has the best burgers ever and is a great place to stop for a meal if you're dashing around looking at properties in the area and missed lunch.

THE CAYES

There are a variety of accommodation options in different locations in the Cayes. There are some stylish resorts in San Pedro, though most of them are to the south or the north of town. It's best to stay in San Pedro so you get a feel for the town. If you're pressed for time, stay in a hotel. But if you are not in a rush, stay in a condo so that you can sample what it's like to live here (for example, going grocery shopping).

© VICTORIA DAY-WILSON

Water taxis leave for the Cayes from the Marine Terminal in Belize City.

Ambergris Caye Accommodations

Blue Tang Inn (Barrier Reef Dr., tel. 226-2326 or US/CAN toll free 866/881-1020, www.bluetanginn.com, US$159–219 high season, US$99–179 low season), a three-story hotel on the beach, is centrally located in San Pedro. A variety of accommodations are offered with kitchens. There is a pool on the premises.

Belizean Reef Suites (Coconut Dr., tel. 226-2582 or 330/544-4302, reservations@belizeanreef.com, www.belizeanreef.com, US$160–385 per night for a four-night stay) are condos, ideally situated in the middle of town on the seafront with a beautiful view. Bars, restaurants, supermarkets, and banks are all within walking distance. There is no swimming pool, but just down the beach is a swimming area next to Ramon's Village, as well as piers to dive off. The condos are clean, tidy, and well run. There is a maid and full washing facilities. You can book for a minimum of four nights, and there are discounts if you stay for five nights or more.

Spindrift Hotel (Barrier Reef Dr., tel. 226-2174 or 226-2018, spinhotel@btl.net or spindrifthotel@yahoo.com, http://ambergriscaye.com/spindrift/, US$53–150) is in the center of town on the beach. Spindrift rooms are more of a budget option and vary from economy to patio to beachfront.

Stylish, beautiful, and luxurious, **Victoria House** (tel. 226-2067, toll free 800/247-5159 or 713/344-234, info@victoria-house.com, www.victoria-house.com, US$215–1,995 high season, US$185–1,615 low season) is an award-winning, gorgeous hotel on the beach south of town. There are villas, thatched cabanas, suites, and rooms. Prices vary depending on the package or type of accommodation.

SunBreeze Hotel (Coconut Dr., tel. 226-2191 or 226-2345 or US/CAN toll free 800/688-0191, sunbreezehotel@sunbreeze.net, www.sunbreeze.net, US$170–225 high season, US$140–195 low season) is on the beach in the center of San Pedro. The SunBreeze has a wonderful pool and an excellent restaurant.

Ambergris Caye Dining

Centrally located in San Pedro, **Estel's-by-the-Sea** (Barrier Reef Dr., tel. 226-2019, chazzwor@yahoo.com, http://ambergriscaye.com/estels) is by the sea. There is a veranda for dining or you can eat on the beach. A simple place with a sand-covered floor, this place has loads of charm. The menu is varied, breakfast is delicious, and the staff are helpful.

From humble beginnings in 1974, **Elvi's Kitchen** (Pescador Dr., tel. 226-2176 or 226-2404, elvi@btl.net, reservations@elviskitchen.com, info@elviskitchen.com, www.elviskitchen.com) has grown and offers a varied menu with good food and good service.

Wild Mango's (Barrier Reef Dr., tel. 226-2859) offers good food on the beach by an award-winning chef. Latin-Caribbean dishes with a twist and seafood are served here. The ceviche is good.

Blue Water Grill (Coconut Dr., tel. 226-3347, info@bluewatergrillbelize.com, http://bluewatergrillbelize.com) is located at the SunBreeze Hotel overlooking the beach. This is one of the best restaurants in town, serving seafood with a good wine list. Pasta and pizza are also available, and sometimes sushi.

At **Fido's Restuarant and Bar** (18 Barrier Reef Dr., tel. 226-2056 or 226-3176, info@fidosbelize.com, http://fidosbelize.com) there is a variety of food, but the chef specializes in Japanese food using Belizean seafood. You'll be spoiled for choice at this large restaurant on the beach in central San Pedro. There is live music every night, a Belizean Art Shop, and a jewelry shop.

Caye Caulker Accommodations

Caye Caulker Casita (Front St., tel. 226-0547 or 622 3608, amandabadger@gmail.com, www.cayecaulkercasita.com, US$75–120 per night, US$500–1,195 per week) features a variety of beautifully built and decorated, self-catering accommodations around a small pool, set in a beautiful tropical garden. Prices vary depending on season, type, and size of accommodation. There is a minimum stay of three nights, or five nights for the larger accommodations.

Iguana Reef Inn (tel. 226-0213, iguanareef@btl.net, www.iguanareefinn.com, US$145–425) offers luxury accommodations on the seashore with a pool. There is a penthouse with a kitchen.

Not far from the Split, **Caye Reef** (Front St., tel. 226-0382 or 610-0240,

© VICTORIA DAY-WILSON

Signs show distances to major cities across the world from Caye Caulker.

escape@cayereef.com, www.cayer-eef.com, US$105–240) targets a home-away-from-home feeling with comfortable rental condos, which include all modern amenities and a pool.

Located in the southern part of town, a short walk from the center, **Barefoot Beach Belize** (tel. 226-0205, barefootbeachbelize@gmail.com, www.barefootbeachbelize.com, US$49–145) is clean, colorful, and has its own pier with hammocks for relaxing. There are rooms and suites. The cottage, bungalow, and cabana have kitchens and are fully equipped with all amenities.

Built round a pool, **Seaside Cabanas** (tel. 226-0498, info@seaside-cabanas.com, www.seasidecabanas.com, US$84–169) is on the sea front in the center of town. It has its own bar.

Caye Caulker Dining

The Rainbow Bar and Grill (tel. 226-0281), on the beach about halfway up between the dock and the Split, is the only restaurant built over the water, catching the wonderful breezes. It mainly serves fresh, grilled seafood.

Femi's Café & Lounge (Front St., tel. 622-3469, www.aguallos.com/femis-cafe), north of the dock closer to the Split, is a lovely restaurant on the beach. Some tables have swings—what a great idea! The menu features a mixture of traditional fare, Mexican food, and seafood, and the food is excellent and a very good value. Look for the specials on the blackboard.

Havana Nights (on the beach in front of Popeye's Resort, no phone), south of the dock, is a wonderful restaurant. Prices are reasonable, service is excellent, and the food is delicious. There is usually a buffet if you can't make up your mind over the menu. There are great vibes at night with Cuban live music and wonderful atmosphere.

Syd's Restaurant (Middle St., tel. 206-0294) serves very good Belizean and Mexican food at great prices. While it's not on the beach, there is a shaded patio at the front with tables.

Habaneros (just south of the front dock, tel. 226-0487) is more upscale than the others and serves good, international cuisine with a good wine list.

STANN CREEK
Hopkins Accommodations

All Seasons Guest House (Village Rd., Hopkins Village, tel. 523-7209, ingrid@allseasonsbelize.com, www.allseasonsbelize.com, US$75–89 per night, US$400–500 per week, US$1,200–1,500 per month), located at the south end of the village, is a small, pleasant place to stay. There are also fully-furnished apartments with all amenities.

Hopkins Inn (Hopkins Village, tel. 523-7283, hopkinsinn@btl.net, www. hopkinsinn.com, US$50–100) is a B&B on the beach with breakfast included. The owners know a lot about the area.

Tipple Tree Beya (on the beachfront in Hopkins Village, tel. 520-7006, http://tippletreebelize.com/, US$30–60) is a good value, with simple and clean rooms in a wooden building near the south end of the village.

Beaches and Dreams Hotel (south end of Hopkins Village, tel. 523-7259 or 635-3996, vacation_belize@yahoo.com, www.beachesanddreams.com, US$75–119) has various wooden cabins in different layouts as well as a great restaurant with amazing food.

Hopkins Dining

Baracuda Bar and Grill (south end of Hopkins Village, tel. 523-7259 or 635-

© VICTORIA DAY-WILSON

a house by the sea close to the Sittee River, Stann Creek

3996, vacation_belize@yahoo.com, www.beachesanddreams.com) is the excellent restaurant at Beaches and Dreams Hotel.

Thongs Café (in the center of Hopkins Village, tel. 662-0110) is a great café with basic food.

Chef Rob's Gourmet Café (south end of Hopkins Village, tel. 670-0445 or 670-1529) has very good food and an à la carte menu. You can't miss the red car sign!

Innie's (southern part of Hopkins Village, tel. 523-7026) is a simple place to try good, local dishes.

Iris Restaurant (near the southern end of Hopkins Village, tel. 664-1410) serves good food in simple surroundings.

Placencia Accommodations

South Waters Resort (Palms Row, Placencia, tel. 620-7320 or 630-8555, southwatersresort@yahoo.com, www.southwatersresort.com, US$85–200), operated by a Belizean family, is on the south beach, close to the dock. You can either rent condo apartments or beach cabanas. The Crows Nest Cafe, Bar, and Grill located on the premises is good, too.

Ranguana Lodge (Placencia, tel. 523-3112, ranguana@btl.net, www.ranguanabelize.com, US$85–90) is set in a lovely garden on the beach in the center of the village.

Miramar Apartments (Placencia, tel. 523-3658, info@miramarbelize.com, http://miramarbelize.com/, US$125–235 high season, US$105–215 low season) offers beautiful, self-catering apartments on the beach in the center of Placencia Village. Rentals are for a minimum of 30 days.

Chabil Mar (Peninsula Rd., Placencia, tel. 523-3606 or US/CAN toll free 866/417-2377, reservations@chabilmarvillas.com, www.chabilmarvillas.com, US$375–650 high season, US$250–575 low season) is a beautiful, boutique resort a short walk from Placencia, with fully equipped villas. Villas vary in location, size, and layout. A minimum stay of two nights is required in the low season (May–Nov.), three nights during the high season (mid-Jan.–Mar. and mid- to late-Apr.), and four nights during peak season (Dec.–mid-Jan. and early- to mid-Apr.).

Seaspray Hotel (Placencia Village, tel. 523-3148, seasprayhotel.placencia-bz@gmail.com, seasprayhotel_belize@yahoo.com, info@seasprayhotel.com, www.seasprayhotel.com, US$25–65) is a good budget option. This hotel has something for everyone, ranging from economy rooms to cabanas with kitchenettes. The owners also have other rentals. It is located on the beach in the center of Placencia and has its own restaurant, De Tatch.

© VICTORIA DAY-WILSON

houses with a view of the sea along Placencia's famous sidewalk

Placencia Dining

De Viners (Placencia Village, tel. 666-1777, devinersbelize@gmail.com), on the beach, in the center of the village, is a British bar and restaurant, which serves delicious food with a twist and exotic cocktails. It has interesting decor and quirky charm. Sit down in one of their bar chairs and you may never leave!

Rumfish y Vino (Placencia Village, tel. 523/3293, rumfish@btl.net, blog rumfishyvino.blogspot.com, www.rumfishyvino.com) is a gastro-bar started by New Yorkers on the second floor of a wooden building with a veranda. Tapas and seafood are served and there's a good wine list.

Just off the sidewalk in a garden on the beach, **Pickled Parrot and Bar** (Placencia Village, tel. 624-2651, pickledparrotbz@yahoo.com, www.pickledparrot-belize.com) is under a thatched roof and serves a delicious variety of food.

Maya Beach Hotel Bistro (Maya Beach, Placencia, tel. 520-8040, info@mayabeachhotel.com, www.mayabeachhotel.com/restaurant.html) serves a combination of traditional dishes with a Belizean twist. The bistro is considered one of Belize's best eateries.

French Connection (Placencia Village, tel. 523-3656, www.frenchconnection.bz) is an upscale French restaurant in the center of the village, serving imaginative continental cuisine.

De Tatch (Placencia Village, tel. 503-3385, seaspray@btl.net, www.seasprayhotel.com/deTatch/index.html), part of the Seaspray Hotel, is an open air restaurant on the beach, just north of the center of town. De Tatch features a Caribbean menu with a great breakfast and a relaxed, laid-back atmosphere.

TOLEDO
Accommodations

With a beautiful view across the sea, **BlueBelize** (139 Front St., Punta Gorda, tel. 722-2678, info@bluebelize.com, www.bluebelize.com, US$75–135) has several one- and two-bedroom apartments with kitchenettes and fully equipped with all modern facilities. Rates vary depending on the size of the apartment.

Sea Front Inn (Punta Gorda, tel. 722-2300, office@seafrontinn.com, www.seafrontinn.com, rooms: US$65–80, apartments: US$375–475 for 2 weeks, US$563–713 for 3 weeks, US$750–1,250 for 4 weeks) lies on the bay in the northern part of Punta Gorda and has 14 animal-themed rooms in landscaped gardens, and a restaurant. All rooms are different. They also have one-bedroom apartments, of which some have full facilities for an extended stay.

Beautifully renovated **Coral House Inn** (151 Main St., Punta Gorda, tel. 722-2878, info@coralhouseinn.com, www.coralhouseinn.com, US$90–100) is the color of coral and is full of unique personal touches, set in a tropical garden with a pool and a bar. There is sea access and four rooms, tastefully decorated with local materials. The inn lies at the southern end of Punta Gorda. Just up the road from Coral House Inn, overlooking the sea, lies Sea Glass Cottage, which can be rented for a longer period (US$125 for up to 3 nights, US$112 for 4–7 nights, US$100 for 8+ nights).

Hickatee Cottages (Ex-Servicemen Rd., Punta Gorda, tel. 662-4475, cottages@hickatee.com, www.hickatee.com, US$75–120 high season, US$75–110 low season) lies a mile outside town on the inland side. There are four cottages, each with a different layout, settled in 20 acres of jungle. The food is good and there's a small pool and bar, as well as a butterfly farm.

Beya Suites (No. 6 Hopeville, Punta Gorda Town, tel. 722-2188 or 722-2956, www.beyasuites.com, US$66–112), winner of the BTB "Small Hotel of the Year" award, lies north of the center of town. It has a variety of rooms and suites, which have modern amenities, some with kitchens or cooking facilities.

Dining

Marian's Bayview Restaurant (76 Front St., Punta Gorda, tel. 722-0129) lies at the south end of Punta Gorda, at the top of a three-story building. The view over the Bay of Honduras is simply breathtaking. Service is excellent and the traditional Belizean East Indian fare and seafood is delicious.

Bamboo Chicken (Front St., Punta Gorda, no phone), close to the southern end of the town at the beginning of the swimming dock, has a distinctive blue color. It has a bar and seating inside, as well as a wonderful veranda overlooking the water. The menu features a variety of delicious food, from traditional choices with a local twist to seafood.

Grace's Restaurant (Main St., Punta Gorda), opposite the BTL office and just up from Mel's Grocery, serves very good Belizean food.

Earth Runnin's and Bukut Bar (Main Middle St., Punta Gorda, tel. 702-2007, bukutbar@hotmail.com) serves Belizean food with some international options. Live music is played here.

Emery's Restaurant (a block off Front St., tel. 702-2929) serves delicious Belizean food and seafood. The service is good as well.

DAILY LIFE

MAKING THE MOVE

At this point you should be considering what official status you want in Belize. If you choose the visitor permit route, you can stay as long as you wish and leave whenever you like with no ties. If you decide that you want to leave Belize, you can do so without ever having invested time in pursuing residency. If you decide to stay, you can get the ball rolling on your permanent residency as soon as the first 12 months are up. After five years, you can apply for citizenship. There are plenty of useful perks if you decide to come as part of the Qualified Retired Person (QRP) Program. Of course, marriage is another option; if you marry a Belizean you can apply for citizenship after one year.

If you have children, you'll need to consider how they will adapt to the new culture and environment. If you're moving with pets, you'll need to contact the Belize Agricultural Health Authority (BAHA) to get the proper forms and requirements for bringing your pet into the country.

One of your final considerations before making the move is what to take with you. There is much available in Belize, but specialty items may not be accessible.

© VICTORIA DAY-WILSON

If there is something you just can't live without, you'll want to bring it with you. Then you'll need to figure out the best way to get all your stuff here.

Immigration and Visas

Moving to Belize is pretty straightforward in that North Americans and Europeans are not required to obtain visas. There are three options to remain in the country. One is to renew your visitor permit every month for a year. This leaves your status rather flexible. You're allowed to rent housing during this period; however, you are not allowed to work—paid or unpaid. In order to work you need to obtain a work permit. The type of permit you require and the type of permit you will receive are directly related to the work you want to do. Some industries are closed to non-Belizeans in order to maintain employment for citizens. Your second option is to apply for permanent residency after a year in the country. This will enable you to work without a work permit and to travel in and out of the country without any restrictions, and after five years you can apply for citizenship. The third option is to come as part of the Qualified Retired Person (QRP) Program, which is controlled by the Belize Tourist Board (BTB).

Which option you choose depends on your circumstances, objectives, and priorities. If you are younger than 45, perhaps with a family, then the permanent resident route opens up options, such as working or running a business in Belize (easier said than done!). You are virtually treated as a citizen. On the other hand, if you are over 45, retired, or in a position to retire, with a proven income of at least US$24,000 a year, you should consider the QRP option, one of the most tax-efficient programs in the region. If you still haven't quite made up your mind and want to give Belize a trial run for a year—time and finances permitting—then the visitor permit option is a good choice with few strings attached. It gives you the flexibility to return home if you feel Belize isn't for you, or it puts you in a position to apply for permanent residency or enter the QRP program, if you'd like to make Belize your home—either full-time or for part of the year.

BELIZE TOURIST PERMIT

After entering Belize (whether as a tourist, on a fact-finding trip, or as a new immigrant), you will be issued a 30-day tourist permit—this is not the same as a visa. North American countries, EU countries, and CARICOM States do not require visas to enter Belize. This is stamped in your passport.

the Department of Immigration in Belmopan

© VICTORIA DAY-WILSON

VISITOR PERMIT AND RENEWAL

Once the first 30 days are up, go to your nearest Department of Immigration office. Try to arrive early in the morning to skip the long lines. You will meet with an immigration officer; explain that you would like an extension on your tourist visa. They sometimes casually flip through your passport and ask how long you are staying and where. Be polite and formal at all times. You will then be given a note indicating the amount you need to pay. Go to the cashier, hand over the note and the money, and you will receive a receipt that you take back to the immigration officer and they stamp your passport. Check your dates carefully because they often add up to 29 days, not 30. Bring another form of ID with you, and an air ticket if you have one. They rarely ask for these, but it's better to be safe than sorry. And that's it—you're free to stay in Belize for another month! Renewing your stamp is very important, as failure to do so will result in a BZ$1,500 fine. This fine can vary. It may be less if you've forgotten and just run over a few days, but it's best not to find out! You can go through this process for six months at BZ$50 renewal fee per month. After six months, the fee rises to BZ$100 per month. When the 12 months are over you can apply for residency.

REQUIREMENTS FOR PERMANENT RESIDENCY

This is a list of documents required to apply for permanent residency which you must present to the Department of Immigration in Belmopan.

- Birth certificates for all applicants
- A completed application form
- A current work permit or trade license (if applicable)
- Documentary evidence that you bought land in Belize or have access to land (if applicable)
- A financial statement proving adequate funds or income to sustain yourself (and your dependents)
- Income tax statement
- Marriage/declaration of support and/or divorce certificates (if applicable)
- A medical examination form (which you can get from any Department of Immigration office). The exam must be performed in Belize and test for HIV and VDRL; include the original test results with the form. Any local doctor can perform the exam on the whole family.
- A police record for everyone in the family over the age of 16. This is best provided by a police station in the vicinity where you have lived for the last six months. This can only be obtained after being in Belize six months. It is in the form of a report, which costs BZ$15 to order, and you will need two passport-size pictures to go along with the application. The report can take at least a month, so try and order it a couple of months before your 12 months are up.
- Three color passport photos of you, your spouse, and children (if applicable)
- Two character references from Belizeans who have known you for at least one year. These individuals are usually ministers, registered doctors, attorneys, the head of a government department, or a justice of the peace.
- Your passport along with photocopies of all pages (evidence that you have been in the country legally for one year prior to application)

COST

The cost varies from US$250–5,000, depending on your nationality. The Permanent Resident Card costs US$150 per person. Other costs include travel to Belmopan, postage, and couriers.

- Citizens from Canada: US$2,500.
- Citizens from European countries: US$2,000.
- Citizens from the United States: US$1,000.

OFFICIAL PERMANENT RESIDENT

In theory, applying for Belizean permanent residency sounds like a fairly straightforward process. And, in some cases it is. In others, it is frustrating and time consuming. It's necessary to make several trips to the Department of Immigration in Belmopan to check on the progress of your application and to attend various appointments.

Pros and Cons

Once you have obtained permanent resident status, there are several benefits: you can seek employment or work for yourself; get a Belizean driver's license; and you can vote in local elections. Obtaining permanent residency is open to anyone, regardless of age, and with it comes a one-time, tax- and duty-free entry of household effects (not including a car, boat, or airplane). The downside is that it can be a costly, time-consuming, bureaucratic, and frustrating process. Having said that, some people do secure it within months, while others are still waiting after a year. Once you have your permanent residency, you can obtain citizenship within five years.

Process

In the run-up to being granted permanent residency, including the first 12 months, you may only leave the country for 14 consecutive days. The application is usually carried out in the name of the husband (in the case of a family), and the same supporting documents must be handed in for the whole family. These are kept together in a file. You will need to provide originals and copies. All forms for your application can be obtained from the Department of Immigration. A final decision will be made when all the requirements are met. While you are waiting for a decision, you need to continue applying for monthly extensions at your closest immigration office. The Department of Immigration says that the process of approval usually takes 8–12 weeks to complete, depending on their workload. If you change address during this period, inform the Department of Immigration immediately. The entire process is carried out at the Department of Immigration in Belmopan. Once residency has been granted you will need to register with the Income Tax Department.

QUALIFIED RETIRED PERSONS (QRP)

The Retired Persons (Incentives) Act was introduced by the People's United Party (PUP) in 1999 and is generally known as the Qualified Retired Persons (QRP) Program. The concept behind it was to create a package which would make retiring in Belize an attractive offer, and thus encourage and increase the volume of people who move to Belize and settle here, earning the government extra income at the same time.

Benefits

The QRP package is not that different from permanent residency, but it does have some additional advantages, such as importing personal effects to Belize with a nominal worth of US$15,000 and means of transport tax- and duty-free. This must occur within a year of officially entering the program. After that, you will have to pay duties and taxes on what you bring in. It also allows participants in the program to earn an income outside of Belize exempt of levies and taxes, regardless of whether the income is from an investment or work performed. People in the QRP are only required to live in Belize one month every year.

Pros and Cons

QRPs may not work in Belize but may stay indefinitely. Their status is similar to that of non-residents, which has other benefits if you have interests in international financial services, including the Offshore Banking Act, the Trusts Act, and the International Business Companies (IBC) Act, which states that people who live in Belize (as residents) may not benefit from such financial services. But if you come in under the QRP program you are technically a non-resident, so you can retire in Belize and continue with your offshore business. The downside is that you still have to pay tourist exit taxes when leaving the country. If you would like to work in Belize, you need to apply for the permanent resident option and not the QRP Program.

To qualify for the QRP, you need to demonstrate an income of US$2,000 per month, which must be paid into a Belizean bank. The income can be an annuity or a pension, which has been generated outside Belize. If you are a couple, you apply as one and therefore the total is US$2,000, not US$4,000. Anyone above the age of 45 qualifies for the program and dependents can be included in the application. Dependents include spouses and children under the age of 18. Anyone up to the age of 23 who is enrolled in a university also qualifies. If a company has granted the pension, the company must prove that they have been in operation for at least 20 years by submitting proof of registration and they must certify that a pension of no less than US$2,000 will be paid on a monthly basis into a Belizean bank. A manager, president, or legal representative of the company must sign this document. Certification of these details is also required by a certified public accountant independent of the company. Two bank references from the company are also required and a document outlining the company's pension scheme. The Ministry of National Security will run a background check on the applicant. Cars shouldn't be older than three years to qualify for duty exemption. Light aircraft are allowed if they weigh less than 17,000 kg and, of course, a valid Private Pilot License (PPL) is required. This can be obtained from the Civil Aviation Department, or the same department can validate an existing license. Any boat is allowed as long as it is for personal use. If you sell any of your items, you will be subject to all taxes and duties.

Requirements

These are very similar to the permanent resident requirements, except that they are processed by the Belize Tourism Board and forwarded to the Department of Immigration. This can sometimes speed up the process. A few small variations in the requirements are: four front and four side passport-size recent photographs of the applicant and dependents; specific proof of income demonstrating a US$2,000 per month or US$24,000 per year income; all the copies of the passport must have a seal from a notary public.

Costs

- Application fee of US$150 payable to the Belize Tourist Board (BTB), submitted with your application.

- Once accepted into the program, a fee of US$1,000 is required.

- US$200 is payable to the BTB for a Qualified Retired Person Residency Card.

- US$750 is payable per dependent entering the program.

Payments must be either cash in U.S. dollars, a U.S. bank draft, or U.S. cashier's check. Personal or company checks are not accepted.

WORK PERMITS

You must have a work permit before you can legally work in Belize. Working without a permit can result in heavy fines from the Belizean government. The process of obtaining a work permit can be time-consuming and bureaucratic. Businesses and individuals that offer the most potential for investing in the country and creating jobs for Belizeans have the easiest time obtaining work permits.

There are two types of work permits. One is the Temporary Employment Permit that applies to investors, people who want to be self-employed or start a business, and volunteer workers. This permit allows you to work in Belize without being a permanent resident.

The other type of permit is an Application for Authorization to Employ Foreigners. The employer needs to submit an application form along with supporting documentation in order to employ a foreigner. The employee needs to have been a permanent resident in Belize for at least six months.

The length of a work permit ranges from three months to one year and is subject to renewal. You have to reapply before the permit expires. In most cases, foreign waiters, vendors, domestic workers, and farm hands will not get work permits. Only Belizean citizens or permanent residents may run a tour company or have a tour operator's license.

It's best not to mail any documents; instead, hand them over in person. Additional documents may be requested from you during the process. Applying for a work permit does not automatically mean you will get one; this is at the discretion of the Labour Commissioner and is not guaranteed. As with most bureaucratic official matters in Belize, costs and requirements can change without notification.

Applying for Citizenship

There are two ways to get Belizean citizenship as an adult. One is through marriage to a Belizean citizen and the other is after living in Belize as a permanent resident for five years. After the five years, you submit an application to the Department of Immigration in Belmopan. Once your application has been processed all adult members of the family (if applicable) will be asked to come in for an interview with an immigration officer one by one. These are usually quite straightforward and involve confirming your identity, where you live, and if you have business plans, and what they are. You can then set a date to take a test about Belize. The government produced a brief pamphlet about Belize's history, politics, and key facts, with questions and answers in the back. This is available at Angelus Press in Belmopan. When you feel you are ready for the test, go back to the Department of Immigration in Belmopan, where you will be asked 20 questions from the pamphlet, which the immigration officer fills in on a piece of paper for you. If you have studied the pamphlet the test is quite easy. After that you are given a date to attend a swearing-in ceremony. The entire process can take between six months to a year.

A Belizean citizenship will allow you to travel to other Commonwealth and

15 Caribbean Community (CARICOM) countries without a visa, as well as most countries in Central and South America.

CITIZENSHIP THROUGH MARRIAGE

To marry a Belizean citizen, you need to get a marriage license from the Ministry of the Attorney General. This can be fairly straightforward and costs US$25. Once you are married to a Belizean citizen, you can usually apply for citizenship after living in Belize for one year after marriage. You do not need to obtain permanent residency first.

REQUIREMENTS

These are very similar to those required for residency, except once citizenship is granted you pay a fee of BZ$300 per adult and BZ$100 per child, instead of the immigration deposit required for residency. When you apply you will need original and copied documents, including: a completed application form, birth certificate, three passport photos, BZ$40 fee, your passport and all pages photocopied, a medical certificate including HIV and VDRL test results, marriage certificate (if applying through marriage), proof of continuous legal residence in Belize for five years (or one year if married to a Belizean), police record, wife/husband's birth certificate (if applying through marriage), and your spouse's certificate of nationality (if applying through marriage). For children you need their birth certificate, two passport photos, proof of continuous legal residence, and a medical examination.

Moving with Children

Belizeans love children and they are welcome almost everywhere. It's a wonderful place to grow up; there is so much to do and so much freedom. Children can wander around freely and play. There are a lot of outdoor activities like swimming, tubing, climbing, and canoeing. Most places in Belize are close to water, be it the sea, a river, a waterfall, or a lagoon. You can't go wrong with children and water! Encourage them to show an interest in the fascinating and diverse nature around them.

It's a good idea to educate your children about which animals and insects to avoid, as children tend to be very curious. If they find something that they haven't seen before, tell them to call you so you can identify it together. How children adapt depends on their habits, hobbies, and to an extent age group. If your children love hanging out at malls, shopping, going to the cinema, eating fast food, and playing computer games, then they will be sorely disappointed. You won't have the variety and availability of items for kids in Belize that you are probably used to.

It is best to discuss the move with your children, encourage them to read up on Belize, ask what they think, and what their expectations are. It will be very different from what they are used to. The majority of the expat population is generally much older, people who have retired and whose children have grown up. There is an increasing number of expat young families scattered about. Post a message on the Belize Forum website and introduce yourself. Find out where other families live so your kids can make some friends. If you want your children to attend a private school you will be limited to the Cayo area (Belmopan) and Ambergris Caye (San Pedro). That's a good way for your children to make new friends and find out what other kids in Belize do for fun.

Primary healthcare is not on par with the United States, so make sure you know where the good hospitals and doctors are and how best to reach them, and keep a comprehensive first-aid kit at home as well as a good medical dictionary. For serious problems, there are good medical facilities in Belize City, Guatemala, and Mexico, or you can return to the States.

There aren't many extracurricular activities or clubs available, though the number is slowly increasing. Again, networking with other parents will come in useful if there is something specific your child likes to do.

CITIZENSHIP FOR CHILDREN

If you receive Belizean citizenship, any children you have under the age of 18 are also entitled to become Belizean, irrelevant of where they were born. You need to submit additional applications to the Department of Immigration for your children. They will then receive a certificate of nationality, which you then submit to apply for passports. Anyone born in Belize automatically becomes a Belizean citizen, regardless of where the parents are from. In the case of citizenship through birth, make sure a registered midwife is present at the birth and a certificate card of live birth is automatically issued by the medical doctor, hospital, clinic, or midwife. Within a month or two of the birth, take the certificate to the Birth Registry, which has offices in all cities and towns in Belize. Within a few weeks or a month you can usually collect the certificate, which you then take to the Central Registry in Belize City to apply for a birth certificate. There are often many people there and few staff on duty; expect a long wait. It's advisable to ask for more than one certified copy at the time to save you coming back should you need to. This process usually takes a few weeks, but for an express fee it can take a few days. You can then apply for a Belizean passport for your child.

DAILY LIFE

Moving with Pets

Transportation of pets into Belize is handled by the Belize Agricultural Health Authority (BAHA). You can find out all requirements from their website, download application forms, and you can also fax, call, or email them. Dealing with the airlines and all their rules and regulations is a bit more complex. Processing is said to take about seven days, but can realistically take anywhere from a few hours to a few weeks. After buying your ticket, submit your import permit application via fax or email to Belize. Ask for a copy of the final permit in case the airline requests it before you leave the United States. You will be asked to pay a small amount for the import permit when you arrive in Belize.

DAILY LIFE FOR PETS

Remember that Belize has a subtropical climate; it is hot and humid. Think about if your pet will adapt to this. Alternatively, if you would like to get a pet once in Belize, there are several Humane Societies who have a host of animals awaiting adoption. Be prepared for the fact that Belizeans rarely treat dogs and cats in the same way as North Americans treat their pets. Pets are generally kept outside; they are not pampered as much and are used more for protection than as a companion. There are a lot of very thin dogs and cats wandering down the road or side streets. You will be shocked by the state of cats and dogs here and the local attitude towards them. However, The Humane Society has great programs (which you can volunteer for) to do as much as possible to help these strays. Mange and venereal disease are endemic. Rabies occasionally surfaces in rural areas, carried by vampire bats and other wild creatures. It is essential that you have your pet vaccinated and on preventative medicine for fleas, ticks, and internal parasites.

There is less variety in pet food than in the United States. You can buy imported biscuits and canned food, but it is very expensive and not always available. Most people buy local alternatives or feed their dogs rice and dog bones from the butcher. There aren't many veterinarians, and among the few vets, some are good and some are not. Vet fees will vary as well. It's important to research your area first. Ask other expats, post a message on the Belize Forum site, or ask the Humane Society.

PREPARING FOR YOUR PET'S MOVE

You can bring dogs and cats into Belize without having to put them into quarantine, but you need to bring a valid International Vet Certificate declaring the

Pooches get a wash in the Mecal River.

pet free of any infectious diseases, fit, and safe to fly, and you must have your pet vaccinated against rabies. Dogs and cats that do not meet rabies requirements (too young for the shot) are to be confined at home until they reach three months of age. Once they are vaccinated against rabies they are confined at home for an additional 30 days. Vaccination has to be done within 14 days of travel. The rabies certificate must be dated one month to one year prior to travel. Belize officials also mention that your pet must not have any visible or open wounds on them. If you are moving your dog to Belize, you must have a valid certification of vaccination against distemper, parvovirus, infectious canine hepatitis, and leptospirosis. Cats may need vaccines for feline viral rhinotracheitis (FVR), calicivirus (FCV), and panleucopaenia. Animals may be required to be revaccinated against rabies upon arrival if certifications are deemed unsatisfactory, in which case they will be quarantined at your expense. A quarantine officer will inspect your pet when you arrive in Belize. If you are going out to the Cayes, you can have your pet in the water taxi or you can fly with Tropic Air. They charge three seats for one dog, each way. Maya Island Air charges only one seat for the dog. You need to notify them in advance that you are traveling with a pet so that they have the appropriate aircraft.

Smaller pets can be carried in the airplane cabin. Pets traveling in the cabin require a reservation to ensure no more than seven pets are booked on any single flight. Checked pets do not need a reservation. Larger pets are transported in pressurized cargo holds. Charges vary depending on the weight of the animal. American and Continental Airlines fly pets into Belize from the United States. There are also cargo airlines that transport pets,

FLYING WITH CATS

When Kristi Rifenbark moved to Corozal from Oregon in 2008, she brought her three cats with her. Here's what she has to say about the experience.

It was a relatively painless process. The hardest part about the whole thing was my cats' reaction to being on two planes and traveling for a day in their carriers. When I crossed the Belize border, I needed an Approved Import Permit, and I was allowed to list all three cats on one permit application. I also needed an International Veterinary Certificate and valid Rabies Vaccination Certificate.

I ran into one big problem at the Portland International Airport (my first airport of the trip). Since I had the cats, I had to first go through screening with each cat, individually, and then go to a special room where the cats had to come out of their carriers and the carriers themselves had to be run through the screening process. I brought a spray called Feliway that was recommended by our vet to calm the cats down a little since we weren't allowed to sedate them (airline policy), so I had sprayed that all over their carriers. At this point, the cats hated us; I wasn't happy about removing them from the carriers and they were freaking out. Cat hair was flying everywhere, and they were trying to find any possible hiding spot they could in this little room.

The security officers said we needed to come with them for additional screening. They were suddenly very serious, and my heart skipped a beat while we followed them out of the room. I needed a full body scan again, and then they searched through all my stuff again. After the scan, they told me that whatever I had sprayed on the cat carriers should never, ever be used again for airline travel. It had set off all sorts of alarms. A little embarrassed, I nodded and we went on our way. I highly recommend that anyone traveling with cats not use this spray when going through an airport. It's called Feliway and made by Ceva. Make sure any pet products you use are airline approved.

– Contributed by Kristi Rifenbark, http://belizedragonfly.com

including AmeriJet, which has a service from Miami to Belize. There are a few regulations to follow. Many airlines do not allow dogs to be checked with luggage. The kennel must be big enough for the animal to stand and turn around in and your pet may not leave the kennel for the duration of the flight. You must have a clear bag of dog food taped to the top of the kennel with instructions should there be an emergency or delay. There must be a water bottle (the gerbil type) that fits on the outside of the kennel door whether your dog knows how to use it or not. The airline will also cable tie the dog in the kennel. Provide some type of pillow or comfy blanket (not mandatory). Label "Live Animal" on each side of kennel with the name of the dog. If temperatures are predicted for less than 45°F at any place of travel, you need a letter from a vet stating that the dog can travel in temperatures as low as 20°F. Other regulations vary by airline. If the pet arrives at the airport and is accompanying the passenger and not considered cargo, no duty will be charged. However, if the pet arrives as cargo with airway bills and other freight or shipping documents, then duty and taxes apply. This comes to 40 percent of the value of the animal, along with a 10 percent sales tax, and a 2 percent environmental tax.

What to Take

Most things are available in Belize, so you don't really need to bring anything except your personal effects. Some things, like major appliances and electric wares, are not of the same quality, and the cheaper brands don't last as long. There isn't a huge choice of luxury goods, items for children, clothing, and sports gear (such as canoes, fishing gear, and diving gear). Expats come and go and you can pick up some good bargains when people leave, but that isn't something you can necessarily rely on. Everything you need here is available; there is nice furniture, appliances, electric goods, and tools. What you won't find is a wide selection, or perhaps the exact model that you want, and quality varies. It's important to work out what you can't live without or what you consider to be a luxury. If you try to replicate your life from back home, it will probably end up costing you more. Try to find a happy medium where you use some Belizean items and some North American items.

Try not to ship anything before you make the final decision to move! The

a local furniture shop in Punta Gorda

© VICTORIA DAY-WILSON

DAILY LIFE

a hardware store in Belmopan

best thing to do is to come out and rent furnished accommodations in Belize for at least six months. Have a look around at locally-produced furniture—you can also have furniture made locally if you provide a design and measurements. The major appliances in your accommodation will probably be from the region, so you will get a feel for those. Look at local art and everyday items like clothing. Travel to areas like Spanish Lookout, Belize City, and Belmopan, and have a look in the larger shops, including Farmers Trading, Midwest Steel, Universal, Caribbean Tires, and Koops Sheet Metal (all in Spanish Lookout); Builders Hardware, Brodies (Belize City), Papis, and Hummingbird Furnishings (Belmopan); Dave's Furniture and Mirab (Belize City). These shops have a bit more variety and range in prices (look around several shops as prices vary for the same items). Ask yourself, what can't I live without? What can I afford? Almost everyone here says they would have packed completely differently in retrospect.

ESSENTIALS

Essential items to consider bringing with you are good quality cotton and linen clothes, and shoes. If you have good large appliances and are using a container to ship furniture, bring the appliances (for Europeans, remember Belize works on a 110-volt system—so any items you bring will need a voltage converter). A small safe for valuables may be useful to have. Other essential items include good bed linens, in particular sheets; a set of good kitchen knives and other kitchenware; kitchen items, like blenders; good quality electric items, like laptops, stereos, iPods, TVs; quality hand and power tools, like drills, saws, sanders, and weed whackers; and hobby items, such as diving gear, fishing gear, canoes, kayaks, climbing gear, and books. If there are specific cosmetics you like to use, bring those because the choice here isn't great and the better brands are expensive. Foodstuffs usually fall into the luxury items category; but, if you have a non-perishable favorite food item that you could not live without (we all have at least one!), then bring a supply with you. Good coffee is a popular item to bring from home. Also, there is a limited and pricey wine selection here. Liquor is not as limited, but all the good stuff is very expensive. It really is best to live in Belize and have a look around to fine-tune that final list of what you will bring with you.

SHIPPING OPTIONS

Moving your possessions to Belize can be done overland through Mexico, by sea, or by plane. If you choose the overland option check on travel advice as there have been security problems with drug cartels. You can drive your own car and possessions. Or, there are people who specialize in offering that service, such as Frank Ehman's company, which provides a trained, experienced, and bonded driver who is familiar with the regulations for transporting and importing household goods through the United States, Mexico, and Belize. You can also have goods driven in by truck in a sealed container or you can ship a container from Miami, Houston, or Camden, Alabama, to either Belize City or Big Creek in Stann Creek District.

SHIPPING AGENTS AND COSTS

Recommended companies include Hyde Shipping, Sterling Freight based out of Cayo, and Belize Logistics in southern Belize. By road or sea takes longer but is cheaper. There are airfreight options, such as Speed Cargo in Miami, and FedEx or DHL. The shipping decision depends on your budget, the bulk and amount of your items, and how quickly you need them. A 20-foot container

© VICTORIA DAY-WILSON

You may choose to visit a shipping office to take care of shipping your items from overseas.

can cost around US$2,500 and a 40-foot container around US$5,000, excluding duties. With containers there are several options such as Full Container Load (FCL) or Less than Container Load (LCL), or you can buy a container and have it driven in (US$3,000–5,000 depending on its condition). Belize Logistics offers a service for smaller items where they consolidate pallets for their clients and split the fee among multiple people. Most services come to Belize on a weekly basis. Ask your shipper about transportation of your goods to the departure destination in America and then from the port of arrival in Belize to your new home.

CUSTOMS BROKERS

It is advisable to hire a customs broker. This may cost money, but it is worth saving you the extra hassle with customs, as rules and regulations change regularly. The customs broker handles most of the paperwork for you and in some cases makes sure that your possessions reach their final destination. Shipping companies can recommend brokers, or you can look on the Belize Customs and Excise website or go to the Department of Customs and Excise. Some companies, including Belize Logistics, Hyde Shipping, and Universal Customs Brokers, offer customs brokerage as an extra service. You can do this yourself, but it will be a frustrating, tough exercise. At Angelus Press, you will find customs forms, a guide to completing the forms, and the code of book numbers required to fill in the forms.

the Department of Customs and Excise in Consejo, Corozal

REQUIREMENTS AND CUSTOMS

To clear your personal goods into the country, whether you bring them with you or they arrive later, you will need an inventory of all items, copies of receipts or proofs of purchase for new items (sometimes necessary), all the relevant shipping documents or the airway bill to the customs department if your goods are coming in by air or sea, and official documentation from the Department of Immigration proving that you are a legal resident of Belize.

There is a list which provides rates on goods commonly imported as accompanied baggage on the Belize Customs and Excise website. Customs duty will be calculated based on the declared CIF value (cost of the goods in your country, insurance, and freight). It's probably easiest to keep a detailed inventory with approximate value of which items you will need to pay duty on, and pack your boxes accordingly so the customs officials don't have to go through everything. Belizean citizens and people with permanent residency do not need to pay duty on household items that are over a year old and intended for personal use. Items less than a year old or intended for sale must be declared with proof of purchase. You may need to pay duty on office-type equipment, like fax machines and certain types of machinery and tools, but computers are duty-free. Qualified Retired Persons have a year to import all of their household items duty-free. Be sure to check whether there are restrictions on what you plan to bring in to Belize.

HOUSING CONSIDERATIONS

By now you should have a rough idea of where you think you want to live. My advice: Rent before you buy. If you are serious about Belize, use the renting period to acclimatize and have a look around properties from a buyer's perspective, because in the long run that's what most people do. Take time—at least six months (minimum)—to rent in the area (or areas) that you like. Don't buy immediately, and if possible keep your property back home so you have the option of returning if Belize doesn't work out for you once the honeymoon period is over. Many people have moved to one part of Belize and discovered it isn't for them and moved elsewhere in the country.

Experience different times of year; even though the climate is subtropical across the country and the temperature is more or less the same all year, the rainy and dry seasons are quite different. It the rainy season it can rain for days in some areas, there are more bugs, and it's more humid than normal. If you live near water, it won't be the picture-perfect, turquoise, clear waters of the dry season: the sea often becomes a bit darker due to the increase of

© VICTORIA DAY-WILSON

water flowing in from the rivers, and the rivers become less clear due to the disturbance and increased volume of water. It's drier and hotter during the dry season and this becomes apparent in the plants, which are less verdant and abundant. There are more tourists around in the dry season (peak time) than in the wet season.

Have a look around various properties in the area. If a property is remote, think of additional transport and fuel costs, access to utilities, and whether you want to be so secluded. If it's on an island, think through the logistics of getting things back and forth. If you decide that you would like to buy a plot of land and build your own house, find out about cost of materials, builders, cost of labor, transporting building materials, and which materials are best to use in this environment. Look at a number of houses to see what others have done. Speak to people, everyone has at least one "lesson learned" story to share. You can't beat experience!

The Housing Search

FINDING YOUR HOME

Hopefully by this point you will have researched various real estate agents, communicated with them, and perhaps settled on one or two. There is no requirement for licensing or regulation of realtors in Belize—although the government has said it will pass an act regulating the industry—so a good place to start is with the two largest real estate associations: The Association of Real Estate Brokers of Belize (AREBB) and Belize National Association of Realtors (BNAR). Try to go with an established company with a proven track record. But, keep an open mind. Don't solely rely on realtors; quite a few perfectly respectable people don't sell or rent their properties through realtors because of the hefty commission charge. Take some time to ask around, keep an eye on the Belize Forum website—or post your specific requirement. Some condos have a "try before you buy scheme," and some resorts have fully-furnished, self-catering accommodations that they rent out for long periods. It's also useful to do some networking; try to find out about expat meetings in the area, or popular hangouts. There is a wealth of knowledge that is purely by word of mouth.

PROPERTY MANAGERS

Some real estate agents offer property management services and it is a niche that is slowly opening up in Belize. Like anything in life, there are some good

© VICTORIA DAY-WILSON

clearing the bush with a machete; self sufficiency is key to living in Belize

property managers and some unreliable ones, and there are a few who specialize in property management. What adds to the confusion is the lack of hard and fast regulations in the business. But then that is one of the reasons many people opt to move to Belize! Depending on the property and security, some people do not like to leave their homes vacant for weeks or months at a time. It is not the same as many homes in North America, where it is easy for some people to lock up and leave whenever the fancy takes them. In Belize, most properties require a lot of regular maintenance due to the elements and insects. This is where networking and word of mouth comes in handy; often people will ask around and arrange a one-to-one agreement for someone to house-sit or rent their home while they are away. If this is an area of concern for you, or if you want the freedom to come and go as you like, it may be advisable to look into condos, which are often serviced and managed, and developments.

Renting

As with the rest of the real estate business, there are no hard and fast rules about finding a rental property and what a reasonable cost should be. There are no daily newspapers here and not many classified listings. When we first came to Belize we rented a perfectly comfortable, furnished, clean house in Cahal Pech (a part of San Ignacio). It was a bit noisy since the houses were close together. In retrospect, we probably paid slightly over the odds, but at the time we didn't know better. Costs vary considerably without much rhyme or reason. There aren't many regulations about renting and your deal will be as good as you can negotiate. A good place to start is to ask real estate agents if they know about places that are available and to talk to other expats. If you are staying in a hotel or B&B, have a chat with the owners. They can often help with good advice and they generally know what's going on locally. Some hotel owners have self-catering accommodations that are available for rent or may be willing to cut a deal with you. If you look around in restaurants and other public places, people often post flyers advertising places for rent. The Belize Forum is a good place to ask around. Make sure you carefully look around any properties you may consider renting, and if an agreement is drawn up, read the fine print closely and make sure that there is a clear understanding between both parties.

COST OF RENTING

It's very hard to put exact prices on properties for rent or sale in Belize because they vary so widely. There isn't really a price guide to follow. The best thing is to look at a few and find something that suits you and your budget. The following are examples of what some fully-furnished and -equipped rentals cost per month. In Corozal, a two-bedroom first floor of a private home near the sea costs US$600, whereas a one-bedroom apartment in central Corozal costs US$900. In San Pedro a one-bedroom apartment costs US$1,000; a two-bedroom condo with sea views costs US$1,200 and another two-bedroom place costs US$6,000. There is a three-bedroom house for US$10,000 and a studio apartment for US$1,500. A three-bedroom house in Belmopan is going for US$1,775, while another three-bedroom property in Belmopan costs US$700. A one-bedroom house costs US$500 and a three-bedroom house is going for US$200. In San Ignacio prices vary from US$500 for one bedroom to US$750 for two bedrooms. A three-bedroom house is going for US$4,000 on Maya Beach and a one-bedroom house for US$850 in Placencia Village. It's advisable to try to line up a few potential options before you leave the United States, and maybe stay in a hotel for a few nights until you find an option you're happy with. Alternatively, if you get in contact with someone through the Internet, look at several photos, ask extensive questions like what part of town is it in? Is it central? Is it noisy at night? What is security like? How far are the main shops? What amenities does it have? Are water and electricity included in the price? It's advisable to try and have a look at something in person once you've arrived in Belize and have a better sense of place. There are no fixed agreements; leases generally vary from property to property and are something you handle with the owner or agent of the property.

Buying

Belize's land laws are based on British law. Foreigners can buy and own land of any kind, including beachfront property. Approval from the Ministry of Natural Resources is required for the purchase of an island. All artifacts, whether found on private or public property, must be declared to and registered with the Archaeology Department. Government Sales Tax (GST) of 10 percent only applies to the first-time sale of a new or substantially renovated property. GST only applies if 60 percent or more of the property has been renovated. It can also apply to residential lots being sold for the first time in a sub-division. There is no capital gains tax in Belize. Property taxes are about 1.5 percent of the undeveloped land and are payable on April 1.

TITLE OWNERSHIP

There are three different types of titles to freehold property in Belize: Deed of Conveyance, Transfer of Certificate of Title, and Land Certificate. The Deed of Conveyance is the oldest form of title ownership and is a registered right to ownership of property. It can be converted to a Certificate of Title by applying for first registration. After that, any subsequent buyer will be issued with a Transfer Certificate of Title. A Deed of Conveyance is a valid legal title once an attorney has confirmed that the seller has legitimate title to the property. A Transfer Certificate of Title is a physical title to a particular plot of land. It is more expensive and time consuming to transfer the title on a Transfer

© VICTORIA DAY-WILSON

a Mennonite prefab house being delivered

Certificate of Title than on a Deed of Conveyance, but ownership is secure. A Land Certificate is an absolute title and applies to property purchases in new or specially designated areas. The government is in the process of re-registering all freehold lands under the Registered Land Act of 1987 to achieve an eventual uniform system of nationwide land ownership. However, this will take time, as some areas have to be re-surveyed. If they apply for it, Belizeans are allowed to hold land under leasehold from the government. After clearing the land and adding a structure, a Belizean can then apply for conversion to a fee simple title. Some Belizeans don't do this, so make sure your lawyer checks the title carefully and confirms the property is freehold.

COST OF BUYING

If you're buying, location, size of the plot, whether there is a structure on it, access, and availability of utilities all play a large role in the price. A very rough guide—and it does vary enormously—is US$300 per acre; agricultural land runs US$500–3,000 per acre. Houses sell for US$25,000–750,000 or US$75–150 per square foot. Beachfront properties can be around US$3,000–5,000 a foot, and beachfront building lots go for about US$100,000–200,000. In Cayo for example, a basic Mennonite prefab house without anything additional can cost around US$15,000–20,000; US$20,000 might buy you a half-acre building lot; small farms go for US$25,000–75,000; for US$30,000 you could buy a 15-acre farm with a basic house in a rural area; US$50,000 could get you a small concrete house; for US$125,000 you may get a 50-acre farm with small dwellings; US$250,000 could stretch to a nice 2,000-square-foot house or a 150-acre farm with a house; and for US$500,000 you should get a luxury 5,000-square-foot house on an estate.

BACKGROUND CHECKS, LEGAL ISSUES, AND COST

The buyer and seller sign a sales agreement on the price and any particular terms or conditions. A 10 percent deposit is fairly common. A title search should be carried out by a lawyer to make sure that the seller is the legal owner of the property, that the boundaries are correct (this is done at the Lands Office in Belmopan), and that there are no outstanding issues related to the property such as any liens, unpaid taxes, mortgages associated with it, or any claims on the property at some point in the past. This search will also reveal whether or not there are any forms of restrictive covenant or encumbrance on the property. The title search can take anything from days to weeks. The lawyer will also need to prepare the transfer documents, which vary depending on the type of property, but usually include the First Certificate of Title (the conversion of a Deed of Conveyance to a Certificate of Title once an attorney has confirmed that the seller has good title to the property), the Transfer of Certificate Title, the Deed of Conveyance, and Land Certificate. The transfer is usually accompanied by the original land title, recording or registration fees, and stamp duty. The cost of a lawyer is about 2 percent of the purchase price.

The buyer places the agreed sum in an escrow account which is released to the seller if and when both sides agree. Once the buyer has the papers, they are registered with the Land and Surveys Department; when a receipt is issued, the seller receives the payment. It takes a few weeks for the buyers to receive the new title in their name. Buyers have to pay a government stamp duty, which is 5 percent of the purchase price. The first US$10,000 is exempt. A registration fee for the new title deed is also required. This is usually US$15. The seller covers the property tax charges and the buyer pays for the stamp duty, recording of registration fees, and the real estate charge (if applicable). Title insurance is available here, but few use it. RF&G Insurance provides it.

BUILDING AND RESTORING

If you're planning your dream house, think about how you will go about the construction. You can be involved or you can act as project manager and hire a foreperson, or you can bring in a building contractor. When you are thinking about buying a property or land in Belize, which you either want to restore or build on, make sure it's within your budget. Property may seem comparatively cheap here, but once you start building, the costs add up. It also depends on whether you buy imported or local goods. Many things are imported, as the market here is too small to support full industries. Even if you have a mental image of your dream home, drive around and see what other people have built; there are some interesting houses out there. If your property does involve building, try to do some calculations before you buy. If you need to put in an access road, electricity, or water, find out what the costs are. How flat is your land? Will you need to get a grader in to smooth a patch for your house? Will you need fencing? Think about things like water storage tanks, septic tanks, and water pumps. If you're building using wood, think about preservatives because you will need them: Some people use burn oil (used engine oil), which is probably the cheapest option; others buy protective varnish, which can vary hugely in price and the most expensive is not always the best. Speak to a building contractor and try to get rough costs, price things out in hardware stores, and go to timber yards. If you are using wood, another expensive item is the nails and screws for the wood. There's

Building materials are sometimes sold on the side of the road.

also wear and tear on the tools because the wood is so hard it will break nails and drills. If you're on the coast, maintenance costs will be high due to wear and tear from the elements. If your property is near water and you have a boat (or even if you don't), consider the cost of a pier or dock.

Sapodillo is a hardwood used for building and it is literally a very hard wood. It breaks nails, but lasts a long time, and doesn't get eaten as much by insects. You need to drill a hole in the wood, continuously moving the drill, and then hammer the nail in. Rough costs are $30 per 15-foot post. It's good for building and for fence posts. The bullet tree (aptly named) is another hardwood. The wetter it gets, the harder it becomes. Manchich is a hardwood that costs around $1.75 per board foot, so is Santa Maria at $0.175 per board foot. Teak is good for beams and costs about $1.75 per board foot. Tamay posts are good for using inside; as long as they don't get wet, they can last a long time. Negrito—the black tree—rots if it gets wet. Mahogany and cedar are good for door and window frames. Cement and tin are popular and durable. Tin roofing costs vary as it comes in different grades. If you are using thatch for your roof (nice but high maintenance), bay leaf palm is best, but you need a permit to cut it. It can last a few years. Cohune is cheaper but not very good. Electric wire is expensive, depending on gauge and place of origin.

You're likely to have more maintenance issues than you may be used to—particularly with wood—due to the elements, humidity, and an ongoing battle with insects. If wood is your material of choice—and it does look nice—listen to the locals and to expats who have been here for a long time. They can offer a wealth of knowledge and expertise, and can advise on what wood to build with and what to avoid. Many advise to use cement and then add wood facing to get the look. "Cement is king in the tropics," one builder and developer said to me. If you are building storage for clothes or in the kitchen, try to keep it as open as possible in order to air the items, discourage hiding places for any insects looking to move in, and to avoid too much fungus. Keep checking regularly

BUILDING AND LABOR COSTS

Below are listed a few costs for various building materials and labor. Prices, variety, and availability vary considerably from one place to another, from shop to shop, and from month to month.

WOOD

- Bullet tree BZ$1.75 per foot
- Cedar BZ$2.50 per board foot
- Mahogany BZ$2.50 per board foot
- Manchich BZ$1.75 per board foot
- Negrito BZ$1.75 per board foot
- Santa Maria BZ$0.175 per board foot
- Sapodillo BZ$30 per 15-foot post
- Tamay BZ$1.75 per board foot
- Teak BZ$1.75 per board foot

OTHER MATERIALS

- Barbed wire 16 gauge, 365 yards, BZ$61
- Cement: Cessa and Carib, BZ$12.75
- Cement: Maya 42.5 kg, BZ$14
- Chain link fencing, 4, 5, and 6 feet x 66 feet for BZ$163, BZ$193, and BZ$229, respectively
- Concrete blocks (breeze blocks), 4" and 6" (8" or 16"), BZ$1.15 each
- Electric wire 30 amp for lighting, BZ$0.80 per foot
- Electric wire 55 amp for wall sockets, BZ$1.30
- Metal 2-inch galvanized fence pipe, BZ$2 per foot
- Nails, screws, BZ$4.50 a pound
- PVC pipes, 0.5 inch, 1.5 inch, 2 inch, 4 inch diameter for BZ$0.60, BZ$1.20, BZ$2.40, BZ$6, respectively per foot
- Rebar: quarter-inch per 40-foot length, BZ$4.50
- Rebar: three-eighths of an inch for a 40-foot length, BZ$18
- Rebar: one inch by 40-foot length, BZ$28
- Sand and gravel 7.5 cubic yards, BZ$200
- Tin roofing, 28 gauge, BZ$6.50 per foot
- Wire mosquito netting in a 100-foot by 4-foot wide roll, BZ$229

LABOR

- Carpenter BZ$75 per day
- Electrician BZ$100 per day, or BZ$25 per plug
- Foreman BZ$45-50 per day
- Gardener/laborer/general help BZ$35 per day
- Helper BZ$40 per day
- Mason BZ$75 per day
- Plumber BZ$75

anyway. Leather is particularly susceptible to fungus. Consider open storage options in the kitchen so it's easy to clear away any unwanted insects.

BUILDING PERMITS

Building permits were introduced some years back but have not been fully implemented apart from in main towns. Regulations are likely to tighten up in the future, so it is worth being aware of them. The law regarding building permits has been enacted, but it is a bit vague. This could become relevant in the future if the government focuses more on the law, as the next regime may well do in order to bring in extra revenue. In theory, the steps outlined below are required. If you are building or remodeling, have a look at the Central Building Authority (CBA) website, which is clear and informative and has several documents such as applications, as well as clear contact details. Normally, if you are building in an urban area you would go to the local town hall and speak to the chairperson of the local building authority. If you are building in a rural area, you need to contact the CBA, which is based in Belize City. Normally the process is quite straightforward; the chairperson, who is usually an architect and/or structural or civil engineer, reviews your plans and gives you a permit. The chairperson is then meant to inspect your site a couple of times to make sure it is being built according to plan. A permit for a fairly large building with a pool and some guesthouses costs around BZ$400. The cost varies depending on the type of building.

construction in Hopkins

THE EFFECT OF THE MOON ON AGRICULTURE

Mayan agricultural traditions and practices have been passed down from father to son as long as the Maya have been in Belize. Remijio Tzib, who lives in 7-Mile Village in Cayo District, says his father, Rudolfo, started passing down his farming methods to him when he was 14 years old. Remijio is now passing them down to his four sons. Having heard stories about the effect of the phase of the moon on agriculture I asked Remijio about it.

He says it is one of the important lessons that he learned from his father. "For example," he says, "We know that branches for thatch must be cut when the moon is full. If they are not they catch beetles and worms and other insects that destroy the thatch branches and the roof doesn't last long. Fence posts are another example. If we want fence posts to be 'living' posts (start growing again after being put into the ground for fencing) then we cut the trees for the fence during the new moon. If we want dry posts for the fence we cut the trees when the moon is full and dig post holes during the new moon to prevent the dry posts from rotting in the ground." Grape vines should also be cut during the full moon.

Many crops are also sensitive to the phase of the moon for both planting and harvesting. From experience, Remijio says that plantains should be planted during the last quarter of the moon or the plant will grow too fast and the fruit will split before it is mature. All above ground plants and annual crops that produce their seeds outside the fruit, such as yams, cassava, peanuts, lettuce, spinach, celery, broccoli, cabbage, cauliflower, onions, and grain crops should be planted during the first quarter of the moon. Cucumbers are included in this group also, even though they don't produce their seeds outside.

Generally, the best time to cultivate, harvest, transplant and prune is in the fourth quarter. It is also the best time to plant vine crops to avoid the plants growing too fast and producing less fruit. Harvesting root vegetables and potatoes is best done during a descending moon – third or fourth phase, but most other vegetables are best harvested during an ascending moon – first or second phase. The time to avoid harvesting is the full moon; the reason may be

A property title should include a lot plan. This can be obtained from the Land and Surveys Department, takes about two days, and costs BZ\$30. If the Land and Surveys Department doesn't have a lot plan, you need to hire a surveyor to draw up a new plan. This can take up to three weeks to complete and costs up to BZ\$700. To obtain a building permit, you have to submit an application form to the CBA along with the processing fee, three sets of plans, four site plans, and four location plans. According to the Belize construction permits bylaws, the plans should include a drawing to scale, showing the plot boundaries in relation to adjoining roads, alleys, footpaths, and the position

that crops hold too much moisture for satisfactory storage. According to Remijio's experience, if corn and beans are not harvested at the right time they will catch weevils more readily; peanuts will be wormy. The new moon phase is the best time for trimming grass and weeding crops because there is more activity underground in the soil and the flow of sap in plants is less strong; so growth is retarded during this time. Therefore, it is also a good time for turning under green manure.

Some people think the moon phase effects are hokey, but Dr. Frank Brown of Northwestern University conducted research over a 10-year period, keeping meticulous records of his results. He found that plants absorbed more water at the time of the full moon. That means that during the full moon there is good absorption of liquid manures. He conducted his experiments in a laboratory without direct contact from the moon, yet he found that they were still influenced by it. It was Sir Isaac Newton who established the laws of gravity, which explain how tides are affected by the gravitational pull of the moon. The pull of the moon is stronger than the sun because, even though the sun is larger, the moon is closer to the earth. The strongest effect is felt when the moon and sun pull from the opposite sides of the earth, at the full moon phase, although it also creates high tides when they are on the same side (at the new moon) as well. These same forces affect the water content of the soil, creating more moisture in the soil at the time of the new and full moon. This increased moisture encourages the seeds to sprout and grow.

The phase of the moon also affects cattle. The late John C. Roberson, Sr., well-known cattle rancher, never worked cattle at full moon and castrated them only during a waning moon. He also found out the hard way when he lost three calves in the chute that they should not be worked in corral during a full moon. It is also during the full moon phase that there is an increase in insect activity, particularly slugs and snails, and internal parasites. So if you are not getting satisfactory results from your gardening or crops, maybe you should consult the calendar and schedule your planting and harvesting according to the phases of the moon.

− Contributed by Dottie Feucht. Originally published in the Belize Ag Report, *www.belizeagreport.com.*

of any proposed building(s) on the same lot. Other information that should be included is the layout of sewerage and drainage, and detailed foundation plans, showing each floor and roof with typical cross-sections through the building indicating foundations, each floor, and the roof, with relative heights and levels of the lowest floor of the building and of the adjacent ground. Plans for all water-retaining structures with reinforced concrete detail, where used, must also be submitted.

Once the city council approves the plans, they are sent to the engineering department, which then sends them to the Ministry of Housing, which returns them to the city council. This can take a while as the Ministry of Housing Committee meets only once a month, and it responds to the city council only once every two weeks. The council is responsible for local regulations, while the ministry administers regional regulations. During the approval process, the Building Plan Committee checks that the project is in compliance with zoning, environmental, and fire safety requirements. Construction must begin within six months of the date the building permit is issued. The permit fee covers four site visits to inspect during four different phases. The whole process is said to take 22 days and cost BZ$670, but it is likely to take longer. Fees for residential properties, which are less than or equal to 1,000 square feet, cost BZ$50 plus BZ$0.10 per square foot. Over 1,000 square feet costs $100 plus BZ$0.15 per square foot. There are extra costs for pools of BZ$150 plus BZ$1.00 per square foot, BZ$2.00 per (running) foot of pier, and BZ$0.25 per foot of fencing. To issue a building permit, the city council schedules two inspections, based on the building plans.

HIRING DOMESTIC WORKERS AND MANUAL LABORERS

For general labor, whether domestic or construction-related, it's best to ask around for recommendations. Like anywhere, there are some excellent workers and there are some that won't meet your standards. When hiring laborers, be open to listening and asking for advice because locals often know things

Builders take a break after working on Mennonite prefab houses.

you might be unaware of, like uses for different types of material and when to plant and cut (local practice for landscaping is based on the lunar system and it works). It's important that you control for quality, both to make sure the work is done to the standard you want and the way you asked. Always be polite and patient. Belizeans respond best to suggestions rather than orders. Also keep in mind that local manual laborers are usually much poorer than expats. Some workers may take their time on the job in order to stretch it out over a longer period and earn more. While you may find the differences between hiring help in the United States and Belize frustrating at times, remember that there are many excellent laborers who work very hard and are good at what they do, and most of us would struggle without them.

Housing Expenses

If you aren't on the grid, or don't have access to it, you will need to consider alternatives such as pumping water, a cistern, a bore hole, a solar system, hydro or wind power, or a generator.

ELECTRICITY

If you are not connected but you do have access to electricity, you need to contact Belize Electricity Limited (BEL) to get electricity. This should take about a day. To install electricity, BEL can take about seven days and will charge BZ$100, in theory; though, on the whole, costs vary depending on where the closest transformer pole is. A short distance of about 10 meters would cost about BZ$4,500. The cable cost is extra at about BZ$5 per foot. The first pole is free, then each pole costs BZ$1,000 plus the cost of the cable, which will vary depending on whether it's copper or aluminum. Your electrician will advise you on what's best. BEL decides how many poles are required, depending on the terrain. Some people hook up to the closest BEL pole and then run the electric wires underground through their property because if BEL installs poles on your property it is more expensive and you have to keep a 20-foot radius of ground clear around each pole, which BEL will come and inspect. BEL will do the actual clearing but you won't get a say about how and where it should be done, which can play havoc with your grounds or garden. There are sometimes fairly short power outages for a few hours. Sometimes BEL announces them on their website. Due to fluctuations in power it may be advisable to invest in a surge protector to protect your more valuable electronic equipment.

© VICTORIA DAY-WILSON

water tanks in Placencia

For a fixed phone line or landline, go to Belize Telemedia Limited (BTL). They offer a variety of packages, starting at about BZ$50 and they take about two weeks to install. All times and figures are approximate and subject to sudden change without notification. Services often take longer than anticipated. Be patient! It will happen eventually.

WATER

For a water connection and sewage (if your location is on the grid), contact Belize Water Services Ltd. (BWS). Obtaining this can take around two weeks and cost about BZ$50; installing it takes a day and costs BZ$450. If you're off grid, you need to speak to the nearest village water board chairperson or to the town council water board. The village council controls most water supplies outside of towns. The water fee is usually a flat rate of around BZ$15 per month; though, it varies quite significantly from village to village. If the village council thinks you are using too much water (for example running a lodge), they may put a meter in and charge more.

GARBAGE

Larger towns have a garbage collection service, while smaller villages depend either on a very loose collection service, usually organized by the chairperson of the village, or have none at all. If there is no collection service, you take your rubbish to the city council dump for a small fee or arrange a system of your own, such as crushing cans and dumping them in the foundation when using concrete, using vegetable waste as fertilizer, and burning off as much as you can.

LANGUAGE AND EDUCATION

Belize is an English-speaking country and you can get by perfectly well without learning any other languages. This is one of the many attractions for foreigners who decide to move here. Most Belizeans are bi- or trilingual and only 4 percent speak English as their first language. Belize is made up of many different groups of people who speak a variety of languages, such as the German-speaking Mennonites, the Arabic-speaking Lebanese community, the Chinese community, the East Indians, the Maya who speak three different dialects of their own language, and the Garifuna who speak an Arawak-based language; Creole and Spanish are spoken by most of the population. When speaking to an expat Belizeans switch between Spanish or Creole to English with ease.

All major signs and information, such as directional ones, are in English. There are a few signs in Creole as well. All the major newspapers, television, and radio stations are in English, although a small selection of media is also available in Spanish.

There aren't many young expat families in Belize, and as a result there isn't

© VICTORIA DAY-WILSON

too much choice when it comes to schools. This is beginning to change as younger people and a few families have shown a growing interest in moving here. If you have children, education will be an important issue for you. At the top of the price list are private schools. These follow an American curriculum and tend to have more resources than Belizean public schools. If you are interested in a private school, it will determine where you live, as the few private schools are situated in Belmopan in Cayo and in San Pedro on Ambergris Caye.

The public schools in Belize are less commonly used by expats and often lack resources. The schools are subsidized by the government and are church-run, most often Catholic. Some people opt for homeschooling. There is a lot of choice for homeschooling curriculum, but it's an area that's probably best to research extensively first.

Languages in Belize

English is the official language of Belize, and of the government and the legal system. Children in school are taught in English. English is the lingua franca used by all groups to communicate. But Spanish is more widely spoken. It's useful to at least have a basic grasp of Spanish, as it certainly helps with local interactions.

Creole is a sort of pidgin English, more of a different dialect, though that's a controversial subject; there are those who argue that Creole is a language on its own, and believe it should be taught in schools and become Belize's official language, but then some people feel that way about Spanish. Creole is mostly spoken in Belize City and along the coast. Garifuna is mainly spoken in Stann Creek and Toledo. Kekchi Maya is most common in Toledo; Mopan Maya in Toledo, Stann Creek, and Cayo; and Yucatán Maya in Cayo, Corozal, and

© VICTORIA DAY-WILSON

a humorous English Hot Dog crossing sign, on Front Street on Caye Caulker

Orange Walk. Spanish is predominant in the northern and western districts but is also spoken throughout the country.

SPANISH

The Spanish language probably arrived in Belize with Spanish shipwrecked sailors in 1511. One of the sailors, Gonzalo Guerrero, married the daughter of a Mayan chief; their children were the first known Mestizos in Belize. During this time, the Spanish were trying to colonize Central and South America and claimed sovereignty over the whole area, with the exception of areas in South America that had been given to the Portuguese.

In 1840, the use of Spanish in Belize expanded due to an influx of Mestizo refugees from the Yucatán in Mexico. Most of them settled in Orange Walk and Corozal. In the 1980s, there was an influx of Central American immigrants who were mainly fleeing conflicts and repression in El Salvador, Guatemala, and Honduras. Immigrants from Central America continue to come to Belize. In the 2010 census, there were over 35,000 recorded Central Americans living in Belize. Naturally their first language remains Spanish.

With about half the population Mestizo (also known as Latino), Spanish is rapidly becoming the main language. It is spoken by over 94,000 people, or more than 46 percent of the population (according to 2001 figures). There is also a large population of Spanish speakers on Ambergris Caye and Caye Caulker. Most Belizeans speak English and Spanish.

CREOLE

The Creole people—the offspring of Black African slaves and European settlers—adopted their own language. The Creole language is based in English but borrows from various African languages and Spanish. The Creole spoken in Belize is similar to that used in Caribbean nations. While some linguists classify it as a dialect of English, the National Kriol Council states that it is "separate from English and should be taught in schools alongside English."

Creole has a Caribbean lilt to it with abbreviated English words. It initially sounds strange; you recognize sounds but you can't quite string them together. Over a period of time your ear becomes attuned to it, and as long as it's not spoken too fast you can gain a rough understanding of Creole.

Creoles made up 70 percent of the population until the 1980s and now account for 21 percent of the population according to the 2010 census, down from 25 percent in 2000. This is partly due to the influx of Central American refugees as well as Creoles emigrating abroad, mainly to the United Kingdom and the United States. Creole is also used as a standard term for any Black

DAILY LIFE

© VICTORIA DAY-WILSON

Creole sign in Placencia

person who is not Garifuna, or who has immigrated from Africa or the West Indies, or anyone who speaks Creole as a first language. About 80 percent of the Creole population speaks Creole and English.

Historically, Creoles settled mainly in Belize City, where the majority have remained. There are also communities along the banks of the Belize River in the original logwood settlements, including Burrell Boom, Bermudian Landing,

COMMON CREOLE WORDS AND PHRASES

Good morning. *Gud maanin.*
How are you? *Da how yu di du?*
Fine, thank you. *Aarait (as in, all right).*
What is your name? *Weh yu nayhn?*
My name is... *Ah nayhn...*
How many children do you have? *How much pikni yu got?*
How much does this cost? *Humoch dis kaas?*
What time is it? *Weh taim yu gat?*
It doesn't matter. *Ih noh mata.*
Is that so? *Fu chroo?*
That's not true! *Dat da lone rass!*
Declaration after a good meal: *Belly full, boti glad.*

Shut your mouth, stop your foolishness. *Stap u rass.*
Come here! *Kohn ya!*
That's right! *No True!*
What's wrong? *How you look so?*
We need to talk about this. *Mek we talk.*
Toilet paper *bombo cloth*
Later *layta*
Teach *teech*
Time *taim*
Home *in hoam*
Mule *myool*
True *chroo*
Ask *aks*

Crooked Tree, Gracie Rock, Rancho Dolores, and Flowers Bank. By the 1800s as the colony grew, some moved south to Dangriga and Monkey River.

MAYA DIALECTS

There are three separate Maya tribes in Belize: the Kekchi, Mopan, and Yucatec, and they all speak different languages. The Mopan and the Kekchi migrated from Guatemala. The Mopan belong to a branch of the Yucatec and their languages are similar. The Kekchi are highland Maya who came from the Alta Verapaz region in the 1900s; their language differs from the other two groups.

Although the Maya are scattered throughout Belize, they are concentrated in Cayo, Toledo, Stann Creek, and Orange Walk. The Kekchi make up the majority of the population in Toledo and theirs is the most widely spoken Maya dialect across Central America. Each tribe speaks a different dialect, but the Mayan languages are decreasing as Spanish and English become more commonly spoken.

GARIFUNA

Garifuna is the first language of about 3 percent of Belize's population. It is an Arawakan/Maipurean-based language with elements of Carib, French, English, and Spanish. There are 14,000 Garifuna in Belize today, 4.6 percent of Belize's population, and the second largest Garifuna community in Central America after Honduras. The major settlements are in Punta Gorda, Seine Bight, Georgetown, Hopkins, Dangriga, Barranco, and Belmopan.

LANGUAGE SCHOOLS

There aren't many foreign language schools in Belize as English is the official language. Most people recommend taking Spanish courses in Guatemala. The former capital, La Antigua, is only an hour away from Belize by car or by plane. It is probably easiest to try to find a tutor, take an online course, or use foreign language resources such as the Internet, books, and CDs. Alternatively, carry a phrasebook with you and make a point of learning the basics from Belizeans you get to know. You can also read the Spanish papers, listen to the Spanish radio stations, and watch Spanish TV. You may also ask around or post a message on the Belize Forum for Spanish classes and tutors.

There is a regional language center at the University of Belize campus in Belmopan. It's most popular with students from Latin America who want to learn English, but there are also Spanish courses. The government of Mexico sponsors Spanish courses in Belize City at the Belize-Mexico Cultural Institute, and the Venezuelan Government sponsors courses at the Phillip Goldson Center in Belmopan.

Education

Choosing a school for your child may be a bit tricky in Belize depending on what your needs and expectations are. There isn't much variety for schooling in Belize, though this is slowly starting to change with the increase of younger people and families moving to Belize. What type of school you pick for your child—unless you want to homeschool or use a village school—will largely determine your geographical location. If you're considering a private school, you need to budget for it. The best things to do are travel around and visit the state schools and private schools, and go online to find out more about homeschooling.

There are several options for schooling your children: local elementary state schools, which are free, government-subsidized, and run by the church; private schools; and homeschooling. Some expats have tried all options, depending on the age and requirements of their children, others focus only on homeschooling. In the public education system, parents pay for books, uniforms, and general supplies, and children buy lunch at school. High school costs around $900 (US$450) per year. The government is expected to start contributing towards

© VICTORIA DAY-WILSON

Children line up outside St. Barnabas Anglican School in Central Farm, Cayo.

high school. Belizean state schools are not like American public schools in that they have far less resources, it is compulsory to wear a school uniform, and students are expected to carry out basic chores. As elementary school is compulsory in Belize, there is usually an elementary school in most villages, and the school is often Catholic.

STATE SCHOOLS

It is compulsory for Belizean children ages 5–14 to attend school. Although basic fees are free in elementary school, poorer families struggle to scrape together the money for books, uniforms, and general supplies. For some, high school is financially out of the question. According to the 2010 census, 63,700 children were enrolled in elementary school; that dropped to 17,200 for high school, and then dipped further to 7,400 for university education.

The Belizean school system is based on the British system. There is preschool, primary, secondary, and tertiary education. Preschool starts with two years of infant classes, followed by six standards in primary (elementary) school and four forms in secondary (high) school, which in Belize is sometimes confusingly also referred to as college.

Tertiary refers to higher education, or university. There are three public universities in Belize: the University of Belize, which has campuses around the country, Galen University in Cayo, and the University of the West Indies in Belize City. All have a good reputation. Most expats who have children of university age send them to schools in the United States, as do Belizeans who can afford to.

PRIVATE SCHOOLS

There are few private schools in Belize, so your choices are limited, particularly geographically. There are two private schools just outside Belmopan that follow the American curriculum. One is the Belize Christian Academy (BCA), which has about 235 students from over

© VICTORIA DAY-WILSON

entrance to Belize Christian Academy on the Western Highway outside Belmopan

PRIVATE EDUCATION IN BELIZE – ONE EXPAT'S EXPERIENCE

My name is Laura Gray. I am 41 years old, married to my husband Brian, and we have three children: Corey (son), 15; Hunter (son), 13; and Logan (daughter), 10. After falling in love with the country, we sold everything we had in Mississippi and moved to San Pedro, Belize, on January 6, 2011. We own a small business called Caye Concierge, which caters to visitors to Ambergris Caye, as well as to those who are moving to the island. We take care of everything that they can't take care of from a distance, and we can get our visitors a 5-10 percent discount on most everything they do while they're here.

I also teach part-time at the medical school here on the island. I primarily work with the pre-med students. We love it here and have no intentions of moving back to the States or anywhere else anytime soon. Our oldest goes to Ocean Academy on Caye Caulker (he takes a water taxi every day), and our two younger kids go to Ambergris Caye Elementary School. When we first moved here, all three went to Am-bergris Caye Elementary. We have had an overall pleasant experience with the education system here. Actually, our kids are getting a better education here than they were in the States. What I want to do is to share our experience and the experiences of our children while highlighting the positive aspects of the schools here.

One thing we were very nervous about when making our plans to move to Belize was the educational system. We figured it would be okay, but even if it wasn't and we had to move back to the States, at least our children would have had the benefit of seeing what education in another country was like. We really didn't know where to start as far as choosing a school, but there was one private school that had a page on Facebook, and a phone number was listed, so I called the principal and talked to her, and then when we went down for our preliminary visit we decided to enroll the children. The cost was negligible – US$375 per month for all three. (That's US$125 each.)

15 different countries and runs from kindergarten to 12th grade. Fees run from $3,400 (US$1,700) for elementary school to $3,600 (US$1,800) for high school per year. The Quality School International (QSI) is the first internationally recognized American school in Belize. It opened in Belmopan in August 2011. The school is for children ages 5–13. There are a few private schools in San Pedro on Ambergris Caye: The Island Academy, La Isla Bonita Elementary School (IBES), and Ambergris Caye Elementary School (ACES), all for ages 5–14. Costs vary $50–700 per month per child.

HOMESCHOOLING

Many families do homeschooling using the Internet. There are a variety of curriculum choices. A good umbrella resource with information on homeschooling

After the children (ages 9, 12, and 14) started school, we quickly realized that they were all at least half a year behind their peers in their respective grades. In fact, my oldest son had a very important upcoming test to take for entrance to high school. We promptly got him a tutor. Our children caught up. My son passed his test with flying colors, too. What began as an overwhelming situation turned into several lessons we all learned about the Belize educational system.

First, their system is modeled on the British System. Second, in Belize the teachers have many more expectations of the children than they do in the States. Children are responsible for 11 subjects, and free time is sparse. After-school classes are not uncommon. When my son was studying for his high school entrance exam, his entire class stayed one hour after school every day to prepare. Even the lower grades held after-school classes for various reasons.

Finally, we learned that overall, the Belize system of education is designed to produce a more well-rounded child than the system in the States. While schools in the States are concerned about yearly testing and generally stick to the basics, the schools in Belize do not. Because the mandatory schooling age ends at 14, the schools make sure that every child who exits primary school knows a great deal – far more than the average American student exiting middle school.

We cannot have been more pleased to see that our children were learning more than their American peers, and about many more subjects. Our oldest child is in high school now. While he still keeps up with a large number of subjects, he does have time for two electives: scuba diving and gardening/composting. He and our other children love school here and have each commented more than once on how much more they have learned here.

– Contributed by Laura Gray,
mother of three and part
owner of Caye Concierge,
www.cayeconcierge.com,
San Pedro, Ambergris Caye

and online homeschooling courses is www.homeschool.com. Michelle Leonard, a trained teacher and musician, helps supervise children of all ages through the church in Georgeville in Cayo using the Accelerated Christian Education (ACE) curriculum. The Calvert curriculum is also popular. It's best to check on the Belize Forum and to ask around about homeschooling networks. There are a few families around the country where the parents created groups for a cross-section of ages so that children can also socialize with other homeschooled kids.

UNIVERSITY

There are three main universities in Belize; the University of Belize (UB), Galen University, and the Central America Health Sciences University (CAHSU),

the University of Belize (UB) Central Farm campus

© VICTORIA DAY-WILSON

Belize Medical College. The University of the West Indies also offers courses in Belize. UB's main campus is in Belmopan, but it also has campuses in Belize City, Central Farm in Cayo, Punta Gorda in Toledo, and two research sites at Hunting Caye and Calabash Caye. Galen University is near San Ignacio in Cayo and has a partnership with the University of Indianapolis. CAHSU is a medical school in Belize City with a curriculum modeled after U.S. medical programs. Expats in Belize who have university-age children most often send them to schools in the United States.

STUDY ABROAD

The College Consortium for International Studies (CCIS) offers semester and summer programs based out of San Ignacio in Cayo together with Galen University. Programs include anthropology, archaeology, business administration, environmental science, economics, international business, marketing, and accounting. With the exception of accounting, these courses are dual credits and degrees with the University of Indianapolis. Students can focus on anthropology and archaeology for a semester with several visits to nearby excavated ancient Maya ruins, or on environmental science with easy access to Belize's barrier reef, cayes, rivers, and rainforests.

The Institute for Sustainable International Studies (ISIS) offers winter and summer programs, and custom programs for sustainable and experiential learning in Belize. Courses include anthropology, animal science, environmental science, community development, sustainable development, marine biology/watershed ecology, and international business. Northern Illinois

Galen University, Cayo

University offers summer health studies in Belize focusing on the healthcare system in Belize, health sciences with University of Belize, alternative healthcare, international health, and health issues in a tropical climate. American Universities International Programs (AUIP) offers a cross-section of summer programs focusing on several fields, including tourism, agriculture, anthropology, biology, culture, geography, international studies, and social sciences. ProWorld in partnership with Ohio Dominican University offers a 10-day program in San Ignacio and along the coast. The program covers tropical biology and political and cultural issues, as well as sustainable development projects. The University of Mississippi Archaeological Field School offers a summer program based out of Belmopan. Miami University has a summer program open to majors focusing on Maya culture and covering the subjects of anthropology, archaeology, architecture, art history, education, history, humanities, and sociology.

Toucan Education Programs Limited (TEP) offers service learning placements based out of San Ignacio in Cayo. Programs range from a semester to a year and areas covered include education, health, conservation, community development, and social services. The Environmental Learning Institute offers summer programs covering field biology, field geology, and environmental studies and sciences of Belize tropical coastal ecosystems. The Western Michigan University offers a summer course in tropical biology based out of Cayo. The Cooperative Center for Study Abroad (CCSA) offers summer programs on biology and health science based out of Cayo, with research at coastal sites.

CHESS: A SUCCESSFUL EDUCATIONAL TOOL IN BELIZE

When Dottie Feucht first heard about the Belize National Youth Chess Foundation (BNYCF) at a meeting of the Belmopan International Women's Group (BIWG), she thought of the little village of El Progresso, also known as 7-Mile. El Progresso has over 100 families with lots of children. There is no electricity in the village and not much to occupy the lives of the children. She inquired about how to bring the chess program to 7-Mile and enrolled in a class for people who were interested in teaching chess.

Dottie then visited 7-Mile, received enthusiastic support to introduce the game at the local school, and talked with the teacher, who already knew how to play. He, too, attended the training session. The BNYCF lent four games and teaching materials to the teacher, who now teaches chess as part of the curriculum. The students enthusiastically received the game and they play games during every spare time slot they have – before, during, and after school. The game became so popular that Dottie bought several sets for families because the children wanted to play at home.

The BNYCF, which was founded by Ella Anderson, is a not-for-profit organization dedicated to promoting chess as an educational tool among the disenfranchised youth of Belize. After just four years, supported by dozens of volunteers, chess is now the fastest growing sport in Belize. Children across the country, in the smallest villages from southernmost Toledo to Corozal in the north, are excited to play chess. Students compete locally, regionally, and internationally. The best players compete annually at the Belize Chess Olympiad held at the University of Belize gymnasium with extravagant decorations and pageantry.

The BNYCF holds annual weeklong chess camps at Caves Branch Jungle Lodge, owned by Ian and Ella Anderson. There, students not only learn chess but experience personal growth and team building through rigorous outdoor activity and special, individual attention by the Andersons and teams of volunteers. The BNYCF depends on volunteers to establish clubs, teach the game, coach teams, assist at tournaments and camps, and transport players who don't have the means to get to them.

As a result of the efforts of the BNYCF staff and volunteers, many students who had severe behavioral problems have become model students; grades have improved; planning, critical thinking, and problem-solving skills have been enhanced; creativity and logical thinking have flourished; the ability to concentrate and focus has been stimulated. Needless to say, Belizean teachers are delighted with the program.

Teachers throughout the country are commenting on the significant positive effect that chess has on the children. There is a cultural exchange at tournaments; children make friends from all over Belize. There is eager anticipation to the next tournament, where friendships are renewed and the battle takes place across the 64 squares.

– Contributed by Dottie Feucht and David Coombs, www.belizechess.org.

HEALTH

Considering Belize is in the tropics, it has surprisingly few diseases. Most health problems in Belize are related to the environment and you can prevent them with good old common sense: Be careful about the water you drink; keep your hands clean; and if you have a cut, clean it and keep an eye on it. Wounds develop bacteria more easily and become infected in the tropical climate. Drive carefully, as traffic accidents kill far more people in Belize every year than malaria, insects, and reptiles combined. Pay attention to the sun: Wear sunscreen, a hat, and drink plenty of water so you don't dehydrate. There are many reptiles, insects, and plants that can cause harm to humans, but remember they're not waiting around every corner, and in most cases, insects and reptiles are far more frightened of you than you are of them.

Although there are good doctors and dentists in Belize, the healthcare system is not on par with North America. There is a shortage of doctors and resources in rural areas, and Belizean hospitals and clinics are fine for minor ailments,

A sign near the cemetery in Caye Caulker warns people to slow down.

but for anything serious, most expats travel to Belize City, the United States, Mexico, or Guatemala. Medical insurance is a good idea, as many expats use private healthcare. Pharmacies are fairly well stocked, but prices can be high for prescription medication.

The Belizean Healthcare System

Belize has both private and public healthcare. There is a lack of medical equipment and quite a low number of medical professionals in the public system. Hospitals are often under-resourced, overcrowded, and short staffed, making it a challenging system to work in. There are many volunteer doctors from Cuba, and other medical staff are generally trained outside Belize in Guatemala, Mexico, Jamaica, or the United States. Most Belizeans cannot afford the luxury of private healthcare and rely on the public system, which is free or low-cost for them. The system is divided into four regions to cover central, western, northern, and southern Belize. There is one psychiatric center and eight public hospitals. Each district has one major hospital and numerous clinics in the surrounding villages and more rural areas. There are about 70 public health facilities around the country. Most of these offer basic primary care. The regional hospitals cover what they can in the way of secondary care services such as x-rays, surgery, and emergency services. Tertiary care is only provided at the Karl Heusner Memorial Hospital in Belize City. Other major hospitals include Belize City Hospital, Belmopan Hospital, La Loma Luz Hospital

© VICTORIA DAY-WILSON

Karl Heusner Memorial Hospital, Belize City

(Adventist), the Southern Regional Hospital in Dangriga, Stann Creek, the Northern Regional Hospital in Corozal, Dangriga Hospital, Orange Walk Hospital, Punta Gorda Hospital, and San Ignacio Hospital.

PUBLIC VS. PRIVATE HEALTHCARE

The private healthcare system is quite good, but it is also fairly expensive compared with other Central American countries. Equipment, facilities, and services are better than the public system. There isn't a reliable public or private emergency service.

Most Belizean public hospitals and clinics are fine for basic primary care issues. Among expats who experienced Belizean public healthcare for a minor incident, a few were not impressed, but most had positive experiences. For serious medical problems or accidents, the system is not adequate. Private options include Belize Medical Associates (BMA) in Belize City or going out of the country to Guatemala City or Chetumal or Mérida in Mexico for good and cheaper treatment. Those who can afford it also consider going to the United States.

Private and public healthcare systems run side by side in Belize. The government and the private sector finance the public healthcare system with contributions from donor countries and international organizations. Public healthcare is run by the Ministry of Health and about 5 percent of the country's GDP is put aside for healthcare. It still remains woefully underfunded and underresourced. However, it does offer healthcare to most Belizeans at no cost, or at a very low cost. As most Belizeans cannot afford private healthcare, and certainly

DAILY LIFE

TRADITIONAL BELIZEAN MEDICINE WITH A MODERN TWIST

Dr. Mandy Tsang is a practicing medical doctor in modern conventional medicine and is a trained general practitioner (GP) from Glasgow, Scotland. Her exposure to Maya medicine was merely opportunistic since she was stationed at a Mayan village (Santa Ana Clinic) as a GP working for the Ministry of Health in Belize. She observed that many patients also liked to dabble in a bit of natural medicine, so she picked up on traditional remedies from her consultations with patients. Her private medical practice offers a choice of conventional medicine or natural plant remedies; she does not advocate one type of medicine over the other because she seeks to give her patients a well-informed choice. She does not consider all her knowledge of plant medicine to be categorized as Maya medicine. Some of the traditional remedies were gathered from other cultures.

Dr. Tsang and her husband, Dr. Alessandro Mascia, have a farm in Toledo where they specialize in guinea pig husbandry and growing coconuts. They make coconut oil soap, copal oil, and other medicinal and beauty products. Dr. Tsang describes their lifestyle and her experience working with traditional and Western medicine in Belize.

We make our medical products in small batches and have chosen not to live an economically-driven life. Our philosophy is to do all the things that we enjoy, give up on material success, and not treat life as a money-crazed venture.

I am a medical doctor, originally from the United Kingdom. While working in Mayan villages, it was a challenge bridging the gap between modern medicine and Mayan beliefs in health and sickness. But on the whole, the experience was positive, as I was fortunate enough to learn a few ancient Mayan remedies. While working as a medical doctor at the Santa Ana Clinic in Toledo, I found that it was not uncommon for a Mayan to seek medical attention at the clinic before going to see the bush doctor. Injections were viewed as magical, and the placebo effect of the hypodermic needle was almost instantaneous in curing non-specific complaints of pain or fatigue. Sadly, I found that my scientific medical knowledge was beyond the realms of comprehension for most Mayan villagers, and the next port of call was usually the bush doctor. The Kekchi Maya view of Western medicine can be encapsulated by the words a Mayan woman said to me, "I come to you to treat cold... but for real medicine I go to bush doctor." She went on to explain that only a bush doctor could cure serious illnesses such as snakebites, "dirty blood," and "fright." In some cases, patients would come full circle back to me after seeing the bush doctor, and this was when I was able to catch glimpses of the bush medicine that was used.

PLANT REMEDIES
Copal: After discovering that the Maya use copal resin on skin conditions like dermatitis and impetigo I became intrigued because I actu-

ally saw good results. It was these results that sparked my interest in copal as a medicine. I found it amazing that copal was used in its raw, unrefined form and was used especially for skin infections (bark, leaves, dead flies and all!). We managed to refine and clean up the copal resin to make the oil we now coin "copal medicinal oil." Further research from bush doctors in the Toledo area and medical plant literature confirms the use of copal for skin conditions including eczema, dermatitis, skin infections, burns, and scalds. Furthermore, it has been effective as a muscle-rub and a liniment for arthritis. Copal is also used as incense and can be found in most market places in the country; it is sold in one-pound blocks of resin in its most natural form, with complimentary pieces of dried bark, leaves, and drunken baymen (a type of bumble bee), wrapped in leaf parcels. The Mayan and Mestizo population in Toledo commonly burn pieces of copal on coals for spiritual cleansing. Copal has been used in ancient Maya and Aztec ceremonies as a ritual offering to the gods and so we can see that copal has a long history of use in Mesoamerica.

Cacao: Cacao is grown in Toledo and is one of the main crops in this district; although its principle use is in the manufacture of chocolate we have found its properties useful in soap-making as it produces a hard bar of soap with excellent lathering and moisturizing properties. Whole cacao beans are pulverized and ground finely and added as an ingredient in soap; we decided to use the whole bean instead of extracting cacao butter to give the added attraction of a chocolate-brown soap bar. Cacao is also used in making our luxuriously moisturizing chocolate smoothie lip balm.

Ruda: *Ruta graveolens* is a plant which has medicinal used for muscle and arthritic rub. An alcohol solution rubbed on the temples for treatment of stress and headache. It is also used in the protection of evil eye and envy. Ruda is a common pot plant in Belize and its anti-arthritic properties are commonly used in most Garifuna and Mestizo households; it is a well-known herb and it a common sight to find an alcoholic infusion of ruda in the medicinal cupboard of these households. The fresh herb is macerated and then infused in coconut oil to make the base for our ruda medicinal oil which is used externally for stress.

Coconut Oil: Coconut oil is a good skin emollient. This is probably the most important plant because it forms the base for almost all our products. We use coconut oil which is grown on our farm and we extract the oil by hand by grating the coconut and squeezing the cream out; the cream is then boiled and water allowed to evaporate leaving the finished product which is coconut oil. We use coconut oil in our healing balms, massage oils and soaps.

*– Contributed by Dr. Mandy Tsang,
a general practitioner in Toledo*

© VICTORIA DAY-WILSON

La Loma Luz Adventist Hospital, Cayo

not health insurance, this is an important benefit. For non-citizens, costs vary ranging from nothing to around BZ$40 for a standard consultation.

The majority of public doctors are competent and well trained, but shortages of staff, equipment, and supplies are a reality.

Government and individual patient spending on private healthcare is almost on par with public healthcare and yet only a quarter of Belize's medical professionals work in the private system. It is split into for-profit and non-profit facilities. There are over 50 for-profit clinics and 4 non-profit clinics around the country. There is some crossover between the public and private healthcare systems, as both healthcare workers and the government try to maintain open cooperation, such as sharing facilities. Some staff work in both sectors. Resources are much better in the private system, with more and better equipment, facilities, and services. However, the cost comes straight out of the patient's pocket (or health insurance), and there are no subsidies, so it is more expensive and certainly out of reach for the average population. It is used by wealthier, middle and upper class Belizeans and expats. There is no regulation of the private sector, and no set costs; prices can vary from doctor to doctor. Services can also vary in cost and quality.

MEDICAL INSURANCE

There are two types of insurance in Belize, public and private. Public insurance is run through the Social Security Board (SSB), which anyone working in Belize pays into and has access to. Belizeans must be registered with the SSB from birth, and people applying for Belizean residency, citizenship, or a

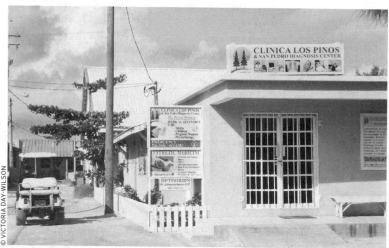

© VICTORIA DAY-WILSON

a health clinic in San Pedro

work permit must also register with the SSB. Registration is free and the SSB will require proof of identity, age, and citizenship. Dependents must also be registered if they are legally staying in the country. Social Security contributions are split between the employer and employee and cover medical expenses for work-related injuries or diseases, and sickness and maternity pay.

Compared with other countries, not that many companies offer health insurance in Belize. There are about 12 companies. Some are Belizean and others are subsidiaries of large international firms. Costs begin at US$30 per person, per month, depending what scheme you opt for. It's best to have a look at what different companies offer and opt for what best suits your needs and your wallet. Having said that, surprisingly few expats have medical insurance. It's a personal and financial choice. Some people feel it costs them a lot more in the long run to pay out insurance premiums compared with occasionally seeing the doctor or dentist in Belize, Guatemala, or Mexico. Others who retired on good pensions with insurance back home sometimes do not opt for insurance in Belize, or their pensions cover them in Belize. The problem with not having insurance is when things go wrong (if you develop a potentially terminal disease, or an ailment related to old age, or get involved in a nasty car accident, or suffer from some other environmental accident).

If you're going to opt for insurance, comprehensive is probably your best option, but that's best discussed with your provider. The other thing to keep in mind is that since facilities are limited in Belize, you may require evacuation to another country. Sometimes group rates are available, some expats opt for a Belizean company; others use a company they are familiar with from home. Bupa health insurance is quite popular with expats. Do your research and ask other expats which companies they recommend. Private insurance isn't regulated in Belize, so read the small print.

If you are going for treatment or a check-up, and you have a Social Security card, take it with you. If you have private insurance, you may need to find out first if they will approve your treatment. If they say no, it gives you a chance to plan financially. Some practices and hospitals require at least partial payment before treatment. If you are using insurance, be sure to send in all your receipts and supporting documentation afterwards. In some cases it takes some time to get your money back.

DENTAL CARE

With the exceptions of a few procedures, all dental work is part of the private sector. There are about 20 dentists working in Belize as well as volunteers who come at various times of year from places like North America. Most dentists will cover teeth cleaning and cavity filling, however there aren't many x-ray machines. On the whole, dental costs are a lot cheaper here than in North America, at about a half or a third of the price, but they vary from practice to practice. Polishing and cleaning costs around $50, but some dentists will quote over $100. An approximate price for a root canal and crown is around $500. Chetumal and Mérida in Mexico are also good, inexpensive options.

TRADITIONAL MEDICINE

Belize has a long history of traditional or "bush" medicine, dating back to the ancient Maya. The most well known Maya healer was Don Eligio Panti from the village of San Antonio in Cayo who lived to over 100. A published authority on the subject is Dr. Rosita Arvigo, who started an apprenticeship with Don Eligio Panti in Cayo in 1983. She studied with him for 12 years and is now a naprapathic physician, herbalist, international lecturer, author, and teacher of Maya medicine. She has lived in Belize for 30 years. There are several books on traditional medicine that are worth reading if you would like to find out more. Some include Dr. Arvigo's books: *Sastun: My Apprenticeship with a Maya Healer, Rainforest Home Remedies: The Maya Way to Heal Your Body and Replenish Your Soul,* and *Rainforest Remedies: 100 Healing Herbs of Belize.* Dr. Arvigo runs the Ix Chel Wellness Center in Santa Elena, Cayo (Ix Chel is the Mayan Goddess of Healing). There are bush medicine doctors across the country, and the Belizeans frequently use them. Dr. Mandy Tsang trained as a doctor in Scotland and lives in Toledo and runs a practice there. She uses a combination of traditional and conventional medicine depending on what the patient chooses and is comfortable with. Many common pharmaceutical medications have plant ingredients, and Dr. Arvigo and Dr. Tsang, and her husband Dr. Mascia, make traditional plant remedies that are sold in most shops in Belize.

PRESCRIPTION MEDICATION AND PHARMACIES

There are a variety of pharmacies in Belize. In most cases you can just walk in and ask for what you want. If you are taking prescription medicine, pharmacies usually ask for a letter from a doctor. You can get that from a doctor in Belize. If you have an existing condition, see

a pharmacy in San Pedro

© VICTORIA DAY-WILSON

a local doctor (costs about $40), bring a copy of your medical records with you, as well as the boxes and leaflets for your original medication, as names and brands vary. Prescription medicines can be quite expensive, specific types aren't always available, and the cost can vary substantially depending on the brand. Check dosages too. Bring an extra supply with you and find out where to obtain your medication in Belize.

DISABLED ACCESS

Belize doesn't really cater much to people with disabilities. Access is difficult in most places and the nature of Belize's attractions makes it a challenging place to get around. Streets are often narrow without much pavement, if any at all. Most entrances are narrow or have steps. There aren't many ramps around.

Illnesses and Preventative Measures

TROPICAL DISEASES

The main diseases in Belize are malaria, Chagas disease (also known as the kissing bug disease), dengue fever, and leishmaniasis. They are known as arthropod-borne diseases, which means they are diseases which can be transmitted to humans from insects. Dengue and malaria are carried by mosquitoes, Chagas' disease is transmitted by the assassin bug, and leishmaniasis by sand flies. Generally, common symptoms are flu-like, with aching joints, headaches, and high temperature. Cholera, typhoid, tuberculosis, and rabies can also be found in Belize but the risk is considered low and immunization helps prevention. You will rarely meet anyone who has lived in Belize who has experienced these diseases, but it's important to be aware of them.

Incidences of malaria have decreased dramatically since the 1980s when the government carried out extensive mosquito eradication programs. Malaria is now rare in developed areas due to eradication. Not all mosquitoes carry dengue or malaria and not at all times of the year (the wet season is the worst), so don't panic if you get bitten. You will more than likely be bitten several times, that does not mean you will become ill. Make sure you have some cream or gel for the bites because they can itch a lot.

The best precautions you can take against malaria are to use Deet (especially at dawn and dusk—the worst periods for mosquitoes), bed nets impregnated with permethrin (make sure they're tucked into your mattress), and screened rooms; burn mosquito coils; stay in air-conditioned or breezy rooms; and cover up arms and legs early in the morning and in the evening if you are outside when mosquitoes are most active. You may ask for chloroquine pills, but it's best not to take them over an extended period of time. Sprinkling citronella essence of oil also seems to deter mosquitoes. Citronella insect repellent balm is made in Toledo by Doctors Mascia and Tsang and is

© VICTORIA DAY-WILSON

an ambulance in Belize City

available locally. Empty any containers of stagnant water or add a few drops of oil, as such conditions are ideal breeding grounds for mosquitoes.

VACCINATIONS

Getting vaccinations and medications, such as anti-malarials like chloroquine pills for malaria and dengue fever, are a personal choice. The only exception to this is that you must get the vaccination for yellow fever if you are coming from a part of the world where it is a problem, like Africa or South America. If you have traveled to those areas, bring your vaccination certificate as proof that you received the vaccine.

Recommended vaccines are hepatitis A and B, typhoid, rabies, measles, mumps, and rubella (MMR) if you didn't have it as a child, and tetanus/diphtheria.

SEXUALLY TRANSMITTED DISEASES

About 3 percent of the population is HIV/AIDS positive and sexually transmitted diseases (STD) can be a problem in Belize. Take normal precautions such as using a condom to minimize risks. If you think you have been exposed, see a doctor.

SUN AND HEAT

It's surprising how many people become ill from the sun. The sun burns and the heat dehydrates. Side effects include discomfort like heat rash, heat stroke,

© VICTORIA DAY-WILSON

The sun in Belize is intense – be sensible.

or more serious consequences like skin cancer. It's nice to have a great tan, but be sensible about it. Wear a hat, stay in the shade, drink a lot of water, start off with a strong sunscreen, and build up your resistance slowly. If you're out on the water all day, wear a T-shirt. Use sunglasses to protect your eyes.

FOOD AND WATER

There are places you can drink the water in Belize and some people do and are fine, but it's best to stick to bottled water, which is widely available. Few people experience trouble with food bought on the street (it's often delicious, so you will miss out by not eating it), but be careful if you have a sensitive stomach. Check that the food is thoroughly cooked and the ingredients are fresh.

REPTILES, INSECTS, AND POISONOUS PLANTS

The best prevention in regard to reptiles, insects, and poisonous plants or corals is to be aware of your surroundings. Keep your eyes open for snakes, scorpions, ants, and spiders. Don't reach out and touch or pick up what looks like a beautiful little insect—it might be poisonous. It might not kill you, but it may hurt. The same applies to corals (it's illegal to damage them anyway, but should you brush against fire coral, you will experience some discomfort).

And, the same applies to a few jellyfish. If you inadvertently touch corals and jellyfish, apply some iodine or vinegar and the pain will pass. If it doesn't, go and see a doctor. Shake out your shoes in case a scorpion has crawled in. Watch where you put your hands. Think about a pile of leaves or logs and the fact that some insect or reptile may have made its home there and won't appreciate you meddling, so poke with a stick first and stay back. Use a flashlight at night. You can't safeguard against everything, but you can save yourself an awful lot of grief by using common sense and, just as important, educating yourself about what's around you.

Find out the names of plants,

© VICTORIA DAY-WILSON

The gumbo-limbo tree (tourist tree) always grows next to the poisonwood tree and acts as an antidote.

birds, reptiles, and insects; you will encounter many interesting ones. If you can't find the information in a book, ask the locals. They won't always know the English name, but it's a start. They will often tell you what you need to know about that particular creature or plant. Familiarize yourself with poisonous plants and creatures so that you can identify and avoid them, and if you don't manage to avoid them, it will be of far more use to a doctor if you can let them know what you think might have bitten or stung you. Don't be frightened, be sensible, and if you have children, teach them what you have learned. Encourage them to be interested, aware, and curious, but ask them not to pick anything up without calling you first. Show them pictures; discuss with them what they should watch out for and why. It is better that they are educated and understand their environment than ignorant and frightened.

A new fascinating world will open up to you. For example, some plants like the poisonwood tree will harm you, but many others will help you, like the gumbo-limbo or tourist tree (red and peeling!), which always grows next to the poisonwood tree and the bark of which acts as an antidote. Find out if you have aloe vera in your garden, and if you don't have it, plant some because it has a variety of uses for soothing sunburns, itchy bites, scalds, and other burns. Did you know potato skins are excellent for burns? As is papaya skin, which is also good for removing sea urchin spines.

© VICTORIA DAY-WILSON

a green vine snake – harmless to humans – wrapped around a heliconia

Not all snakes are bad; there are only nine known highly toxic varieties in Belize (there are about eight in North America), of which only one or two are aggressive. Of the other 59 recorded snakes, some keep down the rodent and insect population, others actually prey on venomous snakes. Three of the most lethal snakes are the coral snake (also found in the U.S.) and two types of Tommy Goff; however, there are other species of coral snake and Tommy Goff which aren't poisonous—look them up and find out the difference. An excellent book full of useful information with close-up color photos of each snake is *A Field Guide to the Snakes of Belize* by Tony Garel and Sharon Matola. It's available in Belize and on the Internet. There are several pamphlets and books with lovely illustrations of snakes in Belize which you can buy in bookstores and tourist shops.

Safety

Security can be a problem in Belize, though some areas experience few problems. Wherever there is such a large economic divide, there will be some crime as in many developing countries. There are robberies and break-ins from time to time and some areas are worse than others. At home, some people have guard dogs and put up a fence and a gate, although depending on where you live this may not be necessary. It's also wise to make sure your phone works and is charged so that in the event of an incident you can call for help. In some places there are also Neighborhood Watch schemes in place.

CRIME

Belize has a fairly high crime rate but this is mainly limited to gang violence in Belize City, which on the whole doesn't affect expats. You are unlikely to experience much crime, and if you do it's most likely to be petty crime like theft. To a certain extent, incidents can be prevented by common-sense precautions. For example, it can be useful to carry photo ID or a photocopy of your passport. If you're traveling by car make sure you lock your car. While traveling around, keep an eye on your bags. If you have valuables, make sure they are kept in a safe place—consider investing in a safe, and insuring valuables. Depending on where you are, don't walk around or drive alone at night, and if you do, try to stick to good roads with decent lighting. Don't flash money around. Trousers with zipped pockets are useful to deter pickpockets. Another deterrent is to look respectable but not affluent. If you're exploring the country and staying in a hotel, check that there are secure locks on your door as petty theft at tourist accommodations has been known to happen. Equally, if you're exploring and considering enlisting a tour guide, check credentials as all legitimate tour guides here are licensed and carry photo ID. It's rare, but there have been a few cases of date rape drugs used on tourists, so keep an eye on your drink.

Avoid traveling in unlicensed taxis. Licensed ones are easy to spot by their green license plates. Both the U.K. Foreign Office and the U.S. State

Department travel advice websites carry relatively current information on security here. In the case of an emergency, call 911 to reach the Police throughout Belize.

POLICE

Police can be slow to react and don't always act in your favor. Belize is a small place and in some cases the police are related or in some way connected to the criminal, so they may not act as harshly as is required. It doesn't help that police are not well paid and lack resources. In addition to the regular police, there are also tourism police in the main tourist areas who wear clearly identifiable and labeled uniforms. In defense of the police force in San Ignacio and Santa Elena, they have done a terrific job of maintaining law and order during festivals and national celebrations when there have been crowds of people, alcohol flowing, and lots of dancing and partying all night. Depending on the nature and seriousness of the crime, you can also report to your embassy if you require assistance.

LAWS

Remember that you are subject to Belizean law while living here. Do not, under any circumstances, get involved in drugs. Penalties are harsher than in North America, and even if you can reach your embassy, they are unlikely to be particularly sympathetic. Penalties include large fines and imprisonment. Possession of unlicensed firearms is illegal and expats have been jailed for this.

Taking photos of official buildings is illegal; check first.

Possession of artifacts that have been obtained illegally without declaration to the government is also illegal. If you buy or find anything you would like to keep, check its providence.

Prostitution is legal in Belize, but solicitation and operation of a brothel are not.

DAILY LIFE

EMPLOYMENT

The Department of Immigration and Nationality set employment policies to protect the Belizean job market, and for this reason Belize isn't an ideal place to come job hunting or to further your career. However, there are jobs available in tourism, construction, medicine, teaching, and real estate, though some of these roles may be seasonal. Remember, if you are offered a local job, it will come with a local salary. Many expats start their own business or buy existing ones, work remotely over the Internet, freelance, take short contracts in the region, volunteer, or are retired. Some retirees focus on projects as an extra income generator.

While Belize encourages foreign investment, some areas are closed off to foreign entrepreneurs. Start by carrying out in-depth market research and by hiring a lawyer and accountant familiar with the ins and outs of employment policies to advise you. You are not allowed to work in Belize unless you are a permanent resident or a citizen. People on the Qualified Retired Person's (QRP) Program are not allowed to work in Belize. To carry out volunteer work

you must also have a work permit. There are quite a few non-governmental organizations (NGOs) and missionaries here. There are a few international organizations like the International Organization for Migration (IOM) and the United Nations Development Programme (UNDP), but their operations are small compared with other parts of the world. Another option for foreigners is to work in the diplomatic corps, which isn't that large as not all countries have representatives in Belize and those who do have fairly small embassies. A few years ago the Americans, Mexicans, and the British built modest embassies in Belmopan.

Starting a Business

A common saying in Belize is, *To make a million dollars, move here with two.* Probably the most common form of work for expats is to start your own business or take over an existing business. This is notoriously hard and most people, even with previous business experience, say that they have never worked so hard in their lives. A business in Belize requires hands-on, full-time attention. Some people focus on one endeavor and are successful, but most find the best way to make ends meet is to have multiple financial schemes. For example, one couple works as landscape artists, runs a B&B on the side, and has a farm. Another expat runs a real estate company, an agricultural magazine, and makes arts and crafts. Another person is a wildlife veterinarian and runs an Internet café as her "day job." An engineer does welding and metal work as well as photography. Most expats work in real estate, arts and crafts, and small tourist-related operations like B&Bs.

© VICTORIA DAY-WILSON

a beach café in San Pedro near the Belize Tourism Board

The most popular industry to go into is the tourism industry and related services, which range from specialized flights for aerial views and photography, cafés, restaurants,

BUSINESS IDEAS

Here is a list of businesses that expats in Belize have started on their own or taken over from another owner. Maybe these ideas will inspire your next business venture.

- agricultural magazine publisher
- art gallery owner
- baker
- bar keep
- bed-and-breakfast owner
- bee keeper
- bookstore owner
- butcher
- café owner
- car mechanic
- carpenter
- ceramics potter
- chocolatier
- curio shop owner
- dairy farmer
- frame shop owner
- geodesic home builder and designer
- graphic designer
- horticulturalist
- hotel manager
- jewelry maker
- landscape architect
- land surveyor
- massage therapist
- meditation instructor
- music teacher
- newspaper publisher
- palm tree exporter
- plant nursery owner
- private veterinarian
- property manager
- screen printer
- shipper and importer
- soap maker
- solar-panel salesperson
- soy ice-cream maker
- stained-glass artist
- swimming pool installer
- traditional healer
- tropical fish exporter
- real estate agent
- restaurant owner
- yoga instructor

Some business are successful, while some aren't. Many people try a variety of things before they find a business that works for them. The trick is to try to identify an unfilled niche in the market, have a practical location, and pitch your prices right. Good luck!

bars, water sports, vacation guide websites, tour companies, resorts, and B&Bs. For most tourist businesses you need to obtain a permit from the Belize Tourist Board (BTB).

It is surprising that people continue to come to Belize to open new resorts when the market is actually quite small. Average occupancy rates are no higher than 40 percent according to the BTB. They are highest in San Pedro and go way above 40 percent in the high season. But in the low season it's so quiet that some people just close down or offer heavily discounted rates. In more remote areas, rates drop well below 40 percent. The fact that many resorts are up for sale, even if they are actively running, is a telling sign of how hard it is to run a resort here. Several owners have only started to see a return after seven or eight years of work.

The government has been trying hard to attract foreign investment and offers a variety of incentives including exemptions from import and export duty, low business taxes, fewer government restrictions in some areas, and full foreign ownership of companies registered and operating here. However, some industries like fishing, sugar cane, and retail are closed to foreigners and reserved for Belizeans. Investment is encouraged in tourism, agriculture, furniture and garment manufacturing, and infrastructure. It's advisable to do some market research, speak to other business owners, and hire a local lawyer and accountant for specific advice. The lawyer and accountant can also help you through the majority of the process of registering your business. Contact the Belize Trade and Investment Development Service (BELTRAIDE) to find out about current investment incentives. As with most things in Belize, there is quite a lot of bureaucracy involved and things move at a slow pace; healthy doses of patience and humor are required, as well as determination and persistence.

RED TAPE

Corporations in Belize are known as Limited Liability Companies (LLCs) and can be formed by anyone. Two directors are required to start a business and the Belize government allows for 100 percent foreign ownership of a company, though it encourages joint ventures with Belizeans.

In order to start a business in Belize you have to carry out a name search at the Companies' Registry in Belmopan and ask for a computerized name search of all existing Belizean company names; this takes a few minutes and is free of charge. You can also contact the Belize Companies and Corporate Affairs Registry by e-mail, telephone, or fax for a fee of BZ$50. Registration of company statutes, memorandum, and articles of association at the Companies' Registry costs BZ$500 for the certificate of compliance, BZ$10 for filing, BZ$50 for registration, BZ$12 (each) for registering the statutes, memorandum, and articles of association, and

STARTING A BUSINESS IN BELIZE

I moved to Belize in 2008 to start a new chapter in my life and build a family business. My mom and I moved to Corozal to open a bar. My parents had a dream to move to a tropical location, which they found in Belize after five years of looking. My dad could not move fulltime to Belize initially so they asked me if I would like to move to Belize with my mom and go into the business with them. I was unhappy with the path my life was taking at that point, so a full dive into this Belize adventure sounded perfect. We moved to Corozal from Oregon and I loved every moment of it. I went through a lot of changes in my life throughout this experience and Belize has been a big influence on that. It is a country full of natural beauty and the Belizeans are some of the friendliest and most welcoming people I have met. Our business – Scotty's Bar and Grill – is currently operating in Corozal.

Going into the process of opening a business in Belize was completely foreign to us. We had lofty ambitions of getting everything set up and going within a few months. Amazingly enough we got it all ready to go within two months. From what I have experienced, Belize is a very easy country to move to and start a business as a foreigner.

Our first step in the process was to get a work permit – a legal requirement. We were misinformed of the specific rules on this when we purchased the business from the previous owner, an expat from Canada. This process was the most frustrating of all and should be the first thing you start to work on if you are planning on opening a business in Belize. The red tape was the worst here. I believe that is because the process involves various departments, and in our experience they do not always communicate well with each other. My best advice is to be proactive (be specific when asking what documents you need because this does change from time to time), and follow up often.

After the work permit there were a few other permits that we had to get to run a business. At City Hall we found out that we needed a trade license and a liquor license (because we planned to serve alcohol) for our restaurant and bar.

The trade license was probably the most simple for us to get. Once the surveyor decides the value of your property they charge you an annual fee. You receive a sticker that you put in a visible place in your business. This only took about two weeks. We then paid the fee to the Treasury (a separate establish-

BZ$14 for registering the directors to act on the company's behalf and takes about two days.

Next, you have to apply to the city council for a trade license. Within a day or so of receiving the application, the city council sends an inspector to visit the site. Along with your application, you will need a certificate of compliance from the Companies' Registry and proof of residency. The city council inspectors submit their findings to the council's trade license board. The

ment), and took our receipt back to City Hall. Make certain that you keep all your receipts (or copies) during the process of obtaining any of these licenses or permits because it can take time to get the actual licenses.

The liquor license was a slightly more involved process. In hindsight this should have been something we immediately started once we knew that our work permit was approved. After a trip to City Hall we got five copies of the liquor license application (they charge you a minimal fee for these). Then we had to contact the local government official in charge of handling this permit, which took a week. We were unable to reach her on her phone and left several messages. So we had to find out where she lived from the people at City Hall. By the time we got in touch with her the deadline had passed to submit applications for the next year so we had to pay a $100 penalty to reapply. We paid the fee, but found out the following year that this deadline was very loose.

The fire chief, health inspector, and police chief all had to come by the bar to inspect and approve the application. Our employees had to take a food handler class within a set amount of time. We had to put an ad in one of the local papers that we were actually applying for a license. We had to attend a meeting where all the business owners who had applied for a liquor license met to find out who had been approved. Essentially we had to wait around until our name was called, go up, get our signed copy of the application, pay the Treasury and then pick up our official license at City Hall.

Trips to the GST (General Sales Tax) office, the Social Security department, and the Labour department were all very simple, but we did have to put some time in waiting in lines. The biggest thing to realize is that things do not move as fast as in the States. There will be a lot of waiting, and you may have to do a lot of follow up with all of these steps. Just make sure you don't let anything fall through the cracks. Be proactive and patient and you will be okay. It becomes frustrating when you assume everything should happen the way you expect it to in the U.S. and the sooner you figure out that you are in a different county that has its own customs and processes, and accept that, the easier the process will become for you.

– Contributed by Kristi Rifenbark, partner and manager in Scotty's Bar and Grill, Corozal, http://belizedragonfly.com

board meets roughly every two weeks to process the trade license applications. After the meeting, you will be notified of the board's decision. If the board approves the license, you will be asked to pay for the license (the cost is assessed by the inspector at roughly 25 percent of the annual rental value of the site), and then a couple days later, your license will arrive. The whole process takes a minimum of 20 days. Afterwards, there will be other details to take care of, like creating a company seal.

Working in Belize

It's not very common for expats to work for a company in Belize, but those who do usually work with multinational companies, organizations, or diplomatic missions. In these cases, the company and the Immigration Department will most likely sort out your work permit for you. Multinational corporate presence is limited in Belize because these companies are often registered abroad or within the International Business Company (IBC) program, in which case they are technically offshore companies. There are many non-governmental organizations (NGOs) in the country; a lot are based in southern Belize, as well as church missions. You will not see an international company presence (or find such jobs). There are organizations like the United Nations Development Program (UNDP) and the International Organization for Migration (IOM) who have small offices in Belmopan, and small diplomatic missions located both in Belmopan and Belize City.

WORK PERMITS

To legally work in Belize, you either need to be a permanent resident or obtain a work permit. Expatriates with the Qualified Retired Persons visa are not permitted to carry out paid work in Belize. Some people work without permits, but if you are caught, both you and your employer can be fined, imprisoned, and deported. The Belizean government has tightened up on work permits in Belize over the last few years in order to protect its citizens, so it can be hard to get one. Businesses or individuals viewed as investors who will create jobs for Belizeans or who are self-employed have the easiest time obtaining a work permit. The length of a work permit ranges from three months to one year and is subject to renewal. You have to reapply before the permit has expired. As with applications for residency, the process can be time-consuming and bureaucratic. You may find yourself visiting the Department of Immigration on a regular basis to keep up the momentum.

Temporary Employment Permit

The Temporary Employment Permit allows you to work in Belize without being a permanent resident. You can apply for the Temporary Employment Permit if you are an investor, wish to be self-employed or start a business, or wish to perform voluntary work. In most cases, foreign waiters, vendors, domestic workers, and farm hands will not get work permits. Only Belizean citizens or permanent residents may run a tour company or have a tour operator's license.

© VICTORIA DAY-WILSON

Guides take tourists canoeing on the Macal River.

Application forms can be obtained from bookstores like Angelus Press in Belmopan or Belize City. Applications must be submitted to the Labour Department (there is one in each district) or to the Department of Immigration and Nationality in Belmopan. Although the Ministry of Labour processes applications for work permits, the permit is issued by the Immigration Department. Officially, the process takes six weeks, but it can take months. Do not post any documents, hand them over in person. You will need:

- A completed application form
- Three notarized passport-size photos
- Valid passport and copies of it
- Bank statement
- Trade license (if applicable)
- Proof of reasonably sufficient funds for the proposed venture
- Application fee, which depends on the level of skill of the applicant, but can range US$50–1,500
- A reference from any local organization, city or village council, or relevant ministry with which the work is related

You may have to attend an interview with the Department of Immigration. In some cases birth certificates and diplomas may be requested, and in the case of missionaries, a letter from the church is required.

Permit to Employ Foreigners

The Application for Authorization to Employ Foreigners is an application form to be submitted by the employer, along with supporting documentation, in order to employ a non-Belizean. The employee needs to have been a legal resident in Belize for at least six months.

Additional documents may be requested during the process. Applying for a work permit does not automatically mean you will get one—that is at the discretion of the Labour Commissioner and is not guaranteed. As with most bureaucratic official matters in Belize, costs and requirements can change without notification, so always start off by checking with the relevant ministry or department what the exact requirements are. Sometimes, the goal posts will continue to move, even though you have been told different. This is standard; smile, be patient and polite, and eventually your papers will come through.

The employer of the applicant needs to submit:

- The application form along with three passport-size photos
- Valid passport of the applicant
- $20 stamps
- Proof that the applicant is competent for the job

The employer should pay the application fee which can vary depending on the level of skill of the worker. Professional workers fees are US$1,500, technical workers US$1,000, religious or voluntary workers US$1,000, entertainers US$500–750, and agricultural laborers US$100. They also have to prove that no suitable Belizean could be found for the job, and have to advertise the position locally for at least three weeks. After everything has been submitted, the employee and employer are interviewed by a labour officer. After that, the application is passed to the Department of Immigration.

TAXES AND REGULATIONS

Before starting business, a company must be registered for a business tax at the Income Tax Department and with the General Services Tax (GST) authorities by presenting a relevant certificate of compliance. You will then receive a Tax Identification Number (TIN) for your company in about two weeks. The cost is BZ$150. Final registration will not be confirmed until a few weeks later. Operations can begin during this time, but the company must withhold the payable taxes. Failure to do so results in penalties and interest costs. All employees must be registered with the social security authorities. Confirmation of registration will take a few months.

You need to pay the business tax if you earn BZ$75,000 or more in a year from a business, or BZ$20,000 or more a year from a profession or vocation. Anyone who is self-employed, in partnership, running a company, or a sole proprietor must file a tax return on the 15th day of each month showing revenue receipts from all sources with a calculation of the tax due. Remittance of the tax due must accompany the return filed. The amount ranges from 0.75 percent to 25 percent of gross revenues, depending on the industry. This can be done at income tax departments and sub-treasuries in Belize City, Belmopan, Corozal Town, Dangriga, Orange Walk Town, San Ignacio, Punta Gorda, and San Pedro. Failing to pay tax or to pay it on time results in a fine, the amount of which varies depending on the circumstances. Failure to pay any tax can result in jail. There is a useful and detailed tax guide on the Belize Income Tax website (www.incometaxbelize.gov.bz). You will also need to pay a 10 percent General Sales Tax (GST). If you're buying an existing business, make sure that all taxes have been paid in full by the previous owner by getting a Certificate of Clearance from the Commissioner, or you could be held liable for them.

LABOR LAWS

Belize has strict labor laws and it is advisable to find out about them in order to avoid potential problems. If you are hiring labor, you have to apply for an employer number from the Social Security Board. The minimum wage is BZ$3.10 per hour or BZ$25 per day for manual workers. Employees are entitled to 16 days sick leave at their basic rate of pay if they have worked 60 days in the last 12 months. Pregnant women are entitled to 30 days of sick leave for pregnancy-related problems. Vacation is two weeks a year. You have to pay PAYE and social security for your workers. Social security payments per week range from 5 percent to 6.5 percent of the employee's salary depending on how much they are earning. Termination of employment after six months requires three days notice or payment in lieu. Six months to a year requires a week's notice or payment in lieu; a year to two years requires two weeks' notice or payment in lieu. The average work week is six days or 45 hours with paid overtime at a rate of time-and-a-half or double-time on Sundays or holidays. The laws on labor change from time to time, sometimes without notification, so it is best to check with the Labour Department and Social Security Board first.

The Labour Department issues a booklet called *Labour and You,* which is a guideline for employers and employees. The Social Security Board website (www.socialsecurity.org.bz) is also a useful source of information. Belize has nine trade unions and an umbrella organization, the National Trade Union Congress of Belize (NTUCB).

The citrus industry is one of Belize's biggest earners and employers.

BUSINESS ETIQUETTE

As with most things in Belize, business is not as formal as in North America. Office workers dress semi-casually; shirts and pants for men and skirts for women are the norm. Sandals are fine, but not flip-flops. Always address colleagues, business partners, or business acquaintances by their title, not their first name. It is common practice to have a general chat before getting down to business. Decisions tend to take a long time and several meetings to reach. While punctuality is appreciated, people are not as fastidious about it as in North America.

There is a small pool of skilled labor here. Unfortunately, in the past there was a bit of a brain drain to the United States, but Belizeans are starting to trickle home.

Volunteer Opportunities

There are a variety of options for volunteer work, including small community outreach programs helping women and children, and less fortunate members of society; helping families who are struggling because a member of the family has HIV/AIDS (still a taboo subject here); senior homes and orphanages; working with animals, like stray cats and dogs at the Humane Society, or the rescue and rehabilitation of birds, particularly parrots, at Belize Bird Rescue; fundraising for a variety of causes; helping in schools, libraries, and hospitals or clinics; and volunteering with archaeological, conservation, educational,

THE BELMOPAN INTERNATIONAL WOMEN'S GROUP

Saying yes to a move from Wisconsin to Belize when my husband was offered a position as Deputy Country Director with the American Bar Association's Rule of Law Initiative was a no-brainer. We packed up a few suitcases, shipped a dozen boxes to our freight forwarder, and headed to Belmopan – sight unseen. The head-spinning first weeks after our move belied the snappy confidence with which we'd made such a decision. Adjusting to life on foot in the intense heat and sun of a Central American "spring" (March–May) was a sweaty, sunburned slog. Thankfully, we got to know our neighbors in that same time and they invited us to happenings around Belmopan. One such gathering was the monthly meeting of the Belmopan International Women's Group (www.belmopaninternationalwomensgroup.org). As the temporarily unemployed half of a couple new to town, I was eager to make friends. The Women's Group was as eager to welcome me as a member and, most recently, as Secretary of the Executive Committee. The friendships and community created through working and playing with this group could make anyone far from home feel at home.

Affectionately referred to by its members as "the BIWG," this dynamic group of women offers the friendliest and most direct path to volunteer opportunities in Belmopan and surrounding villages in the Cayo District. Founded by the wife of a British diplomat, the group has galvanized around the goals of community building among women and local outreach. Lively monthly meetings of the BIWG may include members hailing from Belize, the U.K., Canada, the U.S., India, Iran, Venezuela, New Zealand, France, Italy, Suriname, Holland, Argentina, Spain, Columbia, El Salvador, Mexico, and Brazil. Held the first Wednesday of each month, visitors are enthusiastically welcomed and invited to enjoy a lunchtime libation from host venue Corkers bar or wonderful homemade sweets and savories donated by the members for each meeting.

The variety of projects supported by the BIWG reflects the spirited and vital interests of its members. Members assist with feeding programs, school library projects, HIV/AIDS outreach, supplying toiletries to a domestic violence shelter, cancer treatment support, improvements to the local maternity ward, clothing for newborns, birthday celebrations for an area children's home, funds for emergency pediatric care, or funds for school fees. The avenues for volunteer service through the BIWG are well established and supported by knowledgeable members who are always happy to welcome a new set of hands. The BIWG is an invaluable resource for locals and visitors seeking new friendships, fulfilling volunteer work, and a global community in little Belmopan.

– Contributed by Susan Walker

VOLUNTEER OPPORTUNITIES IN BELIZE

There are many opportunities for volunteering in Belize. Here is a sampling of a few well-known organizations.

ANIMALS

- **SAGA Society Belize** (http://sagahumanesociety.org) in San Pedro helps homeless and suffering dogs, cats, and other animals on Ambergris Caye.

ARCHAEOLOGY

- **Programme for Belize** (www.pfbelize.org) is a Belizean-run organization which manages the 260,000-acre Rio Bravo Conservation and Management area. Volunteer opportunities in conservation and archaeology are available at its two research stations.

COMMUNITY OUTREACH

- **The Cornerstone Foundation** (www.cornerstonefoundationbelize.org/volunteering) is based out of San Ignacio and works with cultural and community outreach programs.

CONSERVATION

- **The Belize Audubon Society (BAS)** (www.belizeaudubon.org) works in many aspects of conservation and also manages parks and protected areas.
- **Belize Botanic Gardens** (www.belizebotanic.org) in Cayo runs garden projects for those interested in horticulture and agriculture.
- **The Belize Zoo and Tropical Education Center** (www.belizezoo.org) looks after orphaned, rescued, donated, and rehabilitated wild animals.
- **Birds Without Borders** is a research, education, and conservation or-

and missionary institutions and organizations. Rotary and Lions Clubs are also very active across the country.

You must have a work permit to carry out volunteer work in Belize. If your organization is not sorting this out for you, you need to go to Angelus Press in Belmopan or Belize City to get an application form, which you then take to the Department of Immigration along with three notarized passport-size photos, a valid passport and copies of it, a bank statement, and a reference or letter from the relevant organization. The application fee starts at about US$50, but it is best to go to the Department of Immigration and check on the latest procedures as they can change without warning.

There are many interesting opportunities for volunteering in Belize. There are also different kinds of volunteer work. Although you are giving up your

ganization which works with the Belize Zoo and is coordinated by the Zoological Society of Milwaukee County, Wisconsin (www.zoosociety.org/Conservation/BWB-ASF/).

- **Green Reef Belize** (http://greenreefbelize.org) is based in San Pedro and has several projects to protect Belize's marine and coastal resources.
- **Itzamna Society** (www.epnp.org) in San Antonio works with the local Maya community in the protection and conservation of the environment.
- **Monkey Bay Wildlife Sanctuary** (http://monkeybaybelize.org) is an environmental education center near the Belize Zoo which works with conservation and community service projects.
- **Toledo Institute for Development and Environment (TIDE)** (http://tide-belize.org) in Punta Gorda focuses on conservation in Toledo District.

EDUCATION AND DEVELOPMENT

- **The Mount Carmel High School Belize** (http://mchsbenque.org) in Benque Viejo del Carmen is a Catholic school where volunteers can teach.
- **Young Women's Christian Association (YWCA)** (http://ywcabelize.org) works with sports, arts, and other programs, and helps women and girls in Belize.

WORKING WITH CHILDREN

- **King's Children's Home** (www.kingschildrenshome.org) looks after orphans and abandoned, neglected, and abused children in Belmopan.
- **The Scout Association of Belize** (www.scoutsbelize.org) sometimes has opportunities for volunteers, especially those with scout experience from their own countries.

own time and labor for free, that doesn't mean the volunteering will be free of charge. Generally, there are two types of organizations that offer organized volunteer opportunities. The first is for-profit outfits, for example, a travel company that hooked up with a conservation project. This sort of volunteer option can run into the thousands of dollars for the volunteer. The second type of organization is non-profits, such as non-governmental organizations (NGOs) and charities; these usually ask for a contribution towards room and board, and will be grateful for any donation you can give.

ORGANIZED VOLUNTEER WORK

There are many organizations which you can work alongside for set periods of time, which can vary from weeks to months. The organized programs tend to be structured and fulltime. Often you will be living onsite and therefore paying a small contribution per day towards food and accommodations, as well as transportation. Living conditions may not be what you expect. Fees vary from organization to organization, but a rough starting point is around US$25 per day.

To go about finding an organized volunteer opportunity, identify a field of interest, and research opportunities within that field in Belize. You can either do this with an organization based out of Belize or an international organization that works in several countries. Places to start your search are to ask your church group (if applicable) or your local charity if you work with one. There's a wealth of information on the Internet, and you could also post a message on the Belize Forum asking for suggestions and advice. GoAbroad. com (www.goabroad.com/volunteer-abroad/search/belize/volunteer-abroad-1) has a varied list of organizations that offer volunteer opportunities. These can be on the mainland or marine projects.

INDEPENDENT VOLUNTEER WORK

If you would like to help out in your local community (which is a good way to get involved in the community and to get to know people) but would prefer a more flexible structure and not to pay for donating your time and labor, then independent volunteering is something you should consider. You will find that wherever you end up in Belize, there are a variety of causes you can help with right on your doorstep.

The best way to get involved is to ask around if you're not sure what you want to do, or if you have identified a cause you would like to help, go and offer your services. This is an open-ended way of volunteering, but can still be quite time consuming. Work can range from hands-on assistance to administration and fundraising. For most grassroots projects, which generally rely solely on donations, a spare pair of hands is always welcome.

NGOS, CHURCHES, AND MISSIONARY WORK

An internship with a non-governmental organization (NGO) could provide useful experience towards a future career. There are many NGOs working in all fields in Belize, many of which are grassroots projects that involve community outreach programs. These are often a good way to integrate your existing knowledge or areas of interest with your desire to get involved in a local community. In some cases there are paid positions depending on your level of experience and what the NGO requires; in others, an internship is a good starting point for graduates or people who want to try something new.

Some of the larger NGOs operating in Belize are listed on the Commonwealth Network website www.commonwealth-of-nations.org and on the Belize Net website www.belizenet.com.

If you are a missionary or interested in working with the church in Belize, there are several similar opportunities, which are most often coordinated as organized volunteer work. Alternatively, check with your church to find out about how to get involved in missionary work in Belize. There are also some Rotary and Lions Clubs volunteer projects in Belize.

DAILY LIFE

FINANCE

Belize is relatively inexpensive when compared with North America, although it is one of the most expensive countries in South and Central America. How much you can get by on will depend on where you choose to live, whether you choose to buy local or imported produce, and where your children attend school. Whether life is cheap or expensive is largely up to you. If you try to replicate your lifestyle in North America or Europe, you will probably end up paying even more than you did there because so much is imported here and therefore much more expensive than back home.

To live economically but comfortably here, and to have some money left over for the fun stuff, you will need to find a compromise between buying local and importing your favorite items from abroad. You will also need to make decisions about your use of electricity versus gas. Communications are more expensive than in North America because of a lack of choice and infrastructure.

© VICTORIA DAY-WILSON

Belize bank notes

CURRENCY

The Belize dollar is pegged at 2:1 with the U.S. dollar and both currencies freely circulate. You may pay in U.S. dollars and receive change in Belize dollars. Double check prices to make sure they are in Belize dollars so that you're not surprised by the cost. Belize dollar bills come in 100s, 50s, 20s, 10s, 5s, and 2s. There are one-dollar coins, 50-, 25- (also called a shilling), 10-, 5-, and 1-cent coins.

Cost of Living

If you're wondering how much you will need to live in Belize, it's a good idea to take your final figure and double it. If possible, try to have a financial reserve to cover two or three years while you are adjusting to the move. Belize might sound cheaper, but moving from one country to another and getting established is always a costly process. There are inevitably hidden costs that you hadn't thought of, or higher costs you didn't expect.

HOUSEHOLD EXPENSES

Belize imports most of its electricity from Mexico so it is expensive. How expensive it is depends on your lifestyle. Running lots of North American

BUDGETING FOR BELIZE

Here are some factors to consider when drawing up a budget to move to Belize:

- Will you keep a property in your home country and what will the associated costs be?
- Do you have things to put into storage?
- Factor in travel costs back and forth over a long period.
- Will you be shipping in a container to Belize or have any other type of additional moving costs of personal effects?
- Are you moving with pets?
- If you have children and want to put them in a private school, include that in your budget.
- Will you be bringing items that you will have to pay duty on?
- Consider the cost of renting and hotels when you first get here, as well as eating out.
- Work out what your budget is for a property.
- Consider what type of property it might be – is it remote? In that case you need to figure in costs for wear and tear on vehicles, gas, alternative utilities such as solar or generators, and a water source.
- Are you buying land? Consider building costs, permits, and labor.
- Are you buying a house? Will you be remodeling it?
- If you are buying on or near water, will you need a boat?
- Consider all additional costs of buying property such as estate agents, taxes, lawyers, and registration. Don't just look at the baseline figure.
- What will your initial status in Belize be and what will that cost you (QRP, visitor's permit, permanent residency)?
- If you are thinking about starting or buying an existing business in Belize, carefully calculate those costs and all associated costs such as licenses, taxes, and permits.
- Consider costs of mobile phone services. If you will be making many international calls, consider what type of Internet system you may opt for, whether to install a landline, and whether to get a post office box.

appliances and using an air-conditioner will keep your bill high. Butane costs about BZ$10–15 per week. A gas cooker will save you a lot; electric cookers are expensive to run here and the price of gas is reasonable. Gas tumble dryers will also save you money. A conservative bill for a small, basic house for two people that use a stand fan intermittently, a TV, laptops, refrigerator, microwave, and lighting comes to about BZ$70 a month. A modest typical expat

Many people buy local produce at the markets.

home for two people that run all appliances comes to BZ$70–120 a month. A bigger house with a family of four may run BZ$160–300 per month. The cost of water ranges BZ$2–70 per month, as charges differ from area to area.

Petrol here is expensive at around BZ$11.74 per gallon for regular, compared with BZ$6.21 in Quintana Roo, Mexico, and BZ$9.72 in Peten, Guatemala. Premium is around BZ$12 per gallon, and diesel about BZ$10 per gallon. For infrequent use of a vehicle and short trips, say about 400 miles a month, fuel costs will come to around BZ$150. Of course that depends on what type of vehicle you have and if you use gas or diesel.

COMMUNICATIONS

Mobile phone charges vary depending on use and if you make the best of the monthly offers. Both Smart and Digicell (which belongs to BTL) offer packages once a month where you can raise your credit (with a limit of BZ$50) and get double for free; so you may pay BZ$20 and get BZ$40 worth of credit. Or, if you pay the maximum BZ$50, you can get triple credit; in other words, you pay BZ$50 and get a total of BZ$150 worth of credit. Shops in towns usually advertise this on the day before and the day of the sale and you will receive a text telling you which date is "double-up" day. Modest, infrequent use of phones runs about BZ$50 per month. Internet with Hughes (which you pay in the U.S.) runs to about BZ$60 per month, depending on what package you have. BTL also offers Internet, but they block Skype, which saves a fortune if you are making international calls. Fixed lines vary depending on what package you opt for and can be obtained from BTL starting at around

BZ$45 a month. Cable TV costs BZ$40 and up per month, depending on what package you have.

FOOD AND ALCOHOL

Modest weekly grocery costs for two can run about BZ$300 and depend on whether you are buying expensive imported goods or local products. There are a variety of local brands, which are a fraction of the price, that are just as good, if not better, than the imported ones. Shop around because the same product can vary by as much as BZ$5 from store to store; products come and go as well. Try local food. There is excellent BBQ chicken sold on the side of the road for BZ$5; you can order take-away or eat there. If you ask for it, they will throw in coleslaw or potato salad and a tortilla for BZ$8. There are delicious little meat pies, vegetarian pies, tacos with shredded chicken or bean paste, cabbage, onion, and cilantro on corn or flour tortillas, conch or lobster fritters, and tamales sold from bikes or the backs of cars on street corners and in car parks. You usually get three for BZ$1, unless you're in Belize City where it's the other way around. Fresh fruit juices are also delicious, refreshing, and usually cost around BZ$3. Street vendors sell bags of fruit and coconut juice for BZ$1. Eating out on the low end costs around BZ$10 per person, mid-range about BZ$30, and the high end starts at BZ$50.

Alcohol can be a sticking point depending on your preferred tipple. Belikin beer is very good and costs around BZ$3. Local rum is also very good, but the better quality spirits are imported and expensive, reaching up towards the BZ$100 range and above. The same applies to wine, of which there is not a huge variety.

OTHER LIVING EXPENSES

If you have children in private school, costs vary between BZ$50 and BZ$700 per month per child.

Domestic help or a laborer or gardener costs BZ$25–35 a day.

A visit to a doctor costs around BZ$40. Dentists vary, with quotes for cleaning and polishing ranging BZ$50–125. Repairing a capped tooth can cost around BZ$70.

Banks

There are five commercial banks in Belize and numerous offshore banks. Caribbean Bank (formerly Barclays) and ScotiaBank, are large multinational banks with branches in Belize. Alliance Bank, Belize Bank, and Atlantic Bank are based in Belize. They are all regulated by the Central Bank of Belize in accordance with the provision of the local Banking Act.

It is almost impossible to exchange Belizean dollars outside the country. Currency regulations limit the amount of dollars one can take out of the country to US$10,000 per year. Some banks, like Atlantic, offer safety deposit boxes for BZ$220 per year for a small one, or BZ$350 for a large one, as well as a non-refundable deposit of about BZ$150.

OPENING AN ACCOUNT

Opening an account isn't as straightforward as opening a bank account in North America. You need to fill out an application, provide your passport, proof of address, and a letter from your former bank confirming your banking relations and stating your banking details. Regulations can change, so it's best to do your research and speak to the banks first. You also need an official residency status. That doesn't apply to opening an offshore bank account. Internet banking is catching on but is often limited to paying bills and transferring funds between accounts within your bank. Most banks accept international wire transfers for a significant fee. Most people rely on their

© VICTORIA DAY-WILSON

Altantic Bank on Caye Caulker

main bank accounts abroad and just keep a small amount in their bank accounts in Belize.

CREDIT CARDS AND ATMS

Most places take major credit cards such as VISA and MasterCard. There are ATMs in most places with the exception of remote areas or small villages. If you're traveling around and relying on ATMs to draw cash, it pays to draw extra if you are going to a smaller or more remote area in case there isn't an ATM there. If you're relying on cash for day-to-day purchases, try to use small bills as people often don't have change for larger amounts.

ATM in San Ignacio

© VICTORIA DAY-WILSON

Taxes

On the whole, most people who aren't earning money from the Belizean economy do not pay income tax here. There is no capital gains tax and no inheritance tax. Those in the Qualified Retired Person (QRP) Program are exempt from income tax but are not allowed to work in Belize either. Pension income is also tax-exempt. Property taxes depend entirely on the type of property and vary from 1 to 1.5 percent of the value of the undeveloped land. Property tax in rural areas is based on land value, rather than the developed value of the property, to encourage development. Belize law allows you to avoid income taxes altogether by transferring income and assets (though not real estate) into a Belizean International Business Corporation (IBC). Dividends to you from the IBC are not taxable.

If you are employing anyone for more than eight hours a day you will need to pay the social security tax. There are offices across the country who can advise you on this or you can look at their website. If you are a QRP shipping within the first year and according to regulations, you won't pay import duty,

© VICTORIA DAY-WILSON

Social Security Board in Belize City

but others will on certain items. When you buy property you will be subject to a 5 percent value of the property Stamp Duty. You will indirectly pay the goods and services tax (GST), which is normally included in the price of most goods and services at 12.5 percent of the total value. It's a bit like value added tax (VAT) or sales tax. If you are running a business you will need to pay business tax and income tax. If you are employed in Belize you will need to pay income tax, which is charged at a rate of 25 percent, and for residents of Belize, the first $10,000 of their annual income is exempt. Americans living in Belize are supposed to declare anything they earn while in Belize to the IRS, even if it is only local and related to the Belizean economy. You are not liable for tax in Belize on income earned outside the country.

COMMUNICATIONS

The quality and cost of communications vary depending on where you live in Belize. In some rural areas, mobile phone signals can be so poor that people rely on email, or will find one point on their land where they get decent reception. The way to get around that is to have an Internet connection and use email, use your cell phone when you're in an area with good reception (perhaps when you're in the closest town doing your shopping), or get a fixed line from Belize Telemedia Limited (BTL). This may take some time but is a bit more reliable than the cell service. It is worth paying for decent Internet if you are home schooling, have family and friends abroad you want to stay in regular contact with, or have business and domestic affairs outstanding in your home country, such as property management or paying bills; all these transactions can now be handled over the web. Most banks offer Internet banking, and there are several bill-paying services online. If you have an Internet connection a great way of communicating is to use a voice over Internet application (VoIP) like Skype. There is no sign-up or installation charge.

© VICTORIA DAY-WILSON

Internet Access

The downside to getting your Internet access through Belize Telemedia Limited (BTL) is that the company tries to block Skype. So if you sign up for BTL Internet, you won't be able to use Skype. If you try to call a BTL number from Skype, you will probably have trouble getting through. In order to use Skype, you need to use a satellite Internet service such as Direct TV, Hughes, or Starband. Hughes is good and Computer Ranch in Spanish Lookout is very helpful and will install it for you for around US$2,000. You pay the bills in the United States. This can easily be done over the Internet. Costs are around US$120 per month for unlimited use. Starband is now offering its SOHO satellite Internet service for about US$150 per month. The downside to satellite Internet is that it can slow down when there are heavy clouds or drop out completely during a thunderstorm. It is advisable to unplug your connection at the wall, as with all electrical appliances, if there is lightning. The other thing to be aware of is how much you download. Be careful because if you exceed your bandwidth you will be "FAPed"—notified that you have exceeded Fair Access Policy—and you can lose your Internet access or it will significantly slow down for about 24 hours. It's best to discuss these issues with your provider and whoever installs it.

Other options include Internet packages from BTL and SpeedNet. They offer a DSL service that is one megabyte up by two megabytes down and costs about US$250 per month. BTL also offers wireless Internet starting at

© VICTORIA DAY-WILSON

a cyber café on Caye Caulker

US$125 per month. Unfortunately, it is a shared service, so the more people there are online, the slower your service will be. There are cyber cafés and wireless hotspots in most places in Belize for around BZ$8–10. If you are in a restaurant or hotel, ask if they have the service.

SKYPE

There are several voice over Internet applications on the market, but Skype is the most common. Type "Skype" into Google and download it from the Internet and install it on your computer, a task that takes a few minutes and is fast and easy. Some laptops have built in mikes and speakers, which can be sufficient for communicating. But, headsets are quite useful especially if there is background noise or you want to have a private conversation. If you are calling from computer to computer anywhere in the world there is no charge. For minimal charges you can also use Skype to call fixed lines and cell phones. Another great feature about Skype is that you can add people to the call—great if you're talking to several family members. You can also send files over Skype.

Telephone and Postal Services

TELEPHONE

To call the United States from Belize dial 00 + 1 + the area code + the number. The international dialing code for Belize is +501: To call Belize from North America dial 011 + 501. Belizean phone numbers are usually seven digits long. There are no area codes, but the first number denotes the district: Belize—2, Corozal—4, Stann Creek—5, Cayo—8, Orange Walk—3, and Toledo—7. Cell phone numbers start with a 6. Belize Telemedia Limited (BTL) and Speednet Communications are the two main phone providers in Belize.

public phone in Placencia

LANDLINES

BTL provides different fixed line packages. As well as fixed lines, you can now get fixed wired. The best thing is to go to a BTL office and inquire about the latest deals. Calling the U.S. from Belize ranges BZ$0.49–1.15 per minute, depending on whether it's peak time or not and whether the call is more or less than five minutes. BTL has a special discounted service known as 10-10-199 for international calls, which ranges BZ$0.33–0.58 per minute.

MOBILE SERVICES

The main phone providers in Belize are also the main cell phone providers: Belize Telemedia Limited (BTL) has a mobile service called DigiCell and Speednet Communications has a subsidiary called Smart. Phones and SIM cards are easily available. You can either set up contracts for US$50–75 or use a top-up card. This can be done from a shop, over the Internet, or from your mobile phone. Keep track of the date you purchase your credit because values less than BZ$30 expire in 30 days and values of BZ$30 or more expire in 90 days. Look out for the monthly double-up deals: You will be notified via SMS and shops advertise the day before and on the day of the sale. On double-up day, you can buy credit and get double the value. So if you pay BZ$20, you get credit valued at BZ$40. If you pay BZ$50, you get triple credit—BZ$150. If you bring a mobile phone from abroad, don't rely on it to work unless it's a GSM 1900Band. In some cases you can go to BTL and ask them to try to unlock your phone. I think the easiest option is to buy a local phone, which starts at BZ$100, and a SIM card for around BZ$20.

© VICTORIA DAY-WILSON

post office in Belmopan

DAILY LIFE

QUICKSILVER IN AMBERGRIS CAYE

Dr. Dianne Lawrence runs a service called Quicksilver that provides new-comers with a variety of services to assist with moving to and living on Ambergris Caye. The only bonded courier business on the island helps with paying bills, banking, tax payments, and getting set up for the move to the island. Quicksilver Go Phones has cell phone rentals to keep in touch locally and internationally. They also offer a private, reliable mail service, providing local addresses and daily delivery to established, convenient locations. And they have a yard maintenance service (Island YB – aka Yard Bo), which includes bug and pest control to keep your property trimmed, chopped, groomed, and free of bugs.

POSTAL SERVICES

To get a post office box, you need to go to the post office and request an application. Hand in the completed application with some form of ID, such as a passport or driver's license, and a utility bill showing your current address. If you are applying for a post office box for a business, the same steps apply, except you also need to show a certificate of incorporation from the Belize Registry or a trade license. For a deposit of BZ$40 you will receive two keys and a small P.O. Box; for a larger box, the deposit is BZ$80 per year. Fees are payable in advance and renewal of rental is due in the beginning of each year. Once the process is complete, P.O. boxes are supplied on a "first come, first served" basis, if there aren't any immediately available. Mail within Belize is fairly reliable and can take a few days. There is a service called Domestic Speed Mail, which delivers your mail faster and offers a tracking service within Belize only. Charges cost BZ$4–15 depending on the weight of your mail. International mail is a different story and can take anything from a week to months, or completely disappear. It's best to use FedEx or DHL for any important or valuable items, or anything that needs to be delivered quickly. However, those shipping services are expensive. Another option is to use the international United States Postal Service (USPS).

VIRTUAL MAILBOX

One way to handle all forms of mail which may come to you in America is to set up a virtual mailbox. There are several companies offering this service, including Mailbox Forwarding. It is a remote virtual mailbox service that provides you with a U.S.-based mailing address. You can receive and view all your mail online. This is also useful for online shopping for vendors who will only ship within the U.S. You will be notified by email when you have mail, whether it's UPS, FedEx, a bill, or anything else. You will see the envelope and can decide if you want it shredded, scanned, or forwarded. Costs vary range US$14.95–59.95 depending on which services you need.

Media

There are a variety of national and regional TV news stations, radio stations, weekly and monthly newspapers—but not daily ones—and a variety of publications on the web, including TV and radio stations' websites. There is often a political slant or bias towards either the United Democratic Party (UDP) or the People's United Party (PUP). Most media is Belizean-owned and Belizean-run with a few expat exceptions, such as *The San Pedro Sun, Belize First* (online), and the *Belize Ag Report.*

NEWSPAPERS

There are four national newspapers. *The Amandala* is a weekly newspaper with the greatest circulation in Belize. It is quite independent and outspoken and leans towards the PUP. Although a national paper, it is based in Belize City and tends to focus on politics and crime from a Creole angle and doesn't always represent the multi-ethnic mix that makes up Belize. *The Reporter* is another good weekly national newspaper which has been running since 1967. It has a similar focus to *The Amandala* and is also based in Belize City. It tries to be objective and impartial. The weekly *Belize Times* and *The Guardian* tend to represent the PUP and the UDP, respectively. Other regional newspapers

© VICTORIA DAY-WILSON

There are a variety of printed newspapers in Belize.

include the *San Pedro Sun,* run by expats in San Pedro; *Ambergris Today,* now only available online; *The San Pedro Daily*; *Caye Caulker Chronicles*; *The Toledo Howler,* produced quarterly; *The Placencia Breeze,* published by the Placencia Chapter of the Belize Tourism Industry Association; *The Star Newspaper,* a Cayo-based publication; *El Chiclero,* published monthly in Benque Viejo Del Carmen, Cayo; and the Spanish *Estereo Amor.*

Also published in Cayo is the *Belize Ag Report,* which is an independent bi-monthly agricultural publication available free of charge in some shops and also online. The *Belize Ag Report* has all kinds of interesting articles about animals and plants, targeting everything from large scale agricultural enterprises to anyone who's trying to grow some plants in their garden. It's interesting and full of useful tips.

WEBSITES

Online media includes Belize First, which covers travel, news, and life in Belize; Belize Magazine; Belizean; and Capital Weekly. Belizenews.com is a useful website which links to all major news sites in Belize.

RADIO

Radio stations include LOVE-FM radio (89.9, 95.1, and other frequencies), which also has a TV arm and airs easy listening music and news; Spanish stations Estereo Amor and Oye; and More FM, which leans towards younger listeners. KREM-FM 96.5 is popular too. WAVEFM is slightly more orientated towards the UDP.

CABLE AND SATELLITE TELEVISION

Belizeans love TV. The most popular local channels are Channel 5, which started in 1991, and Channel 7, which leans towards the UDP, operating out of Belize City. CTV3 presents news affecting the north of Belize from Orange Walk Town, and Plus TV and Open TV run out of Belmopan.

There are several cable TV stations, which cost on average BZ$40, with about 90 channels, including common North American ones such as HBO, Cinemax, SyFy, Showtime, STARZ, ABC, CBS, CNN, NBC, and FOX. Arab, Mexican, Indian, and Chinese pay-per-view channels are also available. If you live remotely, you can get satellite TV. Signal quality is quite good and the satellite footprint of most American TV signals covers Belize. C-Band, Direct TV, Dish Network, and Hughes are available satellite providers. Most people opt for a 6-foot dish in order to get good quality service; others go for an 8- or 10-foot dish. It's cheaper to buy satellite TV receivers in the U.S. and have a local dealer install and provide the dish and setup. Installation costs around BZ$4,000.

TRAVEL AND TRANSPORTATION

There are a variety of ways to enter Belize. Check with the Department of State for travel advice and the latest entry requirements or the Foreign Commonwealth Office (FCO) if traveling from the United Kingdom. You can also check with the British High Commission in Belmopan, the U.S. Embassy in Belmopan, the Embassy of Belize in Washington D.C., or the Belizean Embassy in London. For the latest travel advice on health, check the U.S. Government Centers for Disease Control and Prevention (CDC). You need a machine-readable passport valid for at least six months. EU and CARICOM nationals, Americans, and Canadians do not require a visa.

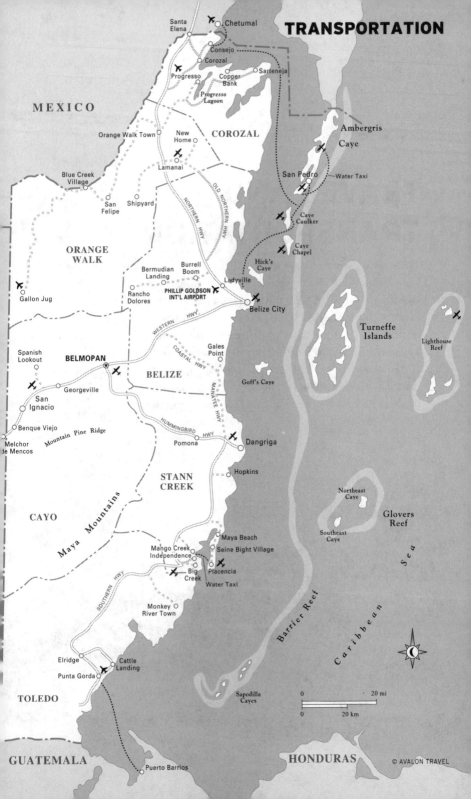

Getting There

AIR

The most common way in is by air to Philip S. W. Goldson International Airport (PGIA) in Ladyville, 10 miles from Belize City. Several international airlines have daily flights. Flights tend to be more expensive during the high season (December–April). U.S. airlines that fly direct to Belize include American Airlines, Continental, Delta, and US Airways. TACA—the El Salvador airline—also has flights from Houston. Prices vary, US$550–1,200 depending on when you are flying and from where. Most flights go from Dallas, New York, Charlotte, Los Angeles, and Atlanta, with Houston and Miami being the most common places of departure. Airports of departure can vary in the low season. If you're flying from Canada, you can sometimes get direct flights from Toronto, otherwise you will need to catch connections to the U.S. through Montreal, Toronto, Vancouver, and Ottawa. From Canada prices range C$930–1,600.

From the UK, most flights leave from London Heathrow to the U.S. and occasionally Canada. There are no direct flights as of 2011, so you have to change planes in the States. In the U.S. times between changing flights can vary from a few hours to 48 hours. Sometimes you have to change more than once. Prices vary, £500–1,300. When you fly into the States, even if you are just in transit, you have to have an Electronic System for Travel Authorization (ESTA), which you can obtain from an American embassy or online. This is normally a quick and easy process completed in minutes. In a pinch, you can apply online for the ESTA at a cyber café in the airport just before catching your plane. Ideally though, it's best to have your papers ready when you get to the airport. When you get to the U.S. airport you have to go through immigration, collect your bags, and check back in again. This can take time and queues can be long; plan accordingly.

AIR AND BUS THROUGH MEXICO

A cheaper way to get to Belize is to fly to Cancún, Mexico. You can catch a Maya Regional plane from there to San Pedro, Chetumal (just north of Corozal in Mexico), or Belize City. Make sure you have some Mexican pesos and a Spanish phrasebook if you don't speak Spanish. Alternatively, catch a taxi for about US$30 from the airport to the ADO bus terminal and then a bus to Chetumal (about US$30). The trip takes five hours, the service is excellent, and the buses are very clean—if not a bit chilly (very effective air-conditioning, so bring something warm). If you like, you can stay overnight in Chetumal at the Hotel Ucum (US$42), or Los Cocos or the Holiday Inn (over US$100). (Chetumal is near Playa del Carmen and Tulum, both nice beach vacation spots.) Once in Chetumal, a taxi to the hotel from the bus station runs about US$3. From Chetumal, there are buses to Belize City and Corozal. The bus to Belize City costs about US$16, takes 3–4 hours, and is direct. There is also the San Juan Express, which leaves at 5 A.M. and runs straight to Guatemala and will drop you off at the border town of Benque Viejo if you're headed towards Cayo. It costs BZ$50 and takes about six hours.

A direct ADO bus service started in 2011 runs from Belize City to Cancún. The service leaves Belize City at 8:15 P.M. and arrives in Cancún at 7 A.M. It takes eight hours and costs BZ$79. People can board the buses in Belize City, Orange Walk, and Corozal only if their final destinations are Merida or Cancún in Mexico. Anyone wishing to travel within Belize will not be able to take this bus. In the other direction, the bus leaves Cancún at 10:15 P.M. and arrives in Belize City at 6:30 A.M. Your last option is to take a taxi from Chetumal or Cancún to your destination in Belize. This costs US$200–400 depending on where you are going and which taxi driver you manage to strike a bargain with! Once in Belize City, those who do not want to continue on buses can take a taxi to Philip S. W. Goldson International Airport or to the Municipal airport (flights are often cheaper from here) and catch internal flights with Tropic Air and Maya Island Air, which fly to most places in the country fairly cheaply.

All of the buses in Mexico leave fairly regularly, sometimes as often as

A Tropic Air plane takes off from San Pedro.

once an hour or every half hour and are generally reliable. Your bus will stop at the border where you hop out and go through Immigration; Immigration charges a US$20 exit fee on the Mexican side and stamps you in to Belize. If you're coming in on a tourist permit and staying for longer than 30 days, you will need to renew the permit (BZ$50) at your closest immigration office before the date stamped in your passport. Before you leave Mexico, you will be given a green card, called a Multiple Immigration Form, which is a Mexican departure registration. Do not lose this, as you will need it when you come back across the border from Belize to catch your plane out of Mexico. Once in Belize City, you can catch a taxi to a hotel or to the Marine Terminal where you take a water taxi to the Cayes, or catch another bus which will take you on to your final destination. The process sounds longwinded but it is actually quite easy and saves money (if not time!). The Mexican ADO terminals and buses are cleaner than many I have encountered in the UK. There are a few small cafés where you can get basic food or drink. Some have Internet access, and there are a few ATMs. As with most places, watch your luggage.

OVERLAND TRAVEL

You can drive your car from the U.S. through Mexico to Belize. Check travel advice first, as in 2011 there were problems in northern Mexico between government forces and drug cartels. The roads are paved and the trip takes 3–4 days. The shortest route to the border crossing into Belize between Chetumal and Corozal is from Brownsville, Texas, into Matamoros, a distance of 1,257 miles via Tampico, Tuxpan, Veracruz, Villahermosa, and Chetumal. Other border points include McAllen/Reynosa (1,267 miles), Laredo (Texas)/Nuevo Laredo (1,413 miles); El Paso/Ciudad Juárez (1,988 miles), and Nogales (Arizona)/Nogales (2,219 miles). Lodging is available in larger cities. Along the way, you will have to pay up to US$12 at tollbooths—check your change and watch out for speed bumps! Roads are not well signed and it's easy to get lost, so it's best to avoid city centers. It's advisable not to drive after dark. You may be stopped for inspections. You will need pesos, so make sure you change enough money in the United States because most places will not accept any other currency, and credit cards are not always accepted. Speaking Spanish is an advantage because few people will speak English.

You will need Mexican car insurance, which you can either buy online or at the border crossing, a valid driver's license, passport, credit card in lieu of posting a cash bond to prove you will not sell the car in Mexico, original vehicle title, proof of ownership (vehicle registration), and a temporary importation permit for your vehicle, which must be secured when you enter Mexico. You

There are many bumps on the roads in Belize.

will also be required to pay a Mexican tourist fee of US$20. Make sure you have all original documents and two copies of each. When you enter Belize, you must have the Mexican temporary entry permit canceled at Mexican customs. When crossing the border, if you plan to stay, make sure you tell the customs broker that the vehicle will be staying in Belize when you pay the duty because when you apply for Belize license plates, you need to show paperwork proving that permanent duty has been paid. If you don't have that documentation, it can cost you around BZ$150. If you aren't staying in Belize, you will be given a temporary permit that lasts 120 days. The duty is the same either way.

You may bring in personal items (don't bring a weapon or ammunition because you will create a world of problems for yourself). If your items exceed the value of US$1,000, you should use the services of a customs broker at the U.S.-Mexico border. Listing all your items and their value may save time and money. If you aren't coming in as a Qualified Retired Person (QRP), you will be subject to duty and tax on your vehicle. Even if you are a QRP, this will apply to you if your vehicle is older than three years. The amount varies depending on the number of cylinders and type of car, but can be anywhere between 20 and 80 percent of the book value. You also need to buy Belize car insurance from brokers at the border. Three months' worth costs about US$100. Depending on where you are, there are two places to register your vehicle once you are in Belize. One is at the town hall, if you live in or close to a town; the other is at the Ministry of Transport, if you live in a remote area. When you apply for Belize license plates you will sometimes be told that they have run out, in which case you are given a note explaining this that makes you legal until you get plates.

Getting Around

DRIVING

There are no four-lane highways in Belize. The highways are two-lane roads with no pavement as such, few lights, not many directional signs. Zebra crossings are a rare sight and so are traffic lights (and parking meters), but the road network is pretty basic and it's hard to get lost. There aren't many gas stations in rural areas, so plan ahead and carry some extra fuel. Also make sure that you have a spare tire and the tools to change it. There are quite a few buses on the road, as well as agricultural vehicles, motorbikes, and Mennonite horses and carts. Many people bicycle. You will also notice quite a few pedestrians along the roads, occasionally on horseback, and, during the school year, kids going to school neatly turned out in their uniforms. You will encounter quite a few speed bumps, potholes in places, bridges, and police checkpoints, usually checking to make sure your insurance and road license are up-to-date and in order. Be careful when driving in Belize: The driving tests are not very rigorous so the quality of driving is dodgy to say the least, and there is quite a bit of drinking and driving. Despite the threat of a fine of BZ$50, few people wear seat belts. Car accidents are one of the main causes of death in Belize. Pay attention and drive carefully.

There are four main highways in inland Belize. Two of the four start in Belize City and you will see little road markers with a number on them. This indicates how many miles you are from Belize City and is also used as

a gas station in Belmopan

DAILY LIFE

© VICTORIA DAY-WILSON

EXPAT STORY: DRIVING THROUGH MEXICO

My husband Michael and I, both retired, came to Belize after applying in advance for the Qualified Retired Persons (QRP) Program. We drove our 2005 6-cylinder truck to Belize. When we arrived in Belize we did not have an official status yet, so we checked off the 30-day visitors box at customs. In one month we went to the border crossing and were told that we checked the wrong box and would have had six months to register our truck. We had to pay a BZ$500 fine for checking the wrong box.

The vehicle must be three years old or younger to qualify for the QRP Program customs exemption. The value of the vehicle depends on condition and how many cylinders it has. We were shocked that our truck was appraised for approximately US$12,500, which resulted in us being required to pay 47 percent of the value. The cost was almost US$6,000. It is a good idea to bring lots of money with you. We were a tad short and had to take a cab back to the bank in San Ignacio. You have to hire a broker at the border as well. We have had lots of other hassles, but still love Belize.

Before we departed for our travels through Mexico, we checked the United States embassy and State Department travel advisories regularly. The advisories are quite detailed and provide good advice about traveling through Mexico. The point of departure we used was Brownsville, Texas. There is a newer border crossing there, which is kind of bleak, called International Bridge. Upon our arrival we learned that we should have made advance arrangements for vehicle clearance at the border crossing 72 hours before or pay US$500 to expedite the waiting time. Our fee was finally waived after we waited all morning.

Some people form caravans to travel closely with other vehicles. The journey took three days and we saw only one U.S. vehicle the whole time. Driving through Mexico is mostly on two-lane roads with several large trucks and many buses. Each checkpoint was heavily barricaded and protected with armed soldiers. There were several armed military convoys all along the way. The police stations were also heavily barricaded. The best advice is: Do not travel at night. The traffic is slow going – travel is about 40 mph until you hit the super highways in the south. It is easy to get lost, as there are not many highway signs present. We closely followed a detailed map and planned ahead to stay in city areas, as there are few to no accommodations in most towns.

Once we were on the toll roads the travel was much faster. The toll roads are much better (and felt safer) than the non-toll roads, but they were expensive. Bring plenty of pesos for gas and tolls. American money is generally not accepted. As we were approaching the Belize border we realized there were no hotels for several miles. The few we found were closed and the driving was through wilderness. So in this area we did have to travel after dark. We reached the Belize border at approximately 9 P.M. and decided to stay in Chetumal, the last city in Mexico, until the next morning. There are a lot of scam artists at the border – beware and only deal with the border officials wearing uniforms.

– Contributed by Mary Loan

a directional tool; for example, people will advertise their shop or house as being at or near Mile 28 on the Western Highway. The main highways are the Northern Highway, from Belize City to Corozal in the north of the country; the Western Highway, from Belize City to Benque Viejo in Cayo District on the Guatemalan border to the west; the Hummingbird Highway, from near Belmopan to Dangriga; and the Southern Highway, from close to Dangriga down to Punta Gorda in the south of Belize. On the whole, the highways are quite good. Unpaved roads vary, some are graded regularly—particularly in the dry season—and are fine, and others are so bad they become impassable during the rains. Generally, it's best to have a four-wheel drive vehicle. There is a lot of wear and tear on vehicles here and maintenance becomes a high and regular cost. You can rent cars, but it's expensive at around BZ$70–125 a day. If you haven't brought a car with you, buy one locally if you plan to stay. Avis, Budget, Hertz, and Thrifty, to name a few, have franchises in Belize, along with local companies like Crystal, which also sells used cars. While the buses plow most of the main roads and highways, you will need independent transport to get around to see the sights, to hunt for property, and to visit people, as many live off the beaten track. In case you end up wondering about the varied colors of license plates in Belize, government plates are blue and diplomatic corps are red on white.

PUBLIC TRANSPORTATION

Public transportation is quite good, fairly reliable, frequent, and cheap across the country. Most buses are old school buses from America, many of which have been painted in bright colors. A bus ticket to San Ignacio from Belize City costs BZ$7, and from Belmopan to San Ignacio costs BZ$3. There are a few express buses, which travel direct, but most buses stop randomly along the way, which means the trip can take a bit of time. If you're not in a rush it's a great way to see the country and experience the people. Music is always played on the buses and varies from Spanish ballads, to reggae, mainstream pop, and punta rock. Most people chat away (mainly in Spanish) or sing along. It is a far cry from the serious, unsmiling faces hiding behind their newspapers on the daily commute in the Western world. On the whole, people are friendly and helpful. The bus conductor always helps people off the bus with their shopping, assists the elderly, and guides little children down the steps or hands them to their parents. If it's a long-distance bus, say from San Ignacio to Belize City, it will stop briefly at the Belmopan bus terminal, where food, drink, and newspaper vendors board the bus to sell their goods. Passengers can also get off the bus. Most of the bus terminals have public restrooms.

© VICTORIA DAY-WILSON

a water taxi docked at Caye Caulker

They look a bit battered from outside but are generally quite clean. A woman stands at the entrance and for 25 cents gives you some toilet paper before you enter. There are usually a few kiosks selling a variety of drinks and food in the bus terminals.

Taxis in Belize often have a sticker or a sign and always have green number plates. In some cases you will find set prices, in others you will need to bargain politely. There are no meters in the taxis and sharing rides is common. A taxi from the airport into Belize City costs around BZ$50. Within town there is a usually fixed rate of BZ$5–10.

BOAT

For those who live along the coast or on the Cayes transportation is entirely different. Many people have their own boats. Parts of the Cayes are only accessible by boat, like getting from the far north of Ambergris Caye to San Pedro. There are frequent water taxis from Belize City to the Cayes. They go back and forth regularly and cost BZ$10–15 one-way depending if you're going to San Pedro or Caye Caulker. The boats are quite big, partially covered, fast vessels with outboard engines. From Belize City they take about 30 minutes to Caye Caulker and 75 minutes to San Pedro. You can catch them at the Marine Terminal close to the Swing Bridge on North Front Street. There are a few shops and a couple of cafés at the terminal. Taxis wait outside. The water taxis also go between San Pedro, Caye Caulker, and Chetumal, as well as between Corozal and San Pedro. There is another water taxi, which travels around Ambergris Caye, making stops at popular places on the island. There

Golf carts are one of the main forms of transport on the Cayes.

is also a water taxi called Hokey Pokey between the village of Independence/ Mango Creek and Placencia Village.

BICYCLES AND GOLF CARTS

For those living on the Cayes or on the coast in places like Placencia Village and Hopkins, golf carts are the most common mode of transportation, along with bicycles and walking. You will see few cars. Golf carts can be rented or bought and are the fastest, easiest mode of transportation in these areas.

PRIME LIVING LOCATIONS

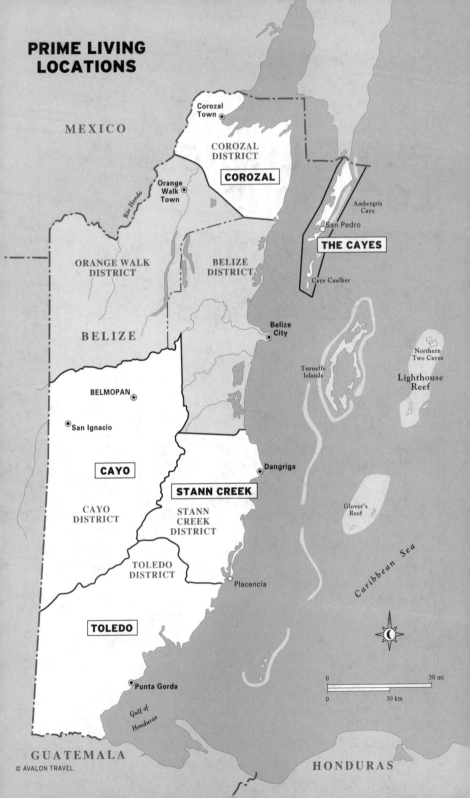

PRIME LIVING LOCATIONS

MEXICO

Corozal
Town

COROZAL
DISTRICT

COROZAL

Rio Hondo

Orange
Walk
Town

ORANGE WALK
DISTRICT

BELIZE
DISTRICT

Ambergris
Caye

San Pedro

THE CAYES

Caye Caulker

BELIZE

Belize
City

Turneffe
Islands

Northern
Two Cayes

Lighthouse
Reef

BELMOPAN

San Ignacio

CAYO

CAYO
DISTRICT

Dangriga

STANN CREEK

STANN
CREEK
DISTRICT

Glover's
Reef

TOLEDO
DISTRICT

Placencia

Caribbean Sea

TOLEDO

Punta Gorda

Gulf of
Honduras

0   30 mi

0   30 km

GUATEMALA

HONDURAS

© AVALON TRAVEL

OVERVIEW

There is something for everyone in Belize, whether you want a rural or urban location, jungle or beach, serenity or hustle and bustle. You can island hop or live on the mainland. Despite its small size, Belize is a beautiful and diverse country. *Because* of its small size, you can get around fairly easily and quickly. People inland sometimes take a weekend break at the cayes or on the coast, and vice versa. Some people move to Belize, settle in one part and then move to another. Quite a few have started off in Corozal and ended up in Cayo or elsewhere. Others have spent time on the cayes and then come inland to Cayo. Which part of Belize suits you depends on your geographical predilection, how much of a social life you want, what your interests and hobbies are, and how much you rely on modern luxuries and utilities. That's the beauty of Belize—everyone is different and most find something to their taste.

On the whole, people don't move to Belize for the urban experience because there really isn't one and most are looking to get away from the frantic bustle of city life, preferring a secluded spot in the jungle or by the sea. The urban

centers that are in Belize aren't like those in North America. The few that come anywhere near the description are a lot smaller and have less to offer than you would experience in a big city in Europe or North America. San Ignacio is quite busy and a few expats live there or on the outskirts. Belmopan is tiny, but will gather momentum as it grows. With the establishment of a few diplomatic missions the social life in Belmopan is picking up. Belize City is not so popular due to its reputation of bad security, but it has a bit more variety. Most expats don't live there but do visit occasionally.

Regarding bugs and reptiles, it doesn't matter where you live in Belize; you will encounter vast quantities of them, and they are often worse during the rainy season. They can be a mild irritation, but the variety of flora and fauna makes up for it. How active your social life is also up to you. It's easier to wander into bars and restaurants on the cayes and in Placencia. Of course, the more involved you are within the community, the more people you will get to know. If you have children and want to place them in private schools, that will narrow your living choices down to San Pedro and the Belmopan area.

Corozal

Corozal is in northern Belize, close to the border of Mexico. Its proximity to Mexico is one of its attractions. Just over the border in Chetumal there is access to large shopping malls, cinemas, and good medical care. If you need to stock up on luxuries or have a taste of so-called civilization, Chetumal is a short drive or boat trip away. Most of Corozal is flat with some beautiful lagoons and well-known nature reserves, and has some ancient Maya ruins such as Cerros and Santa Rita. Its main attraction is the long coastal stretch, which dips into the crystal clear turquoise waters of the Caribbean. There are a few small beaches with firm, hard white sand, but mainly there are piers stretching out to sea. Although part of Belize District, Ambergris Caye is close by. A few people are scattered around, but on the whole people live in developments around villages like Consejo. There is a large concentration of expats and quite a few clubs and activities which contribute to a decent social life. There are also some good restaurants in Corozal. The area has the least rainfall in Belize and, allegedly, the fewest bugs!

Cayo

© VICTORIA DAY-WILSON

looking up the Macal River in Cayo

Cayo has a combination of wild, rugged, emerald green jungles covering hills and valleys, reaching down to the Mopan and Macal Rivers. If you have a pioneering spirit, and really want to get away from it all, Cayo is a good place to be. You can buy several acres, live off the grid if you like, and build your own house. The upside to Cayo is that a social life (if you want it), one or two up-market hotels, several beautiful jungle resorts, and a few decent bars and places to eat are not far away. Belmopan is still slowly coming to life, but the twin towns of San Ignacio and Santa Elena are growing and vibrant, and are good places to get most of your shopping done and catch up with people. The Guatemalan border crossing is not far at Benque Viejo and the Guatemalan town of Melchor offers a bit more variety and markets. It's beneficial to be so close to Belmopan for all official requirements. But the real draw is living life on the wild side, away from the hustle and bustle of towns, and in the beautiful, tranquil jungle. It feels like you're away from everything, although your closest neighbors may be five minutes down the road. There are several ancient Mayan ruins: Caracol, Xunantunich, Cahal Pech, and El Pilar. There are some fantastic places to go riding and plenty of spots to go canoeing. Up in the Mountain Pine Ridge are there are waterfalls and caves that will take your breath away. Cayo offers an adventure-filled, outdoorsy way of life.

The Cayes

There are over 400 islands off the coast of Belize, some are close to the shore, others are far out towards the barrier reef. Quite a few have accommodations. Ambergris Caye and Caye Caulker are the largest (but still quite small) cayes and embody the Caribbean dream lifestyle. The pace is slow and laid-back. In parts there are white sandy beaches, plenty of piers, and stunningly beautiful, crystal-clear, turquoise waters. The social scene is good, as most people live in San Pedro or the built-up area on Caye Caulker. Tourism is the mainstay economy for both islands, so there is a large variety of restaurants and bars to cover all budgets and tastes. Belize is also known for amazing diving and snorkeling, and all other water sports are on offer, including sailing and fishing. Access to and from the cayes is quite easy with regular boats and flights to and from Belize City and Chetumal.

Stann Creek

Of all the districts, Stann Creek has something for everyone. It has a stretch of coast that is the closest in Belize to the barrier reef. It has the Sittee River area, which is known for its amazing birdlife and fishing. The river is deep enough for large boats to sail up and down, and the Caribbean is just around the bend. Not far to the west, the craggy, jungle-clad peaks of the Cockscombe Range stretch into the district, including Belize's second highest point after

along the beach in San Pedro, Ambergris Caye

a hammock on a balcony in Placencia in Stann Creek

Doyle's Delight, Victoria Peak (3,675 ft). Beaches are nice in Stann Creek and all manner of water sports are available. Hopkins Village is a social spot with a few restaurants and cafés. Further south lie several high-end resorts. Traveling down the Placencia Peninsula leads to Placencia Village, a wonderful, warm place, popular with tourists. Most of the village is made up of brightly colored, wooden clapboard houses and it has a wonderful beach. To the west of the peninsula lies a lagoon. If you enjoy a social life, this is a good place to be.

Toledo

If you really want to get away from everything, you can't get more remote than Toledo in southern Belize. It has the only true rainforest in Belize, which offers marvelous opportunities to trek and explore caves and rivers. There are several Maya villages where you can stay and get a genuine cultural experience. Toledo has a long coastline stretching to the border with Guatemala and beautiful cayes, which are less visited by tourists and allow you to explore and enjoy the marine life in peace. It receives the highest level of rainfall in Belize and has rich and varied plants and wildlife. Traditionally Toledo has been the least developed part of Belize and few people have bothered to make the trip down south—their loss! Since the Southern Highway was paved, people are becoming more interested in Toledo and visitor numbers are increasing. There is a sizeable expat community living here who wouldn't dream of living anywhere else. Although it is similar to Cayo, there are Cayo residents who go down to Toledo for a break.

BELIZE CITY

On the whole, Belize City is not very popular with expats as a residential area. This is partly due to its reputation of bad security and crime and the fact that most people who move to Belize aren't looking to live in an urban setting. Many want to live by the sea, on the cayes, or in the jungle. A lot of people come to Belize to get away from big cities and all that comes with them. Having said that, Belize City is still the country's hub, although not its capital. After Hurricane Hattie flattened 75 percent of Belize City in 1961, Belmopan, built from scratch in 1967 (at a cost of $24 million), became Belize's capital city in 1970. Belize City is a low-lying city on the coast in the Belize District and its many canals contribute to flooding whenever a storm hits. Belize City has a volatile history; in the 1600s, buccaneers built it on a combination of mangrove swamp, rum bottles, wood chips, and coral. Strategically located at the mouth of the Belize River, it thrived as a result of the buccaneers-turned-loggers who settled there. Spanish raids on the settlement were frequent, and large parts of the town were destroyed by fire in 1804, 1806, and 1856. Epidemics of cholera, small pox, and yellow fever added to the chaos. But the town continued to grow, particularly when there was an influx of immigrants from the West Indies and people fleeing the Caste Wars in Mexico. Riots rocked the city after WWI during the rise of black consciousness and the independence movement, and a catastrophic hurricane almost wiped out the city in 1931, killing 1,000 people. If nothing else, Belize is certainly a city that has persevered against all odds.

The largest urban center in the country, Belize City has over 53,000 people, or 60 percent of the population of Belize District, an increase of 13 percent from the 2000 census. All of the country's ethnic groups are represented in Belize City, including a sizable population of Creoles. There are some tall, modern buildings, interspersed with some old, colonial buildings. But on the whole, ramshackle, wooden structures line narrow streets along muddy canals. There are several bridges in the town, the most famous of which is the Swing Bridge, which is sometimes opened twice a day. Made in England in 1922, it is the oldest swing bridge in Central America, and the only manually operated swing bridge in the world still in use. It spans Haulover Creek, which divides the city into the South Side and the North Side. Traditionally the elite lived on the seafront and the slaves and laborers lived in the backstreets — what is now the South Side. Things are a bit more upscale on the North Side, with some expensive hotels, embassies, and consulates, and some wealthy homes. Expats and well-off Belizeans tend to live in suburbs to the north and west of the city, in areas like Belama and Bella Vista, or along King's Park, West Landivar, and Princess Margaret Street. Prices can run into the several hundreds of thousands of U.S.

dollars for homes in these areas and rentals run $1,600-$3,200 for a two-bedroom flat or condo in places like Renaissance Towers and Marina Towers. The South Side is more commercial with businesses and industries such as banks, supermarkets, and offices.

Even if you don't have a reason to go to Belize City, spend a day here and have a look around. If you're coming down the Western Highway, stop off at the Belize Zoo at Mile 29 – it's worth it! There are more shops in Belize City and they offer a larger variety than what you can get in most areas of the country. Notable shops include Brodies, Dave's Furniture, and Mirab. Although the parliament and government departments moved to Belmopan, there are still several diplomatic missions, lawyers, accountants, banks, businesses, restaurants, private medical facilities, and media organizations in Belize City. Interestingly, some of the larger shops tried relocating or opening branches in Belmopan but they never got off the ground, so most returned to Belize City. The city is also close to the municipal and international airport, as well as the port where cruise ships come in and water taxis depart for Caye Caulker and San Pedro. It has remained the industrial, financial, and transportation hub of the country, and it is the main communications center. There are several good schools, such as Belize Elementary School (private), Saint Catherine Academy for girls, St. John's High School for boys, which many lead-

ers and key players in Belize have attended, the University of Belize (UB), and the University of the West Indies. Good hospitals and medical care include Belize Medical Associates, Belize Healthcare Partners, as well as several other private dentists and doctors.

To experience some culture and get a glimpse of Belize's history, visit the former city jail, now the Museum of Belize, and Government House, a museum and cultural center. The Image Factory is an art gallery showcasing work from some of Belize's leading contemporary artists. Just down from the water taxi terminal is the Fort George Lighthouse, which is where Baron Bliss, Belize's greatest benefactor, is buried. Drop into the Belize Audobon Society, which runs several nature reserves and works with conservation education. The former colonial administration and court buildings are just over the Swing Bridge and are collectively known as the Courthouse. In the same area on the waterfront is the Bliss Center for Performing Arts, which is home to the Belize National dance Company (BNDC) and hosts several cultural events such as concerts, art exhibitions, and plays. Farther down lies the oldest Anglican cathedral in Central America, St John's Cathedral. Almost opposite, on the seafront, is the House of Culture, a beautiful old white colonial building which was originally Government House, the governor's residence when Belize was a colony.

PRIME LIVING LOCATIONS

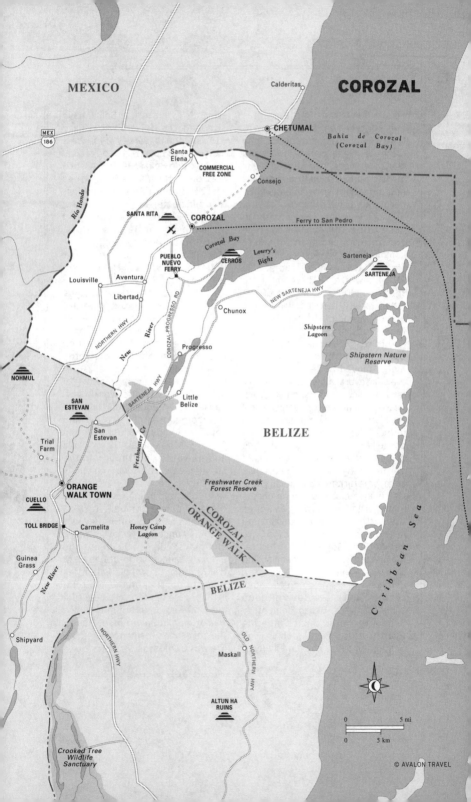

COROZAL

Close to the border of Mexico, Corozal is popular with North American and European expats and lies on the Bay of Chetumal. More Spanish is spoken here, but you can still get by with English. The climate is sub-tropical with less rainfall than southern Belize. It is a short flight or boat trip from San Pedro, a 15-minute boat trip or 30-minute drive over the border to the Mexican town of Chetumal, which offers a variety of goods not available in Belize. It is a laidback place with nice beaches and good access to the sea for swimming, water sports, or boating.

The Lay of the Land

Corozal (pronounced Cor-Roh-ZAHL) is Belize's northern-most district between Mexico and the Caribbean. Corozal Town is the district's capital and lies on the Bay of Chetumal (also referred to as Corozal Bay) between two

© BILL WILDMAN

© LORENZO FORBES

aerial view of Consejo

scenic rivers, the New River and Rio Hondo. It has a population of around 10,000 residents. Ambergris Caye is a short flight or boat trip away. The official Mexican border crossing at Santa Elena and the shopping town of Chetumal are only 9 miles away, and Belize City is 85 miles to the south, down the Northern Highway. There are daily flights and boats to San Pedro.

Property is relatively cheap compared with other popular areas in Belize. It is considered fairly safe and friendly, there aren't that many tourists, and most times of the year are dry and without too many mosquitoes or sand flies. The landscape is mainly flat, swampy savannah or scrub interspersed with sugar plantations. There are several nature reserves and sanctuaries with rich bird- and wildlife, such as the Sarteneja & Shipstern Nature Reserve, Black Howler Monkey Community Baboon Sanctuary, and Crooked Tree Wildlife Sanctuary.

CLIMATE AND CULTURE

Corozal enjoys a warm, subtropical climate much like the rest of Belize but has the lowest rainfall in the country, an average of 60 inches per year.

There is a strong Mexican influence in Corozal and Spanish is widely spoken, though you can get by fine with English. The area is mostly inhabited by Mestizos and Yucatec Mayas who settled in the area after fleeing from the Caste War of Mexico. As with the rest of Belize, Corozal boasts a melting pot of ethnic groups including Creole, Garifuna, East Indian, Mennonite, Asian, and North American and European expats.

Corozal was a private estate before becoming a town in the 1840s. In 1955

PRIME LIVING LOCATIONS

the central plaza in Corozal Town

Hurricane Janet destroyed most of the town. It was rebuilt with a lot of Mexican and Caribbean influence. It has a rich Maya heritage and most of Corozal Town is believed to be built on top of an ancient Mayan trading center called Santa Rita, which is believed to be part of ancient Chactumal, the Maya capital of the area at the time of the first Spanish attempt to conquer the Yucatec Mayas in the early 16th century. Part of it is excavated and lies near the middle of town. Cerros and Lamanai are not far.

Corozal's economy is based on the production of sugar cane, papaya, livestock, and fishing, but earnings from real estate and tourism are increasing. The Free Trade Zone just south of Santa Elena has over 200 outlets and is a source of revenue and employment for the area.

Daily Life

EXPAT SOCIAL SCENE

Corozal is a relaxed, easy-going seaside town popular with expats. There are some good restaurants to choose from, an art gallery, a history museum, and a cultural center. There are several clubs including a yacht club, a gardening club, and a poker club, as well as regular yoga classes. There is also a Rotary Club. On the second Tuesday of every month expats meet at the Purple Toucan at 2 P.M. in Corozal. You bring your own food and the idea is for people to socialize, meet new people, trade information, and buy and sell things.

Property is at a relatively low cost compared with some parts of Belize and

EXPAT STORY: LIFE IN COROZAL

My husband and I chose Corozal three years ago, after visiting Placencia, Caye Caulker, San Ignacio, and Belize City. We were drawn to Corozal because of its proximity to Mexico, supposedly less rainfall, few tourists, and small town, and we found a piece of land that appealed to us tremendously. We bought on a whim, and it was only after we moved that we realized we had made a good decision. I am living here without my husband at the moment; he will retire within the next year and a half (but hopefully sooner). I'm here by myself for the most part. I feel very secure and unafraid, especially because I have two dogs to keep me company, and I sometimes have renters. My mom spends six months out of the year with me, too.

I love visiting Mexico and would cross the border much more frequently if I didn't have to pay the BZ$37.50 each time. I have just applied for my residency, which means I won't have to pay the fee, so I will start enjoying that a lot more. I will visit Chetumal and the nearby Mexican towns to enjoy the shopping and beach, and the casino also beckons me to gamble or dine for supper.

There is a large expatriate community here and they have organized several venues to get together: a friendship lunch, women's group, garden club, darts day, etc. Of those, I only attend darts day, which is held at a good friend's restaurant and bar, Scotty's Bar and Grill in Corozal (best hamburgers and pizza in town, by the way). I have a relatively small group of expat friends that I see frequently because we have a lot in common, but there is no shortage of expats to socialize with. I also have a lot of Belizean friends whom I treasure. I think it is important to immerse oneself in the local culture and make friends.

As for healthcare, luckily I have had no emergency issues. I visited a gynecologist in Orange Walk and found the doctor to be very attentive and professional. I also visited a dentist for a cleaning and have no complaints. The dentist is well educated and allocates time to talk about any concerns she might find. The blood clinic/lab staff is professional and friendly; the pharmacists at the drugstores are very helpful and knowledgeable.

I absolutely love my life in Belize and it has quickly become "home."

*– Contributed by
Donna Goudreault*

there is a sizeable and active expat community, although not everyone lives here all year round. Some come for six months in the year, over the winter months. Most of the expat community is retirees, though that is slowly beginning to change as people are retiring at a younger age or selling their businesses. In 2010, the American Association of Retired Persons (AARP) ranked Corozal a top retirement destination.

There are a variety of options for volunteering in the community. Offering to help at local schools and libraries is always an option, as well as getting involved in conservation. Rotary clubs do a lot of good work, and there is a local soup kitchen. Many people tend to help by supporting a few children or families individually through work or education.

HEALTH

There is good, low-cost medical care across the border in Chetumal and Mérida. As in most towns and villages in Belize, there are a variety of clinics in Corozal and the surrounding villages. The major ones in Corozal include the Northern Medical Group, Bethesda Medical Center, and Corozal Community Hospital. The local hospitals are fine for primary care but for any serious or long-term health issues it may be advisable to go to Belize City, Guatemala, or pop over the border to Mexico where healthcare is relatively cheap. There is a dentist in Shipyard in Orange Walk, as well as a few in Corozal. For pets there is the Northern Veterinary Clinic (NVC) in Corozal.

EDUCATION

There are several state schools in Corozal from preschool through university level. They include St. Francis Xavier Infants Preschool, St. Francis Xavier Primary School, St. Paul's School, Corozal Methodist School, Mary Hill Primary School, St. Paul's by the Sea (Anglican), Corozal Community College, and Corozal Junior College. Francis Xavier for the 5–14 age group is recommended by expats who attended it when they were children. For further education, Corozal Community College (CCC) is considered a good option. Students from the U.S. who have enrolled in CCC have been put back a year, and if returning to the U.S. they have been placed above their year group. The government pays for a school bus that transports students from the surrounding villages to CCC.

Where to Live

Some people live in town or in Consejo Village but most live in developments just outside town like Consejo Shores, Mayan Seaside, Wagner's Landing, and what is known locally as Tony's subdivision or "Gringo Lane." Others areas of interest include Cerros Sands, Orchid Bay, and Progresso Heights.

Consejo Shores was established by Bill Wildman who has done land surveying and a variety of other things in Belize since 1960. It has over a mile of seafront property and is spread over 350 acres, with over 85 established homes. Most original lots have been sold but some are available for resale. Land ownership is held in Absolute Fee Simple Title. All properties are high

a house for sale in Consejo

and dry, averaging seven feet above sea level. Most lots are about half an acre and vary in price, US$33,000–400,000. The best advertisement for Consejo Shores is Bill, who settled here after spending six years searching for the best place to live in Belize. As far as he is concerned, there is no better place to live in the world.

Cerros Sands at La Playa de Cerros Maya community is located 11 miles southeast of Corozal Town. Beachfront, beach view, and channel plots are in the US$18,000–100,000 range. Houses can be built for $157,770–167,770.

Wagner's Landing is a private, controlled-access, gated, waterfront, residential community on the Corozal Bay. The lot has electricity and domestic water delivered to the front lot line. The lot is accessible by a maintained, private road. Wagner's Landing has a private boat ramp into Corozal Bay and a planned, private marina area at the northeast end of the property.

Mayan Seaside is close to Consejo Village and has about 100 lots, most of which have been sold, and several houses have been built or are under construction.

Progresso Heights lies on Progresso Lagoon near Progresso Village. There are many lots on the seafront and inland, all roughly about a quarter of an acre in size. Several homes have been built or are under construction. Prices of lots run US$20,000–26,000.

Orchid Bay is a large, planned development, where lot prices vary range US$40,000–500,000. It lies between Copper Bank and Sarteneja.

© VICTORIA DAY-WILSON

Corozal Town

Getting Around

There are several flights a day on Maya Island Air and Tropic Air from Belize City to Corozal. They go via San Pedro on Ambergris Caye. The flight takes about 20 minutes from San Pedro. The airport in Corozal is about two miles outside of town. There are one or two water taxi services between San Pedro and Corozal. The trip takes about 1.5 hours. There is a boat from Consejo to Chetumal every Wednesday. The trip takes about 15 minutes.

If you're traveling by car, the trip from Belize City takes about two hours along the Northern Highway, which is a good paved road. Quite a few roads in Corozal are all-weather unpaved roads. The road from Corozal to Consejo is good. But, in general a four-wheel drive vehicle is recommended.

Regular buses run up the Northern Highway from Belize City to Corozal and on to the Mexican border town of Chetumal and beyond. A ticket from Corozal to Belize City costs BZ$9. There are several buses to Chetumal from Cancún, Mérida, and Playa Del Carmen. The bus from Cancún takes about five hours, four from Playa del Carmen, and six from Mérida. The bus company is called ADO and operates clean, comfortable, air-conditioned buses. At Chetumal, change buses to cross the border into Corozal.

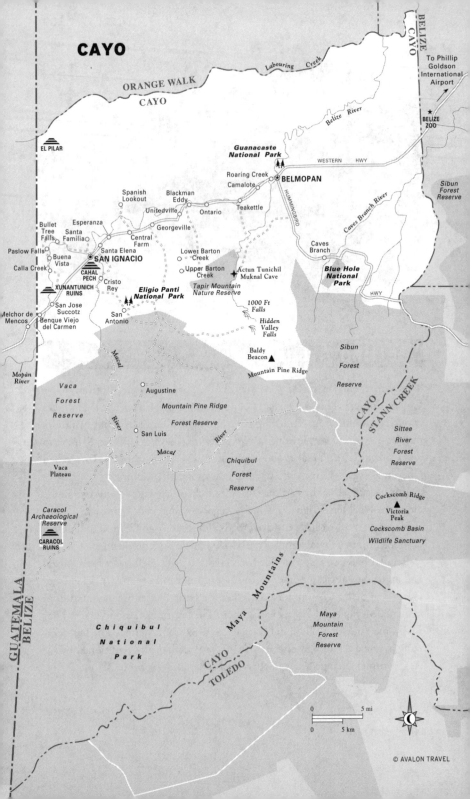

CAYO

If you have a bit of a pioneering spirit and fancy an adventure, then Cayo is for you. A beautiful, hilly area inland at the foot of the Maya Mountains, bordered by Guatemala, Cayo is covered in thick jungle separated by the Macal and Mopan Rivers, which join to become the Belize River. This is the place to buy a plot of jungle, clear some of it, and build your own house. There is plenty of wildlife, rich birdlife, and all manner of weird and wonderful insects and reptiles. The main towns are San Ignacio (known locally as Cayo) and Santa Elena. Cayo is also home to the tiny Belizean capital of Belmopan.

Residents from the coast and tourists both flock to Cayo for adventure and the Mayan ruins. Here you'll find the ancient ruins Caracol (also known as "The Snail" in Mayan), Cahal Pech (Place of the Ticks), Xunantunich (Stone Woman), and El Pilar (Watering Basin in Spanish, as the area has abundant sources of natural water). You'll also find natural wonders such as the Actun Tunichil Muknal Cave, Mountain Pine Ridge Forest Reserve (location of the beautiful Thousand-Foot Falls), Blue Hole National Park, Chiquibul National

© VICTORIA DAY-WILSON

Park and Forest Reserve (home to the largest cave system in the western hemisphere), and Tapir Mountain Nature Reserve. People often say Cayo puts the "turf" in a "surf and turf" holiday.

Large tracts of agricultural land usually covered in citrus trees and green fields intersperse the district, offering the option of starting and living on a farm. For those who prefer an urban life, there is San Ignacio and Santa Elena. The Hawkesworth Bridge (built in 1949) connects the two towns, which are separated by the Macal River. It is the only road-suspension bridge in Belize.

Cayo is popular with expats. Here you get the best of all worlds: stunning jungle, rivers, and ancient ruins, and if you fancy a break or a change of scene, the coast is close by. Property is cheaper here than on the coast, and there are fewer mosquitoes and no sand flies. Some people work in the tourist industry, while others start small businesses. There are quite a few retirees here, as well as adventure-seeking tourists. Quite often, people buy plots of jungle along the Mopan or Macal River and build their dream home. Cristo Rey is a popular area for this.

There are a variety of options for finding a home in Cayo. You can find land with river frontage and build a house; start a lodge, B&B, or resort; or you can live in San Ignacio, Santa Elena, or Belmopan.

The Lay of the Land

Cayo District is the largest in Belize with a population of 70,000, according to the Statistical Institute of Belize (SIB) 2010 census. Cayo lies inland in the western part of the country along the border of Guatemala. It is one of the most popular areas in Belize for expats and tourists alike, and the reason for this isn't hard to see. The Maya Mountains cover more than half the district, pouring over its southern borders into Stann Creek and Toledo Districts. The Mountain Pine Ridge runs through the center of Cayo and the result is that almost everywhere you look there is a stunning jungle-clad vista of rugged peaks in the distance. Sometimes the peaks take on a bluish purple hue, which adds to their mystery. Abundant rivers and creeks run down from the mountains and a series of caves are scattered across them—some still undiscovered except perhaps by old hunters. Mayan ruins, most of which are easy to access, are spread across the district and nestled on high ground among the huge jungle trees; it's likely that there are more that lie undiscovered.

Farther to the north and heading east out of the district towards Belize

the Cayo landscape

District, undulating verdant fields planted with citrus and a variety of other crops, or grazed by cattle or horses, spread out like a blanket interspersed with jungle.

More than 60 percent of Cayo District is protected as a wildlife sanctuary, national park, or forest reserve. The Mopan and Macal Rivers snake through the jungle and connect to feed the Belize River.

The country's capital, Belmopan, is only an hour's drive from the Caribbean Sea, and San Ignacio, the district capital, is only a short drive from the border of Guatemala at the border town of Benque Viejo del Carmen.

San Ignacio, also known as Cayo, was at one time isolated between the Mopan and Macal Rivers with no roads to get there. It became known as El Cayo, the Spanish word for island. The population in Cayo District is largely Mestizo and Creole, with some Lebanese and Mopan, as well as a fairly large Chinese population. A sizable Mennonite community resides near San Ignacio in Spanish Lookout. Once a terminal for the chicle and timber trade, Cayo now relies on tourism and agriculture for its economy. The primary crop is citrus. Oil has been discovered and is exported by the Belize Natural Energy (BNE) Company, which has its headquarters in Spanish Lookout.

There are two major highways in the district: The Western Highway runs from Belize City to the Guatemalan border, and the Hummingbird Highway starts in Belmopan and ends at the juncture of the Coastal Road and the Southern Highway in the Stann Creek District. There is a paved road out to Spanish Lookout off of the Western Highway. Most other roads in the district are unpaved dirt roads that vary in quality. Some are graded regularly and can

PRIME LIVING LOCATIONS

be accessed in the wet season; others are less well maintained and can be tricky to navigate even in a four-wheel drive vehicle during the rains.

CLIMATE

While a few degrees cooler than the coast due to a slightly higher altitude, the climate in Cayo is subtropical. It's warm and humid. The average temperature is 79°F. The coolest month is January and the hottest is May. It does get a few degrees cooler up in the Mountain Pine Ridge, and on a cold evening in the rainy season, you may need a light sweater and a thin blanket or duvet at night. Average temperatures in Cayo can reach 88°F and drop to 66°F.

The whole month of May can pass without any rain, but in June–November, it can sometimes rain for days. There are dramatic thunderstorms (it's advisable to unplug your satellite connection because of the lightning), and the ground becomes very muddy. The wet season is interspersed with dry and sunny days, when everything dries up again.

The day starts early for most when it is still cool and crisp and you can get the majority of your chores out of the way before the heat really sets in. The dry season runs February–May, and the wet season June–November. During the wet season temperatures are around 88°F.

Belize lies in the hurricane belt, though it rarely experiences the full impact of a storm. Cayo seems particularly well protected because of its inland location and high elevation, and when there are hurricane warnings, many people head up here.

LANGUAGE AND CULTURE

Walk through any town in Cayo and you will likely hear Spanish, Creole, and English spoken. Most people speak English, but it is useful to know some basic Spanish and to learn some key phrases in Creole. If nothing else, it shows an effort to integrate.

The Creole population became a minority in Cayo after an influx of people moved to Belize in the 1980s, seeking refuge from instability in other Central American countries. As a result, the majority of the population is now Mestizo, and Spanish is widely spoken.

Daily Life

EXPAT SOCIAL SCENE

In Cayo, expats come from all walks of life. Quite a few are birders, writers, retired professors, and artists. If you're looking for an active social scene, then it's best to be in San Ignacio or Belmopan. Many people who move to Cayo like their space and privacy but enjoy dropping in on each other for the odd drink or party. Most people know or know of each other, and as in any small community, gossip is rife. Social mixing is influenced by economic and professional status as opposed to purely by nationality. It's a very multinational scene. If you live remotely, a good way to keep your finger on the pulse is to join a Belize Forum: There is a lot of useful information and dialogue about personal experiences at www.belizeforum.com/belize. The Belmopan International Women's Group (BIWG) is also a good place for women new to the area to meet other women.

More expats are moving to Belmopan due to the rise of diplomatic missions and non-governmental organizations (NGOs). With more people, the social scene is becoming more active with several activities for children such as dance, karate, and golf lessons, as well as a library. There are social programs organized through the church in Georgeville three times a week. It gives children who are homeschooled an opportunity to mix socially with their peers. A youth group and various other activities are in the planning stages.

There is a lot of day-to-day interaction with the local population in Cayo. You will get to know people who you will greet in the street, at a café, or while out shopping. Saturdays are very busy in San Ignacio because of the thriving market on the banks of the Macal River, where all manner of goods are sold. People also bump into each other while shopping for building materials and general supplies in the Mennonite village of Spanish Lookout.

VOLUNTEERING

There are plenty of options for volunteer work with a variety of worthy causes, such as helping the elderly, victims of domestic violence, and people with disabilities; lending a hand in health clinics; looking after abandoned animals; and organizing community projects and fundraising. There are opportunities to donate food and clothes, subsidize school tuitions, and provide educational supplies. There are also opportunities to work as a fee-paying member on conservation expeditions through field study centers and with archaeological teams. There is an active Rotary Club in San Ignacio, with 28 members and a focus on education, and another Rotary Club in Belmopan.

OPENING AND RUNNING A RESORT IN CAYO

My husband Alan and I honeymooned in Belize in 1998 with only a tent, a rented four-wheel drive vehicle, an axe, and a map of questionable accuracy. I am a former special education teacher and school administrator and my husband Alan was the owner of a private investigation firm in Florida. We fell in love with the country and its people, and continued coming back to vacation in Belize on a regular basis. After several years of courtship with Belize, we decided to take the leap and stay on more permanently, starting first in a tent with no running water, no electricity, and only a rough idea of starting a citrus farm. Five years and many ideas and learning experiences later, Table Rock Jungle Lodge opened for business on the Macal River, five miles south of San Ignacio in the Cayo District.

We found the local labor force eager to help, hardworking, honest, and easy to work with. I must also note that Belize is especially friendly to its female entrepreneurs. Despite being a Central American nation, there is little in the way of male chauvinism, and many, if not most, businesses here are owned or run by women. We learned very quickly that despite these advantages, Belize definitely has its challenges to starting and running a business, as there is no such thing as a Home Depot or mega box store

around the corner – or anywhere in the country for that matter. Many items that we needed in order to get started were not be available from one day to the next. For example, there may not be a single store in town or in the country that had deck screws or the right color of paint during the week we needed them. Supplies often had to be ordered and shipped from the United States, which at first was a logistical nightmare.

We later learned how things work here and this process became easier, although still quite costly. Dealing with local regulations and government bureaucracy can be equally mind-numbing and time-consuming, as can communications and Internet services. As an expat there are endless hoops to jump through in order to run your business, such as obtaining and maintaining work permits, immigration visas, corporate bank accounts, and taxes. While regulations can be as stringent as in the United States for a small business, the overall costs are much more reasonable for the employer.

Having initially come to Belize to experience the abundance and beauty of the natural surroundings, especially in the Cayo area, we ended up staying and starting our business here because of the amazing and beautiful people that make up Belize. We draw such positive

The Octavia Waight Centre in San Ignacio is a home for the elderly that accepts volunteers. If you want to work with animals, the Belize Humane Society in Belmopan welcomes help with abandoned or maltreated animals and provides a good vet service and advice. The Belmopan International Women's Group (BIWG) has a membership of 110 women, some of whom are overseas members. The BIWG provides a forum for women to network, meet new people, and serve many good causes in the community, which don't usually

energy from living in this sparsely populated, ethnically and religiously diverse country, which includes Mestizo, Mayan, Creole, Mennonite, Anglo, Chinese, Lebanese, and East Indian inhabitants who practice Catholicism, Episcopalism, Pentecostalism, Taoism, and some of the old Mayan beliefs.

Purchased as only thick jungle and an abandoned farm, Table Rock was hewn out of the rainforest and has continued to develop since the first walking trail was carved out by machete in 2002. We have worked to make Table Rock Jungle Lodge unique by preserving the natural surroundings, keeping the number of rooms limited, employing local villagers, and by replenishing one of Belize's earliest natural resources—the mahogany tree. All this hard work has paid off: We received the distinction of Belize's Small Hotel of the Year, we won the Belize Green Business Award, and we are a Trip Advisor Travelers' Choice and Certificate of Excellence Winner.

We've been asked what were some of our biggest learning experiences. From learning how to live in the jungle with just tents and coolers to making our own electricity and supplying our own water, our Belizean education has been a true adventure. We have learned more than we ever wanted to know about living "off the grid," and now have an almost inexhaustible knowledge of Mayan and Mestizo culture, local medicinal plants and herbs, and the use of local products and techniques for building construction. We have also learned one of the most important lessons Belize can teach, which is, "If you come to Belize without patience, you will learn it; if you come to Belize with patience, you will lose it."

When asked by family and friends what our business plan was when we announced our intentions to move to Belize, we answered, "The business plan is that we get to live there. The rest will work itself out." We now celebrate birthdays, holidays, anniversaries, funerals, and births in our adopted village of Cristo Rey. While we have suffered hardships, such as the death of our first child who was born prematurely and only survived for one month, we have also celebrated inexplicable joys such as the birth of our second son, Samuel, just recently born right here in San Ignacio Town. We look forward to continuing our life here and raising our son as a Belizean. And while we know that there will continue to be hardships and difficulties, we will not fight our rugged life in Belize, but learn to dance with the unique rhythm of each day.

– Contributed by Colleen Spring, www.tablerockbelize.com

PRIME LIVING LOCATIONS

attract the attention of larger organizations. They hold a meeting at Corkers Restaurant in Belmopan on the first Wednesday of every month. There is a membership fee of BZ$30, which goes towards their outreach projects in the Cayo District.

The Cornerstone Foundation in San Ignacio works on a variety of community outreach programs, including helping people with food, health programs, literacy, and women's projects.

The George Price Centre for Peace and Development in Belmopan works on conflict resolution and strengthening communities in a peaceful and constructive manner. In Belmopan there's also a children's home—Marla's House of Hope—that provides care for neglected and abused children.

HEALTH

There are several hospitals in Cayo District. The larger ones are the Western Regional in Belmopan and La Loma Luz Adventist Hospital in Santa Elena. For clinics, there is the Cayo Family Clinic and Pharmacy on Bullet Tree Road, and the Mopan Clinic in Benque Viejo del

© VICTORIA DAY-WILSON

You can volunteer at the Octavia Waight Centre for the elderly.

Carmen. A dermatologist from Belize City visits every Saturday.

Most doctors are from various countries in Central America. The healthcare is fairly good for basic issues. There are also various clinics, doctors, and pharmacies scattered around town, as well as rural clinics. There is a clinic in Spanish Lookout that is run by the Mennonite church and is staffed entirely by Mennonite women who have been trained as EMTs and midwives.

For more serious medical problems, most people go to the Karl Heusner Memorial Hospital (state) or Belize Medical Associates (BMA, private) in Belize City, or to Guatemala City, Mexico, or North America. Have a look around hospitals on your fact-finding trip. Don't count on a good, functional 911 emergency system.

The famous Maya healer Don Eligio Panti who lived to the age of 103 came from the village of San Antonio in Cayo. One of his nieces, Maria Garcia, runs a guesthouse here and is also president of the Itzamna Society, a local organization that protects local environment and culture, and she offers courses in medicinal plants. Don Eligio passed on his skills to Dr. Rosita Arvigo, who operates the Ix Chel Wellness Center in Santa Elena. It is open year round, but Dr. Arvigo is usually only there in the winter.

There are also traditional Chinese medicine options like Mr. Chen, a Taiwanese acupuncturist at Mile 25 on the Western Highway, and a Philippine herbalist in Armenia, on the Hummingbird Highway.

EDUCATION
State Schools
San Ignacio and Santa Elena have four main schools and one university. Sacred Heart College (Catholic) is the biggest primary and secondary school in San Ignacio, followed by Faith Nazarene Primary School. Across the river in Santa Elena are the Eden Seventh Day Adventist High School and the Saint Ignatius High School (Catholic). Just outside San Ignacio in Central Farm is Galen University and a University of Belize (UB) campus.

Private Schools
Just outside Belmopan lies the Belize Christian Academy (BCA), a private school with about 235 students from over 15 different countries. It runs from kindergarten to 12th grade. The school provides a bus to and from the Cayo area and Belmopan. All students are required to pay a non-refundable application/testing fee of US$25. There is an enrollment fee of US$275, and annual fees run from US$1,700 for elementary school to US$1,800 for high school. The Quality School International (QSI) is the first internationally recognized American school in Belize. It opened in Belmopan in August 2011 and teaches children ages 5–13.

Homeschooling
Many families in Cayo homeschool their children using the Internet. There are a variety of curriculum choices. A good umbrella resource with information on homeschooling and courses can be found at www.homeschool.com. Michelle Leonard, a trained teacher and musician, helps supervise children of all ages through the church in Georgeville using the Accelerated Christian Education (ACE) curriculum. The Calvert curriculum is also popular.

Where to Live

There are quite a few options for where to live in Cayo. Locations vary depending on if you want privacy and seclusion, in which case buying a plot on the Macal or Mopan River is a good option, particularly if you like the jungle environment. To be really remote and in a slightly cooler climate, you can head up to Mountain Pine Ridge. The beautiful Hummingbird Highway that connects Belmopan to Dangriga in Stann Creek District is another popular area. The highway gently winds down towards the coast through thick lush rainforest and citrus plantations with places like the Blue Hole National Park alongside. At Mile 29 you'll find an anti-gravity spot where your car goes backwards uphill—it never fails to amuse and fascinate!

You can buy a house or buy a plot of land and build a house. You can buy a wooden prefab house from the Mennonites at Spanish Lookout. Houses in both San Ignacio and Santa Elena reflect the local design—wooden clapboard, sometimes on stilts, or cement with a tin roof—as most of the inhabitants are Belizeans. Most homes are small. The majority of expats who move here haven't come all this way to live in urban areas and tend to buy large tracts of land on the outskirts of towns, in the surrounding rural areas, or in remote parts such as Mountain Pine Ridge. Even expats running businesses in urban areas rarely live centrally.

You can live in any of the small villages along the Western Highway between San Ignacio and Belmopan. If you are more of a social person and prefer an urban life, there is the option of living in the twin towns of San Ignacio and Santa Elena. San Ignacio and Santa Elena have a single town board and are expected within the next few years to become one Cayo city. A popular part of San Ignacio is up on the hills of the town in the Cahal Pech area.

Although technically the capital of Belize, Belmopan is a bit of a one-horse town that wasn't incorporated as a city until 2000, but the social life has picked up since the U.S. embassy was completed in 2008. If you are running a business or attached to an embassy or aid group, Belmopan is the place to be. Do bear in mind that urban in Belize is not the same as urban in North America. The towns are small, and there isn't much in the form of arts and culture. There are no major bars, nightclubs, malls, or restaurants.

SAN IGNACIO

Nestled among the Maya Mountains in the heart of Cayo, on the west bank of the Macal River, San Ignacio lies 72 miles from Belize City, 22 miles from Belmopan, and 9 miles from the Guatemala border. Like the rest of Belize,

© VICTORIA DAY-WILSON

San Ignacio town center

it is a melting pot of ethnicities and cultures, with Mestizos, Maya, Creole, Garifuna, Mennonites, North Americans, Europeans, Indians, Chinese, Lebanese, and other Central Americans.

Spread over several hills, San Ignacio is a small town (relatively speaking) with about 20,000 residents. It's a hustling and bustling town which has grown rapidly over the last few years due to a combination of foreigners moving in—both from North America and Europe, as well as other Central American countries—and tourists using it as a popular base from which to explore the delights of Cayo's caves, rivers, jungles, and ruins.

Just above San Ignacio, a short walk up the hill, lies Cahal Pech (Mayan for Place of Ticks), one of the main ruins and the name for the suburb surrounding it. It's amazing to have something of such ancient historic importance virtually in the center of a busy 21st century town!

Quite a few expats live in or on the outskirts of San Ignacio and Santa Elena because there is more of a social life than in rural areas, roads are good, and access to most things is easy. People living in town are also on the grid for power and water, and have better phone reception than some outlying areas. It's easier and cheaper to pop into town to meet people or do some shopping. One thing to take into account financially when deciding whether to live in town or outside is the cost of fuel, which is high in Belize. Regular gas costs BZ$11.74, premium BZ$12.03, and diesel BZ$10.35. Of course properties are smaller in town, so if space and seclusion appeal to you, there are larger tracts of land in more rural areas. And some tracts are not that far out of town, so you can have the best of both worlds.

There are a variety of restaurants and cafés in town, ranging from the high-end San Ignacio Hotel on the hill to the basic backpacker budget options, as well as several places to try local cuisine. Burns Avenue, the main street in town, lined with a choice of cafés and eating venues, runs above the Mexican-style plaza where the buses to Belmopan and Belize enter. In the middle of town, at one end of Burns Avenue, several streets meet and form a large intersection. Along these different streets lie a variety of supermarkets, banks, butchers, bakeries, estate agents, medical clinics, the post office, gift shops, domestic appliance shops, and shops which sell a little bit of everything.

Going down towards the Macal River, you'll encounter the market, which is open every day of the week. But Saturday is the market day—as much a chance to socialize and catch up on gossip as to stock up on wares. Like the town, the market has grown and is now one of the biggest in Belize with wares ranging from fruits and vegetables, to spices, clothes, bread, eggs, and even puppies. The colorful scene is enhanced by the variety of people: Traditional Mennonites in their straw hats rub shoulders with Mestizos, Mayas, Creoles, and foreigners. Tourists wander around with cameras and backpacks; locals mingle and chat. Sometimes music fills the air as school bands practice at the entrance of the market. Alongside the market is the other bus stop from which local district buses leave to San Antonio, Benque Viejo del Carmen on the border, and Spanish Lookout. Parked alongside the buses are cars and wooden Mennonite carts with the horses grazing close by in the shade. And alongside this bustling colorful scene, the river—broad and shallow—snakes by, always enticing you to jump in and cool down.

Across the river run two bridges connecting Santa Elena and San Ignacio. Coming into San Ignacio is the low wooden bridge and leaving is the higher Hawkesworth Bridge. This is the starting point for the annual four-day La Ruta Maya Canoe Race to Belize City, held in early March to commemorate Baron Bliss—a Brit who bequeathed about two million dollars upon his death in 1926 to what were then British Honduras and her people because he liked it so. Despite its tranquility, the section of river running through town is always a place of action, filled with people cleaning their cars or washing horses, kids playing in the water, adults cooling off, and canoes with tourists or locals passing by. When driving home after a long, hot day of shopping, I never tire of the beautiful view upriver over the Hawkesworth Bridge. It is wild and peaceful; the river is deeper and cuts a swathe through the lush green jungle. It almost seems impossible that you just left town. I think all heads turn when crossing that bridge.

We sometimes get up early and hop in the canoe and go into San Ignacio via the river. It's a beautiful way to go shopping! It takes a bit longer but the journey is worth it. The river is peaceful and tranquil at that time of day, and there is more wildlife visible. The plant life is incredible and viewing it from a canoe provides a different perspective. Once in town, someone has to guard the canoe until you load it up with your shopping and paddle back upstream. Back on the river, the hustle and bustle of town is left far behind and the natural beauty and serenity of the river and jungle take over.

the Hawkesworth Bridge from the Santa Elena side, with San Ignacio in the background

SANTA ELENA

Santa Elena is basically an extension of San Ignacio: Together they are one town divided by the Macal River. Santa Elena has some larger supermarkets, as well as clinics, pharmacies, and local roadside eateries. But, across the river, San Ignacio is where most people tend to shop and where the market, soccer field, and the most facilities for tourists are located. There is one basic hotel in Santa Elena: The Aguada. The Ministry of Education, Ministry of Works, and Social Security Office for San Ignacio, Santa Elena, and the surrounding area are in Santa Elena. The police station, Lands Office, and mayor's office are in San Ignacio. The fire station recently moved from San Ignacio to Santa Elena due to easier access through traffic. Most people pass through Santa Elena and very few expats live here. One could argue that parts of San Ignacio are more upscale and, deservedly or not, Santa Elena has a poor reputation for security.

BELMOPAN

Belmopan is Belize's young capital city and was created after the devastation of the former capital (Belize City) by Hurricane Hattie in 1961. The government moved here in 1970, but the unofficial capital and main hub remains Belize City. Belmopan is an unexceptional place, not what you'd expect of a capital. It's fairly flat and spread out, but following the addition of several diplomatic missions and international organizations, it is slowly growing and the social options are increasing.

At Belmopan you can turn off the Western Highway and head down the Hummingbird Highway—the most beautiful road in Belize—which culminates in Dangriga in Stann Creek District. The road winds through rugged hills, covered in thick jungle broken up by the occasional citrus farm. A nice place to stop is Blue Hole National Park. (Belize has two Blue Holes—one in the sea and one on land; this is the one on land.) This area along Hummingbird Highway is a good place to buy a small citrus orchard, and several expats have settled along it.

Most expats who live in Belmopan work with diplomatic missions or organizations like the United Nations. Houses tend to be comfortable with nice gardens, not that different from what you would expect in an upscale urban area in Europe or North America. Belmopan is generally a safe area to live, however most of the expats—mainly American embassy employees and other resident embassies—live around the U.S. Embassy area. Some people who run businesses in Belmopan choose to live on the outskirts.

Belmopan is a small but sprawling town. Unfortunately there are no real parks in Belmopan, and for some reason no big trees! It is a bit hard sometimes to find a suitable place to spend quality time outdoors. The "international" community is very small but very well integrated and welcoming. Most of the social activities revolve around dinner with friends at their houses and a party every once in a while. There is only one club, called La Cabana, where there is good music until late. There is no cinema, no tennis club, and no shopping mall. There is one restaurant called Corkers, which is about the only decent place to have dinner. There is a big Chinese restaurant and a pizzeria. There is also a slightly wider choice in the supermarkets than in San Ignacio and Santa Elena.

ALONG THE MACAL AND MOPAN RIVERS

People with a lust for adventure often choose to live along the Mopan or Macal Rivers, which meet at Branch Mouth, just north of San Ignacio, and become the Belize River. Many open resorts, lodges, and B&Bs offer cave tubing along the rivers or other trips to caves and ruins, or they arrange trips for their guests through tour operators in town. Idyllic as it may sound, opening and running these establishments takes a lot of hard work, time, energy, and money, not to mention perseverance in the face of stiff competition in this fairly small market. Many people have worked on their resorts for years before seeing a return. But some of the results are beautiful. It's worth driving around and stopping off at various lodges for a drink just to see the creativity and individuality brought forth by everyone's different dreams and tastes.

swimming in the Macal River

In some cases—and increasingly now as more people have moved, built homes, and then sold them—you can get a jungle, river-front property with a house on it. However, there's still plenty of jungle to go around and several large tracts of virgin bush waiting to be developed. As the area's popularity has risen over the last 10 years so have the prices.

One old-timer who came to Belize in 1973, and has lived in different parts of Cayo ever since, thinks life in Belize is easier these days. When she and her husband first started, they needed a generator for electricity and they hauled and pumped water. Her experience was that those who were practical and could fix things made it; and those who couldn't often didn't. I would say that is still true to a large extent. She added that back then there was more bush and fewer people, which led to a tighter community as people had to rely on each other. The lifestyle was different. People had no phones and then in the 1980s people relied on 2 Band Radios for a BZ$100 licensing fee.

Ironically, back then the roads were better as they were regularly maintained by the Forestry Department. Many roads now are quite rough and can become hard to navigate in the wet season even though they are graded once a month. Car maintenance becomes very expensive when you live outside town.

Cristo Rey, San Antonio, and the Mountain Pine Ridge

The Mountain Pine Ridge and the villages of Cristo Rey and San Antonio are south of San Ignacio. The main road leading here from San Ignacio (via the Hawkesworth Bridge and through Santa Elena) is only partly paved and can be a hard, bumpy ride in the dry season and a slippery one in the wet season.

© VICTORIA DAY-WILSON

a home in the jungle on the Macal River

The government has been promising for years to pave the unpaved sections since there is a fairly high volume of traffic on the road and it leads to many resorts and several expat homes, but that promise has yet to materialize. One man, who owns property along the road, paved his section of road because he got fed up with the poor road.

I do always think that arriving at your destination is worth traveling on the bad road. After a drive through the dark, cool jungle, surrounded by the sounds of exotic birds and the stunning array of colors, you arrive at your house and relax, listening to the river bubbling away, and the irritations of the road soon melt away—until you need to go shopping again!

Steep forested hillsides tumble into the Macal River, which has a mind of its own. At some times of the day it can be a deep roaring torrent with a strong current and at other times, a shallow slow meandering river. During the rains it can rise as high as 40 feet. Most people build their houses slightly higher up to avoid flooding and also because all land 66 feet up from a river or seafront in Belize is declared public land. The hillsides have a wild, rugged beauty.

The area from Cristo Rey up into Mountain Pine Ridge, with its stunning waterfalls and caves along the east bank of the Macal River, is a popular area to buy a plot of jungle with river frontage or to rent a house from someone with an existing plot. Beyond San Antonio there are no villages, but there are tourist lodges and secluded homes. Due to previous isolated incidents with theft and hijacking, there is a ranger checkpoint at the entrance to the Mountain Pine Ridge Forest Reserve where you must sign in and a Belize Defence Force (BDF) escort is offered as a precaution.

Farther down Chiquibul Road lies Mountain Pine Ridge Forest Reserve, which is higher up and slightly cooler than San Ignacio and the surrounding villages. Land up here is often on a 100-year lease, but some land bordering the reserve may be available. The soil is not as rich as lower down in the valley and a few years ago the area's pine trees were decimated by a beetle but they are gradually returning to normal. The area is mountainous, remote, and off the grid. Stunning rivers and waterfalls run through beautiful caves in this area. Some expats live here and enjoy its beauty and isolation.

Santa Familia to Benque Viejo del Carmen

Heading west out of San Ignacio towards the border town with Guatemala, Benque Viejo del Carmen, are the villages of Santa Familia, Bullet Tree Falls, Paslow Falls, Buena Vista, Calla Creek, and San José Succotz which lie along the Mopan River. The land along the Mopan River changes and is generally flatter with undulating fields of livestock or crops interspersed with jungle. And as with anywhere in Cayo, hazy blue hills in the distance form a beautiful backdrop.

Bullet Tree on the Mopan River is an area where many artists settle, as is Paslow Falls outside Bullet Tree. The village is named after the profusion of bullet trees in the area, so called because they have one of the hardest woods of all the trees in the rainforest. So many of these trees are still standing because, until recently, people struggled to cut them down.

Just across the river from San José Succotz lies the ancient Maya ruin of Xunantunich, which has a stunning panoramic view if you have the energy to climb to the top of it! An old hand winch ferry will carry you and your vehicle across the river. These lovely old ferries are in use all over Belize.

Areas along the road toward Benque and along the Mopan River are becoming increasingly popular with middle-class Belizeans and expats due to the close proximity with Guatemala and some nice resorts. Although most of the roads are unpaved, they are good. In most places the Mopan River is wide and shallow. The border is easy to cross and on the Guatemala side is a market town called Melchor, which, while not necessarily much cheaper than Belize, offers a wider selection of goods. It also has good, basic dental and medical care at a cheaper price than Belize. For more serious health issues, you need to head to Guatemala City.

SPANISH LOOKOUT

Heading east towards Belmopan is the Mennonite community of Spanish Lookout, also an area where oil has been discovered and the headquarters of

© VICTORIA DAY-WILSON

Mennonite houses in Spanish Lookout

the Belize Natural Energy company (BNE). The oil is exported and Belize imports fuel for local use. There is no refinery to process the oil in Belize. Most of the Mennonites living in Spanish Lookout are progressive and use modern machinery. It is one of the best and closest places to go for building supplies, prefab houses, car parts, and anything out of the ordinary. Along with the Lebanese, the Mennonite community is one of the driving forces behind Belize's economy.

Driving into Spanish Lookout is always a bit of a culture shock as all the trees are cleared and have been replaced by idyllic green pastures with horses or cows grazing behind tidy fences. Everything is meticulous, neat, and clean. As you drive towards the heart of the settlement, large stores—some with mirror glass windows—line the main road. It's a bit like clicking your heels and finding yourself somewhere in North America. Stop at Western Dairies for a cooling and delicious ice-cream—they are arguably the best in Belize!

WESTERN HIGHWAY VILLAGES

Many villages line the Western Highway between San Ignacio and Belmopan. This section of the Western Highway is fairly unremarkable, as are the villages. The land is quite flat and cultivated in some places. There is scrub with a combination of neat citrus lines, green fields with cows or horses, a bit of jungle, and several creeks. All around, the Maya Mountains provide a stunning backdrop. Several expats choose various areas to live along this road or slightly inland from it.

Central Farm is Belize's agricultural center and home to the Taiwanese agricultural mission, Caribbean Agricultural Research and Development Institute (CARDI), which conducts agricultural research and training, and one of the University of Belize campuses. There is also an airstrip here. Expats often buy land around Central Farm. At Georgeville you'll find Chiquibul Road, which leads to Mountain Pine Ridge and the Barton Creek area, known for its beautiful waterfalls and caves. At Mile 60 lies Unitedville, the headquarters of Pepperland—home to Hot Mama's, the famous Belizean habanero hot sauces. At Blackman Eddy—so called because apparently the first settler there was a Black man called Eddy, also possibly because of all the eddies here—is the turn-off to Spanish Lookout. If you are hungry, Wolf's Place in Blackman Eddy serves the best burgers in Belize and is a great place to relax and enjoy good food. Peter and Petra Wolf also offer lodging, activities, and hammocks to rest those travel-weary feet. Following Blackman Eddy are Ontario Village, Teakettle Village (which used to have a bad reputation for security but has changed recently as more foreigners have moved in), and Camalote. Just before Belmopan lies Roaring Creek, where there is a golf course (one of the few in Belize). Foreigners generally avoid Roaring Creek as it is regarded as a less secure area. The same goes for Esperanza, just northeast of Santa Elena.

PRICES

Cayo District is the most expensive inland area, and, within Cayo, San Ignacio and Belmopan are the most expensive. It's hard to quote average prices

© VICTORIA DAY-WILSON

a house for sale in San Ignacio

specifically for property in Cayo as prices vary enormously depending on which estate agent you are dealing with, the location of the property, the type of property—land with or without river frontage, developed or not, with or without habitable buildings, or a smaller plot with a house. Prices also vary depending on access and what kind of access—none, seasonal, or year-round—and whether there are water and electricity connections. Therefore, there is no average acreage price. One estate agent quoted acreage prices of US$1,000–23,000, with river frontage at about US$10,000 and house prices at US$50,000–1 million. There are also hidden costs to take into account. For example, you may find a beautiful, large, lush, jungle-covered plot of land with river frontage at a very reasonable price; but, before you decide to buy, add up the cost of access, water, sewage, and electricity (if there isn't any), as well as clearing the land and building a property. Most people find they spend a lot more than they anticipated.

Houses and the land they are built on can vary, US$80,000–500,000 depending on the type of building and location. A house in San Ignacio costs US$75–150 per square foot, depending on the materials and how well the house is built. On top of that you need to add the cost of land. Again, the final price will vary vastly depending on construction, location, and utilities. Mennonite, wooden, prefab-house shells without interior finishing cost US$2,835–16,200. Plots of under 50–100 acres along the Hummingbird Highway can cost in the range of US$1,000–2,000 an acre. These properties usually have some road frontage and electricity. Larger, accessible plots are in the region of US$500–1,000 an acre. Rental properties in Belmopan range from US$500–1,000 per month for a three-bedroom furnished house or an apartment in a compound with a pool to US$3,000 per month for decent, bigger houses with a garden—normally the ones that the ambassadors live in. Of course, you can pay much less for something else. You can buy a decent three-bedroom house for about US$100,000.

Getting Around

Two major highways run through Cayo. The Western Highway runs between Belize City and the Guatemala border at Benque Viejo del Carmen. The Hummingbird Highway—Belize's most scenic road—starts just after Belmopan and ends in Dangriga in Stann Creek District. Part paved and part dirt roads lead off to areas such as Spanish Lookout, San Antonio, Cristo Rey, and

© VICTORIA DAY-WILSON

the paved part of the Hummingbird Highway to San Antonio

Bullet Tree Falls. Parts of these roads can be hard to access during the rains and wear and tear is a problem in the dry season. Expect a high turnover on vehicles, and budget for regular maintenance. A four-wheel drive vehicle is advisable, but local buses do access most outlying villages on a fairly reliable schedule every day from San Ignacio. If you live on the Macal River, you can travel into town by canoe.

PRIME LIVING LOCATIONS

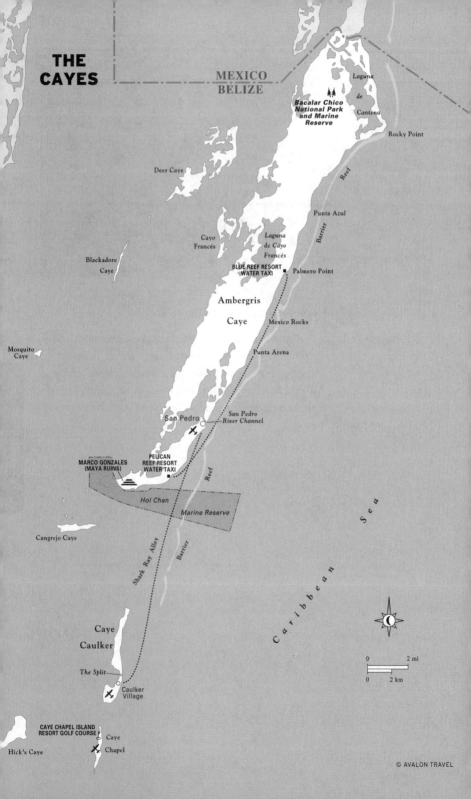

THE
CAYES

MEXICO
BELIZE

Bacalar Chico
National Park
and Marine
Reserve

Laguna
de
Cantena

Rocky Point

Deer Caye

Punta Azul

Cayo
Francés

Laguna
de Cayo
Francés

Barrier

Reef

Blackadore
Caye

BLUE REEF RESORT
WATER TAXI

Palmero Point

Ambergris

Caye

Mexico Rocks

Mosquito
Caye

Punta Arena

San Pedro

San Pedro
River Channel

MARCO GONZALES
(MAYA RUINS)

PELICAN
REEF RESORT
WATER TAXI

Reef

Hol Chan

Marine Reserve

Cangrejo Caye

Barrier

Shark Ray Alley

Caribbean

Sea

Caye
Caulker

The Split

Caulker
Village

0   2 mi

0   2 km

CAYE CHAPEL ISLAND
RESORT GOLF COURSE

Caye
Chapel

Hick's Caye

© AVALON TRAVEL

THE CAYES

The two main cayes that expats like to settle on, which are also among Belize's main tourist attractions and sources of income for the government, are Ambergris Caye (pronounced am-BUR-gris or am-BUR-grease KEY) and Caye Caulker. These beautiful palm- and mangrove-fringed, idyllic islands lie just off the coast of Belize surrounded by turquoise seas and white beaches. There is a Caribbean feel to both islands, with wooden buildings painted in all the colors under the sun. The pace on the islands is laid-back and relaxed. There is a local slogan of "no shirt, no shoes, no problem." There is excellent diving, snorkeling, fishing, and all manner of other water sports at the Belize Barrier Reef. There is an abundance of colorful, tropical fish in all shapes and sizes just beyond the islands. You are never more than a short walk from the sea on either island. The sea water is warm, the climate is good, there are good transportation connections, and the people are friendly. There are a variety of good bars and restaurants as well as a fairly active expat social scene. With such a laid-back vibe, idyllic surroundings,

© VICTORIA DAY-WILSON

and relaxing comfortable way of life, it is hard not to get sucked into permanent vacation mode.

The Lay of the Land

Belize has over 400 islands, of which Ambergris Caye and Caye Caulker are the largest. Both technically belong to Belize District even though they are closer to the shore of Corozal District. Both islands lie toward the northern tip of Belize's waters with Ambergris Caye lying just below Mexico's Yucatán Peninsula. It is believed that the narrow channel called the Boca Bacalar Chico Channel separating the Ambergris Caye from the Yucatán was dug by the ancient Maya Indians to facilitate a trading route between the Bay of Chetumal and the Caribbean. If that route had never been dug, it's possible that Ambergris Caye would be a part of the Yucatán Peninsula and belong to Mexico. The islands are surrounded by the Caribbean Sea and smaller cayes, and lie less than a mile from the Barrier Reef. There are three major marine reserves, the Caye Caulker Marine Reserve, Hol Chan Marine Reserve, and Bacalar Chico National Park and Marine Reserve. There are several lagoons scattered across Ambergris Caye. Both islands are a short flight or boat ride from Belize City, Corozal, and Chetumal.

AMBERGRIS CAYE

Ambergris Caye is 25 miles long and its width varies from as narrow as a few hundred feet to as wide as 4 miles. The main town on the island, San Pedro,

looking out over the piers from a condo in San Pedro

San Pedro

is about 1.5 miles long and 1 mile wide. There are three main streets, known as Front Street (Barrier Reef Drive), Middle Street (Pescador Street), and Back Street (Angel Coral Street). A sandy beach lies along the ocean side of the island and mangroves stretch along the mainland side. North of the center of town lies an area known as San Juan, which is where most of the island's workforce lives. They come mainly from Belize and Central America. Just after San Juan is Boca del Rio (Mouth of the River), which lies just before the channel that cuts the island in two. This is a nice sandy place to go swimming with a small park for children. In 2006 a bridge was built to cross the divide, but prior to that a ferry was used. The northern part of the island is more sparsely populated, but closer to the bridge are several condo developments and expat residences, as well as resorts. In the far north, known as Basil Jones, lies the Bacalar Chico National Park and Marine Reserve. To the south of San Pedro lies San Pablo, also a popular area for resorts and homes.

CAYE CAULKER

Caye Caulker is five miles long and less than a mile wide. There are three main streets, known as Front Street (Avenida Hicaco), Middle Street (Avenida Langosta), and Back Street (Avenida Mangle). In 1961 Hurricane Hattie divided the island in two. Local word has it that the channel—known as the Split—was deepened and widened with a bit of human intervention too. With sandy areas and deep turquoise waters, the channel is the best place on the island to go swimming. Unless you go early in the morning, it is usually packed with visitors and some locals, and there is a bar that plays very loud music. There is no bridge

the Split on Caye Caulker

over to the north side of the island and any travel between the two sides is by boat. The north side is mainly covered in mangroves and not very developed. There is local speculation that someone will start operating a ferry between the two sides. The area from the airstrip to the southern tip of the island is a reserve and mainly swampy mangroves. There are a few homes in that area.

CLIMATE AND CULTURE

The climate in the cayes is mild, like the rest of Belize, with average temperatures as high as 88°F in March–October and as low as 66°F in November–February.

The earliest known inhabitants of Ambergris Caye were the Maya. During the Classic Period (300–900 A.D.) they are thought to have had a major trading center on the island with a population of around 10,000. The whalers and buccaneers who followed in the 1600s are the ancestors of some of the island's population today. Originally the islanders worked on coconut plantations and earned a living off fishing. In 1847 immigrants escaping the Caste Wars in Mexico joined the existing island inhabitants. Today tourism on the island accounts for Belize's biggest economic gain, which goes to the government in Belmopan mainly in the form of taxes. It is a sore point with some islanders that not enough of this hard earned currency is pumped back into the island.

The islanders are called San Pedranos and include Creole, Maya, Mestizo, Central American, Chinese, Lebanese, North American, and Europeans. English, Spanish, Creole, and Maya are all spoken, but you can get by fine with just English. Ambergris Caye has the country's largest concentration of expats and is the most popular area in Belize for expats to move to. There is a Latin culture of strong family values, so children are looked after and are able to run around and play. San Pedranos love festivities and celebrate all of Belize's national holidays, including Independence Day, St. George's Caye Day, and Garifuna Day, with gusto. The holiday specific to the island is the Costa Maya Festival. Now in its 20th year, the festival is held in August and is the only one of its kind in Central America. The festival promotes the culture of Central American countries, celebrating food, dance, music, and beauty. International artistes and beauty queens fly in from all over Central America to represent their countries. There are beauty pageants, parades, delicious food, a variety of contests. At Easter there are kite contests and Easter egg hunts with food and music. At Christmas there is a lighted boat parade. There are fishing tournaments where you watch the fishermen bring in their catch and give it away. There are always things going on that are fun and engaging for the community; but those who don't get involved with local events are likely to end up bored and stuck on a bar stool.

Known in Spanish as *Cayo Hicaco* (Island of the Cocoplum), Caye Caulker was originally known as Cay Corker by the British, and was a popular stop for sailors to stock up on water and cork bottles. The coconut and fishing industries were the main sources of revenue for the island. Although it has now been replaced by tourism, fishing is still a big industry. Caye Caulker is also known for its tradition of wooden-ship building and sailing races. In the 1800s Mestizo immigrants escaping the Caste Wars in Mexico settled on the island, along with Maya, Creole, Garifuna, Chinese, and North American and European expats. There is also a strong Rastafarian culture.

Daily Life

There are various supermarkets on Ambergris Caye. It pays to shop around and find the best deals, as some are more expensive than others. On the whole, everything on the island is more expensive due to logistics and tourism: Items cost an extra 25–60 percent more than on the mainland. There is a wide selection if you're willing to pay the price. Supermarkets range from enormous, gleaming stores with rows of goods to traditional, smaller, Belizean-type stores, usually run by Lebanese, East Indians, or Chinese. There are several banks, a post office, and a variety of cafés, bars, and restaurants to suit all budgets and tastes. Some of the venues are part of resorts or hotels. There are some interesting shops, including art and jewelry shops, which sell a variety of Belizean items. The artists and jewelers are a mix of expats and locals who live on the island. There are rental golf cart and bicycle services, an airstrip, and water taxis.

The pace is more laid-back and relaxed on Caye Caulker. "Go slow" is the slogan for the island and is applicable to the pace and lifestyle. It is inexpensive compared with many other Caribbean islands and though it is slowly developing, it has retained much of its charm and resisted the onward march of progress. Caye Caulker offers a smaller choice across the board since it is a smaller place. There are a few basic supermarkets, a couple of banks and cyber cafés, a range of cafés and restaurants, and an airstrip and water taxi service. Spare parts or luxuries often need to be sourced on the mainland and couriered in by water taxi or plane.

Expats who are successful on the cayes have self-discipline and understand that a lot of hard work is required, balanced with some time off. Most people work within the tourist industry.

Crime has increased on both islands. There are a few murders a year and the odd mugging. Thieving has always been a bit of a problem, which isn't surprising with the economic divide. Use common sense, don't leave things lying around, lock your door, don't walk in dark areas at night on your own, be aware of your environment—these are simple precautions that apply in most parts of the world. Some people have dogs for protection and there are different neighborhood watch communities.

You will see many golf carts locked; this is partly because theft is becoming an increasing problem. But in the case of golf carts, which generally look alike and most keys are not always individual, it's easy to hop in, drive back

houses and restaurants along the beach in San Pedro

© VICTORIA DAY-WILSON

EXPAT STORY: LIFE ON CAYE CAULKER

Living in Caye Caulker, you get two or three standard questions from guests coming and going: How did you get here, what made you choose Caye Caulker, and how long have you been here?

I arrived here in the summer of 1999 while traveling through Central and South America with a good friend. Our first stop off the boat was a bar called the Sandbox, and we popped in to ask if anyone knew of a hostel as we were only staying for a few days. The bar was nearly empty (in those days there were no summer tourists coming), except for two women sitting at a table drinking beer, killing themselves laughing.

It turned out that one of them was the hostel owner and she was full (only six beds at that time). Her friend offered us her spare room. She lived only about 100 yards away, and we dumped our bags and joined them for a beer. The next two weeks were a blur of hangovers and packing bags, as each night my friend and I would agree to meet at the Sandbox with our bags and get a water taxi out.

It was a perfect way to meet the local barflies and chat endlessly about construction, as the previous summer the island had been decimated by Hurricane Mitch. I felt welcome and at home. We did eventually leave and had a whale of a time getting ourselves into mischief all the way down to Bolivia.

November in London is not much fun, and I really did not want to head back there. So I emailed the Sandbox and asked if I could stay for a while. They said yes, and that was the start of it all. That kind of answers the standard questions: boat, by mistake, and 12 years.

So why stay? Somehow my new friends made it impossible to leave. Yes, I was broke, but there were lots of jobs to do even just for a meal or a beer, as I didn't have a work permit in those days. The locals kind of let me in and I soon became part of the Caye Caulker family. Over time I got my residency and I bought some land; I built a home, then some rooms, and then a three-bedroom home and a pool, and then I bought another lot and built another home. I started a small business where I rented out local and expatriate homes to tourists by the week and it became a huge success.

Having a varied skill set certainly helps here. You have to do a lot yourself. I had never even looked into the toilet tank back in London, and now I am fixing it weekly as the hard water and sea air takes the life and luster out of fixtures and fittings like I have never known. I could tell you all about the great fishing, the beautiful reef, and sailing, but you know about that. These are the things of everyday life on this small island with a population that is growing fast but still retains a village feel, where the four-year-olds who used to call me Miss are now 16 and call me by my name.

I recently sold the business and now run our local Humane Society. I strongly believe in giving back to the place that has taken me in. I have my rental property and I do the odd project for hotels and bars, renovations, interior design, and the like. I married an American who has been here since the late 1980s and we have a couple of cats and a dog. Life is busy, fulfilling, reasonably healthy except maybe for a few too many beers, and perhaps it is my age (getting into my mid-40s now), but the days are too short. I'd like to stretch out my days in Belize for as long as possible.

– Contributed by Amanda Badger, www.cayecaulkercasita.com

to your accommodation, and then realize it's not your golf cart! This has happened to me on several occasions. If you invest in a golf cart, it's best to make it uniquely identifiable, perhaps by painting it a bright color.

Although living the island life may sound like a dream come true, there are downsides and frustrations to living on the cayes. If something breaks down, such as your golf cart or your washing machine, you will often have to source the broken part on the mainland and then have it couriered over before repair work can begin. That process alone can take weeks and cost far more than you anticipated.

EXPAT SOCIAL SCENE

There is a busy social scene on Ambergris Caye. The several bars on the island are the most popular locations to meet up for socials. The age groups on the island span people in their early 20s–60s. Some expats have made the island their home, while others come and go for a few weeks to a few months a year. Some are retired and some run businesses, mainly in the tourist industry. People either start up new businesses or more commonly buy existing ones such as bars or restaurants or businesses that support the tourist industry, like photography, specialty foods, and health and fitness programs. The younger group, people in their mid-30s and early 40s, is increasing in numbers. Most people are looking for a change of lifestyle, freedom, and lack of regulations, and are buying or starting businesses.

On Caye Caulker expats are in their 30s–60s. As on Ambergris Caye, some expats live here full time, while others come and go. There are several expat homes and, more recently, a few condos. Almost everyone on the island works in the tourist industry, which is quite busy even in the low season. Most expats are retirees from North America and a few are from Europe. Social life revolves around bars and trivia nights. During the high season there are more socials, including private parties and festivals like Mardi Gras.

ENTERTAINMENT

Ambergris Caye has a movie theater, aptly named the Paradise Theater, just north of the bridge which is also used for plays and concerts. On Friday nights there is a wine tasting at Wine Devine and Bingo at Lion's Den, on Saturdays there's a BBQ, and on Sunday afternoons at Crazy Kanuks there is a jam session with expat musicians, horse-shoe throwing, crazy golf, and a BBQ. There are also sailing classes, a ladies card club, trivia nights, karaoke nights, a gym, and a dinner club. These events are for expats and locals and are held at various venues in San Pedro. For kids there is a sailing club, summer camps, soccer,

© VICTORIA DAY-WILSON

the Paradise Theater

yoga, and church groups. There are many opportunities for family socials. Parents may have a drink or two and a chat while kids play on the beach.

VOLUNTEERING

There are various volunteer options in Ambergris Caye. You can help out at the local library, in schools, or at the PolyClinic. The Mama Vilma Family Home provides support for victims of domestic abuse and less fortunate children. The Saga Humane Society is very active and always needs volunteers. The American Crocodile Education Sanctuary (ACES) needs help working on their new site and assistance with the collection of scientific data on crocodiles, including catching, tagging, and release. The San Pedro Lions Club is active in the community and help less privileged people.

The Saga Humane Society is also active on Caye Caulker and welcomes volunteers. Helping at the local school is another way to become involved in the community.

HEALTH

Several doctors have private clinics, such as a gastroenterologist, general practitioners, and dentists. There is a government-run PolyClinic, which offers basic primary healthcare and can handle minor emergencies. Although there are doctors on call, it is only open on weekdays until 5 P.M. The doctors are Cuban or Belizean. There is no emergency center. Charter flights are scheduled to fly people to Belize City for any serious emergencies. The airlines are very helpful in such situations. Most people go to the privately-run Belize

SAGA HUMANE SOCIETY

PROMOTING KINDNESS AND PREVENTING CRUELTY TO ANIMALS

The Saga Humane Society was founded in 1999 in response to the animal control measures used in Belize. It was a time when no veterinary services were available in San Pedro Town. A small group of volunteers banded together to do what they could to aid the suffering stray dogs and cats on the streets. After much work and dedication, the first non-profit veterinary clinic and animal shelter opened in Belize. The Saga Veterinary Clinic houses the cattery where there are always plenty of kittens and cats looking for a loving home. Fort Dog houses homeless dogs and puppies that receive treatment and loving care. Saga houses up to 60 animals at any given time until they find a Forever Home.

SAGA HUMANE SOCIETY VETERINARY CLINIC SERVICES

Saga Humane Society operates the only non-profit veterinary clinic on the island of Ambergris Caye. It is a full-service hospital with a veterinarian on staff. Pet owners can make appointments for wellness care such as spay/neuter surgeries and vaccinations, as well as treatment for illnesses or injuries. Our in-house pharmacy has the most important veterinary medications in stock, thanks in a large part to the generosity of volunteers, residents, and visitors.

VOLUNTEER OPPORTUNITIES

As a Saga volunteer, you are important to us! Volunteers help the shelter run smoothly, increase adoptions by being knowledgeable and friendly, and make our animals more comfortable and happier. Volunteering is important for the organization, the animals, and the individual. There is a world of opportunities for you to use your special skills to help homeless animals in our community. We always need volunteers to help care for and socialize our shelter dogs and cats, assist with maintenance and carpentry projects, and help with special events. If you love animals and can give us one shift per week, we can promise you good feelings and fun.

BRINGING YOUR PET TO BELIZE

If you are considering bring your pet to Belize here is a summary of what will be required. When you purchase your airline ticket, make a reservation for your pet with the airline and check the requirements for flying with your pet. Bringing a pet into the country falls under live animal importation and is regulated by the Belize Agricultural Health Authority (BAHA, www.baha.bz). Belize does not quarantine dogs and cats brought into the country. Submit your import permit application to BAHA prior to leaving. It is not a requirement to have the permit in hand when leaving the U.S.; however, it is a good idea to request a copy to be faxed to you before you leave. Please visit their website for complete details and applications.

– Contributed by Saga Humane Society, Board of Directors, www.sagahumanesociety.org

Medical Associates (BMA) in Belize City for serious medical issues. The Saga Humane Society provides a good vet service. A private vet practice called the San Pedro Animal Hospital opened in 2009 and is owned and operated by Laurie Droke, DVM, and Peter "Pedro" Lawrence.

On Caye Caulker there are two doctors, a government health clinic, and a private clinic open during the week. These services are fine for primary healthcare, but anything more serious is best handled in Belize City. There are no dentists, though sometimes American dentists visit for a few days and do work on a voluntary basis. There is a vet who lives on the island nine months a year. The Saga Humane Society can help with contacts.

EDUCATION

Ambergris Caye offers a variety of state and private schools. There are several state-run schools in San Pedro: San Pedro Roman Catholic Primary School, St. Peter's Elementary, and St. Peter's College San Pedro High School. The Island Academy, La Isla Bonita Elementary School (IBES), and Ambergris Caye Elementary School (ACES) are private schools for ages 5–14. Costs range BZ$50–700 per month per child. Other private schools include Holy Cross Anglican Primary School, which requires tuition fees, has volunteer teachers from the United States, and nurses on the staff, and New Horizon Elementary SDA School, which is Adventist.

Being a smaller island, Caye Caulker has fewer options. There is the state and church-run Roman Catholic Caye Caulker Primary School and a fairly new high school called Ocean Academy. The high school has a focus on tourism and marine biology so that local children can go on to find work on the island.

Where to Live

It's best to visit both Ambergris Caye and Caye Caulker and preferably rent for a few months so that you can get a feel for which island suits you. Once you figure that out, the next decision is between oceanfront or lagoon housing. Ambergris Caye is bigger, utilities and roads are more developed, and the beaches are better. It is busier and more expensive, and has more upscale options. However, if you're looking for a small, quiet scene with a slow pace then Caye Caulker may be ideal. If you aren't looking to live on the islands fulltime look into property management companies, as the marine elements can be a nightmare with maintenance.

AMBERGRIS CAYE

The inspiration for Madonna's hit song *La Isla Bonita,* Ambergris Caye is just that—a beautiful island with a lot to offer. There are three main areas to live. These are spread over the north side of the island beyond the bridge, in San Pedro, and down to the southern tip of the island. Where you live also depends on how much you value creature comforts; more people are coming who are willing to live off the grid. Good roads do not run the entire length of the island, nor do water or electricity. There is more breeze on the seafront and therefore fewer mosquitoes, but land is cheaper the farther inland you go. The south has nice beaches and the west side has many coves. If you're going farther than four miles north of San Pedro you need to use a boat as the road is very bad and peters out into non-existence. People have their own boats and there are regular water taxis. Electricity runs 13 miles north up the island from San Pedro and 5 miles south. There is water in San Pedro, but it does not stretch all the way down south and north. People rely on rainwater catchment systems and reverse osmosis.

The island has one radio station, Reef Radio (92.3 FM), and there are two local papers, *The San Pedro Sun* and *Ambergris Today* (online only).

While Ambergris Caye is the bigger of the two islands, it's actually quite small. It has a population of about 20,000. There is a sizeable expat population; guesstimates vary between 500 and 1,000. The main town and hub of activity on the island is San Pedro, which even in the low season is a busy and bustling

FOR SALE
CUSTOM 2ᴺᴰ FLR CONDO
3 BED / 3 BATH
FURNISHED
$399,000.00 USD
226-4545

© VICTORIA DAY-WILSON

condos for sale in San Pedro

LAID-BACK LIVING ON AMBERGRIS CAYE

Do you dream of trading in winter for island life and endless sunsets? Living in a place where walking, bikes, and golf carts are the main transportation? Are you ready to enjoy National Geographic moments daily? All it took was one three-week vacation, and I was answering yes, and planning our move. I was instantly captivated by the colorful, easy-going island of Ambergris Caye, its rich Caribbean history, fabulous views, and friendly people.

The island is very community oriented. There are many organizations such as Saga Humane Society and San Pedro Sailing Club that always need extra hands, donations, and advertising. Volunteering in Belize is a great way to make friends and meet new people. I enjoy promoting fundraisers, and the raffle prizes are always worth buying tickets in support of a good cause. I also give ongoing regular updates about what various organizations are doing and what they need on my blog, www.tacogirl.com.

Sight-seeing on Ambergris Caye is fantastic, with Bacalar Chico National Park and Marine Reserve, a designated World Heritage site, at the north end of the island and Hol Chan Marine Reserve and Shark Ray Alley to the south. Both sites are great places to see wildlife and are accessible by boat in roughly 20 minutes. Marco Gonzalez Maya, a 2,000-year-old Mayan site is also to the south and worth visiting. I love that the beach is in walking distance and a great place for people-watching or quietly sitting on a dock enjoying the turquoise waters of the Caribbean Sea.

When I am looking for an off-island adventure, I sometimes take a water taxi or sail to nearby Caye Caulker Island for lunch. If I want an aerial experience I hop on a puddle jumper for a mainland day trip. Belize offers many great travel options.

Rental apartments come furnished to some degree, which made our move easy. I was glad I packed sheets and kitchen items. Here is a sample of some basic grocery pricing: bananas 4/BZ$1; eggs 4/BZ$1; jar of coffee BZ$10.80; a box of milk BZ$3.50; sugar BZ$0.60 lb; boneless chicken breast BZ$4 lb; snapper or grouper fillets BZ$12 lb; shrimp BZ$17 lb.

Ambergris Caye has a wide variety of restaurants; you can experience everything from delicious, budget-friendly local food to fine dining on the beach. Flautas, tostadas, and tacos are some of my favorite inexpensive San Pedro treats that can be found around town and in the park at night. I can honestly say I still appreciate island life as much as I did when we moved here in January 2006.

– Contributed by Laurie Norton, www.tacogirl.com

PRIME LIVING LOCATIONS

place. The few streets, which were once covered in sand, are now paved and golf carts shoot around everywhere, alongside bicycles and the odd car.

The surprising thing about Ambergris Caye is that it feels and looks much larger than it is. This may be due to the abundance of condos, hotels, and homes along both sides of the island. The main streets of San Pedro are full of people—expats, tourists, Belizeans, Chinese, and Lebanese, among others.

Most of the island is surrounded by a ring of sand and there are plenty of spots where the sea glitters a bright turquoise. As in any marine environment, there is sea grass. In some areas, resorts have been given permission to clear small areas, but it grows in most places and is harmless. You can go to one of the many piers surrounding the island (or build your own pier) and jump into the water, which is crystal clear and clean even at depths of over 20 feet.

If you're looking for a place in the sun with a laid-back lifestyle, then this might be the place for you. Bear in mind that the island is more expensive than the mainland in part because of the tourist industry but also because of the logistics of getting items to the island. Things slow down in the low season, and for several months of the year during the rainy season there is very little business.

Prices

The north of the island is more developed than the south, with larger developments with big homes, but you need a four-wheel drive vehicle once you get two miles north of San Pedro because the road is so bad. In the interior up north, bare land lots go for around US$10,000–12,000 for 50 x 100 feet. Beyond two miles north of San Pedro, homes are clustered together and there is power but no water. The south is less developed with condo projects, there is more seafront availability, and the road is not bad. Typically expats live along the seafront in two-story cement buildings with piers and space in between properties. There is water up to a limit. An eighth of an acre or 5,000 square feet starts at US$99,000 on the seafront. On the west coast, properties cost US$60,000–70,000, and in the far north where there is no road they are US$40,000–50,000. People who don't have good road access rely on boats to get in and out of San Pedro for shopping. There is an area at the back of town where you can tie up your boat.

Prices vary depending on location—the closer you are to San Pedro, the higher the price. Prices also rise with better road access, availability of water and electricity, a larger plot, the quality of beachfront property, and access to the sea. Properties on the sea are sold by linear footage of beach ranging from less than US$1,000 to US$10,000. Properties with utilities tend to cost in the US$275,000–300,000 range. Common lot sizes are 50 x 75 feet, 50 x 100 feet, 75 x 100 feet, 100 x 150 (which is the average size slightly farther from San Pedro), and 100 x 200 feet. A basic 75 x 100 feet lot on the beach costs roughly US$150,000–350,000 depending on how far north or south it is. Another popular option is to buy a condo. A one-bedroom condo on the seafront in San Pedro costs US$200,000 and upwards. The advantage of con-

AMBERGRIS CAYE HOUSING DEVELOPMENTS

There are many developments in various stages of completion across Ambergris Caye. Some are completed, well established, and were built years ago, others are new or have just started construction. Most lie on the seafront; some offer the choice between the coastline and canal lots. It's best to have a quick look at the websites (which aren't always very informative), and get in direct contact with the company involved. Here is a list of some of them:

- **Grand Belizean Estates** (www.grandbelizeanestates.net) and **Coco Beach Resort** (www.cocobeachbelize.com), where prices range US$450,000-700,000, has received some awards and lies just over three miles north of San Pedro. The main contact for the two is **Sandy Point Resorts** (www.sandypointresorts.com).

- **Belizean Shores** (www.belizeanshores.com) is just over three miles north of San Pedro and was completed in 2004.

- **Grand Baymen** (www.grandbaymen.com) is quite new and lies near San Pedro; properties are in the US$100,000-365,000 range.

- **Grand Caribe** (www.grandcaribe.com) is just over two miles north of San Pedro.

- **South Beach Belize** (www.southbeachbelize.com) is a new development with lots at US$90,000-1 million, bungalows at US$150,000-250,000, and villas at US$250,000-400,000.

- **Las Terrazas** (www.lasterrazasbelize.com) has properties that cost US$280,000-700,000.

- **Indigo** (http://indigobelize.com) lies 4.5 miles north of San Pedro and construction is ongoing. Prices are in the range of US$495,000-650,000.

- **Meridian** (http://meridianbeachresort.com) is on the north side of the island.

- **Costa Maya** (www.costamaya-reef.com) is just over six miles from town.

- **Athens Gate** (www.athensgate.net) lies over two miles to the south.

- **Miramar Villas** (www.miramarvillas.net) and **Palm Bay** (www.palmbayclub.net), lie toward the end of the island, 20 miles from San Pedro; properties cost US$45,000-210,000.

PRIME LIVING LOCATIONS

dos is that a property management company takes care of the maintenance, which is extensive on the seafront.

The cost of building a house depends on the distance from town because of the cost of transporting materials. If you are building farther up north or down south, a barge will be used to transport building materials and equipment. A rough cost for building is US$150–350 per square foot. Depending on variables, a beach home can cost around US$600,000 or more. RFG

Insurance will not insure a wooden structure. Bear in mind that if you are on the seafront you will incur higher long-term costs for maintenance.

CAYE CAULKER

Caye Caulker is the smaller island with a population of about 1,800. It is very popular with backpackers, so there are many establishments that cater to that group as well as some upscale accommodations.

Caye Caulker is broken into three main areas, the north after the Split, the main village on the island, and down towards the southern tip. There are a lot of swampy areas on both sides. Heading south there are basic tracks, suitable for golf carts and bicycles, which get flooded during the wet season but are still passable, and there is no water or electricity. In the north there is a road, no water, and an electricity cable, which runs under the sea and brings power. Popular areas are on the seafront in the main village and towards the south past the airstrip.

All the action is at the tip of the southern part of the island, which has the largest concentration of shops, homes, cafés, bars, restaurants, and accommodations for tourists. There aren't many good sandy beaches, but there are many piers jutting out into the water, often with a few colorful hammocks slung under a light cover. The main sandy swimming area is at the tip of the southern part of the island.

Walking and bicycling are the main modes of transport here, but there are

street on Caye Caulker

quite a few golf carts, too, though "traffic" doesn't get as congested as in San Pedro on Ambergris Caye. The three main streets are mostly just sandy tracks. Palm trees and colorful wooden and cement structures line the shore and main lanes. People wander around barefoot or in flip-flops with casual clothes. Many tourists just wear trunks or a bikini and a sarong. The southern part of the island is a nature reserve but around that end there are housing lots for sale, and expats have built fairly large homes, sometimes in concrete and sometimes in wood. House designs are as far as your imagination will stretch.

Prices

As with Ambergris Caye, properties vary in price depending on location—seafront, middle, or lagoon (west side of the island)—access, utilities, size of the lot, and whether there is a structure on it.

The most popular area for expats to buy is on the waterfront in the village just east of the pier where there are good breezes. A lot there can start at US$78,000, but there aren't many available. Another popular area is on the waterfront on the east side of the island. Lot sizes range from 60 x 80 feet to 90 x 90 feet to 50 x 100 feet. A beachfront lot can range between US$17,000 to US$3.5 million—in this case the higher figure is for a resort. A 100-square-foot, three-bedroom house in need of some improvement costs about US$245,000. On an area in the southern end of the village called Bahia Puesta del Sol, lots cost US$17,000–30,000. Houses are in the US$65,000–124,000 range. These are often traditional, wooden, Belizean constructions. There is a property on the north side of the village going for US$210,000; another cement house on the waterfront is on the market for US$499,000. The highest residential listing is a building on the seafront for US$719,000. A three-story cement structure on the southern tip of the island can fetch about US$310,000.

Properties and lots in the north cost US$21,000–445,000. In general, the north is underdeveloped and therefore cheap. You can pick up a beachfront property for US$85,000. Though, you'll need to travel by boat to get back and forth. Perhaps eventually there will be some sort of ferry service. There aren't many properties available, partly because it's a smaller island and partly because there has been less development. At the time this book went to print one real estate agent had 60 listings and had closed 24 deals in eight months. The areas of South Point, Eden Isle, and Bahia Puesta del Sol have power and water, but just south of the airstrip the utilities end. There are properties past that point, and people who live there use solar and wind power, and water collection. It will be a while before power is supplied to that area.

Getting Around

You can get to Caye Caulker and Ambergris Caye by water taxi and by plane from Belize City, Corozal, and Chetumal. Tropic Air also runs charters from Cancún to San Pedro. Flights are relatively cheap and regular from Philip S. W. Goldson International Airport as well as the Belize City Municipal Airstrip. The airstrip on Caye Caulker is in the southern part of the village and in San Pedro it's in the middle of town. Round-trip flights run from about BZ$150 from the international airport and BZ$70 from the municipal airport. The flight to San Pedro takes about 20 minutes and Caye Caulker about 15 minutes. Flights to or from San Pedro stop off at Caye Caulker.

There are regular boats from Belize City to both islands. They leave from the Marine Terminal on North Front Street. The water taxis are run by San Pedro Water Taxi and Caye Caulker Water Taxi. The trips take one hour and 20 minutes and cost BZ$35 round-trip, BZ$15 one way to San Pedro, and BZ$10 one way to Caye Caulker. You can catch a boat between the islands for BZ$10, and it's a 25-minute ride. There is also a boat to Chetumal, which takes one hour and 40 minutes and costs start at BZ$30 for a one-way ticket. On both islands, the main way of getting around is on foot, by bicycle, or golf cart. Bicycles and golf carts can be rented. The Coastal Express is a regular, frequent, water taxi service, which operates around Ambergris Caye and leaves regularly from the Amigos del Mar's dock in the center of San Pedro.

arriving on Caye Caulker by water taxi

STANN CREEK

In the south of Belize, Stann Creek is mainly populated by Maya and Garifuna, with many Creoles and Mestizos. According to the 2010 census, the district had a population of 32,166 people. There is a combination of true jungle and amazing beaches with all the water sports to match, as well as great fishing. Dangriga Town (Standing Waters in Garifuna) is the capital of the district.

Coastal areas in Stann Creek that are popular with expats include the Garifuna village of Hopkins; nearby Sittee River; and the area farther down the Placencia Peninsula with the lagoon to the east and the Caribbean to the west. Moving south along the peninsula are the Riversdale and Maya Beach areas, and, finally, at the tip lies Placencia village.

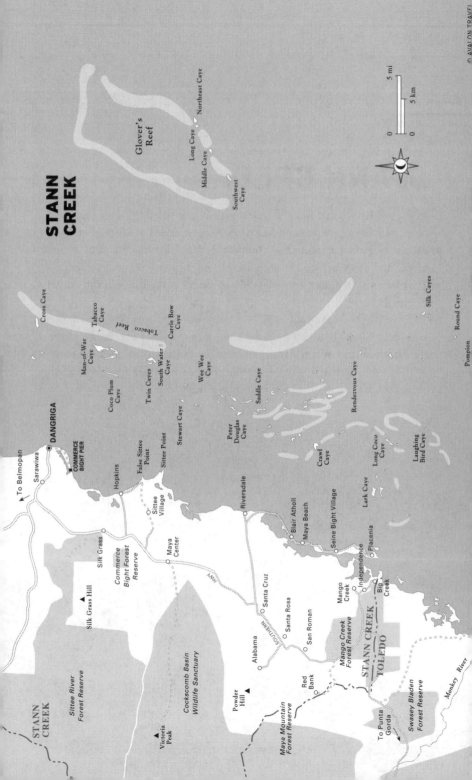

STANN CREEK

STANN CREEK

Glover's Reef

Northeast Cave
Long Cave
Middle Cave
Southwest Cave

0   5 mi
0   5 km

© AVALON TRAVEL

Cross Cave
Tobacco Cave
Man-of-War Cave
Tobacco Reef
Coco Plum Cave
Carrie Bow Cave
Twin Caves
South Water Cave
Wee Wee Cave
Stewart Cave
Saddle Cave
Peter Douglas Cave
Rendezvous Cave
Crawl Cave
Laughing Bird Caye
Long Coco Cave
Lark Caye

Silk Caves

Round Caye
Pompion

DANGRIGA
COMMERCE BIGHT PIER
Sarawiwa
To Belmopan
Hopkins
False Sittee Point
Sittee Point
Sittee Village
Maya Center
Riverdale
Blair Atholl
Maya Beach
Seine Bight Village
Placencia
Independence
Mango Creek
Big Creek

Silk Grass Hill
Silk Grass
Commerce Bight Forest Reserve
Sittee River Forest Reserve
Victoria Peak
Cockscomb Basin Wildlife Sanctuary

STANN CREEK

Southern Hwy
Santa Cruz
Santa Rosa
San Roman
Alabama
Mango Creek Forest Reserve
STANN CREEK
TOLEDO

Powder Hill
Red Bank
Maya Mountain Forest Reserve
Swasey Bladen Forest Reserve
To Punta Gorda
Monkey River

The Lay of the Land

Large agricultural tracts of banana plantations and citrus groves make up part of the landscape. Off the coast are crowd-free cayes and remote reaches of the Belize Barrier Reef. Stann Creek's stretch of coast is the closest to the Barrier Reef in the whole of Belize. Although tourism and fishing have become large contributors to the district's economy, Stann Creek is a major banana and citrus fruit–producing region. There is a deepwater port at Big Creek from where the fruit is exported.

The white beaches of Placencia, a 35-minute flight from Belize City, are popular with tourists and expats alike. The narrow 16-mile peninsula separates the Caribbean Sea and the mangrove-fringed Placencia Lagoon. Before becoming a tourist haunt, Placencia was a fishing village, which was originally founded by English buccaneers in the early 1600s.

Dangriga is the capital of Stann Creek district and is known as the culture capital of Belize. It was originally known as Stann Creek Town. Located within the district are the villages of Alta Vista, Commerce Bight, Dancing Pool, Georgetown, Guana Church Bank, High Sand, Hopkins, Independence and Mango Creek, Kendal, Lagarto Bank, Maya Mopan, Middle Bank, Middlesex, Mullins River, New Home, Pomona, Quarry Hill, Rancho Grande, Red Bank, Regalia, Sarawee, Silver Creek Camp, Silk Grass, San Roman, and Sittee.

© VICTORIA DAY-WILSON

Placencia Lagoon with mangroves

PEOPLE AND CULTURE

Stann Creek is home to the Garifuna, who are direct descendants of a group of African slaves who escaped two ship-wrecked Spanish ships carrying slaves from Nigeria bound for Spanish colonies in America near St. Vincent in 1635. The slaves mixed with the local Carib Indians of St. Vincent. The Garifuna culture developed among their offspring. On November 19, 1802, 150 Garifuna were sent by the Spanish from Roatán, one of the Bay islands off Honduras, to be woodcutters in Stann Creek and Punta Gorda. They got to know the coastline so well that they would smuggle goods to the British whom the Spanish had forbidden trade with. They adopted elements from the Carib language but kept their African musical and religious traditions. Dangriga is also known as a center for music and it is where punta rock originated.

There are six Garifuna communities in Belize. One is in Seine Bight, a village two miles south of Maya Beach and about five miles north of the village of Placencia. Seine Bight stretches about four miles along the Placencia Peninsula. The name possibly originates from French fishermen who were deported from Newfoundland after the British gained control of Canada. Seine is a type of net used by fishermen who dried and salted their catch in the area. Bight is a depression in the coastal line. Garifuna settlers initially arrived in Seine Bight around 1869 and more followed in the 1950s. The population of Seine Bight was just over 800 in 2010. English is spoken, as well as the Garifuna language, which draws from African dialects and Carib, with a mixture of French, Spanish, and English words.

Daily Life

EXPAT SOCIAL SCENE

The social scene in Placencia Village is very active with many people walking along the sidewalk and popping into some of the beach bars for a drink and a chat. People also meet up for coffee in the morning. The northern part of the village is quieter but you are never far from the action if you want it. One of the favorite expat hangouts farther up the peninsula is the Maya Beach Hotel. People hold private parties; they mix through the church and through mutual interests. Some people form small music bands and develop a following; others fish or get involved with other water sports, or volunteer. You can be as social as you want to be. Most people run a small business or are retired. There aren't many young families.

the sidewalk in Placencia Village

© VICTORIA DAY-WILSON

VOLUNTEERING

Many expats volunteer in projects such as library programs in local schools. They also help with functions and fundraising at the Tourism Center, and volunteer with the fire brigade or crime watch. There is also the Rotary Club of Placencia, which does a lot of community work with a focus on education, and the Placencia Humane Society.

HEALTH

At the Placencia Health Center there is one private physician (Dr. Alex), a full-time nurse, several masseuses, a local "healer," and occasionally an acupuncturist. There are polyclinics in Independence and Dangriga. There is a small community health clinic in Hopkins, staffed by a volunteer Cuban doctor and a nurse. For more serious medical issues there is the state-run Southern Regional Hospital (formerly Dangriga Hospital), which has 52 beds and is mainly staffed with Cuban doctors. It provides both primary and secondary care services. Four basic specialties are offered: gynecology, surgical, pediatric, and internal medicine. The Southern Regional Hospital has two main wards: the General Ward and the Maternity Ward. For more serious issues go to Belize City, Guatemala, or Mexico.

EDUCATION

St. John's Memorial Preschool in Placencia Village was founded in September 2009. In 2010 there were 42 children from 3 years old enrolled with two teachers. There is also St. John's Primary (Elementary) School for ages 5–14. Across the lagoon on the mainland in the village of Independence is the Independence High School (IHS), which is for the 12–16 age group, and Junior College Independence for the 16–18 age group. The government pays for school children to catch a water taxi across the lagoon from Placencia to Independence and then to catch buses from there to the schools. Seine Bight has St. Adolphus Primary School.

PRIME LIVING LOCATIONS

In Georgetown, the Georgetown Technical High School opened in December 2010. In 2010 only half of the school's construction was complete. When finished, Georgetown Technical will have 16 classrooms, one computer building, a technical building, a workshop, and an auditorium. The new school is expected to accommodate over 350 students. It's advisable to have a look around the schools that are state and church run.

In Dangriga Town there are five primary schools, two high schools, and a sixth form (final year of high school). Solid Rock Christian Academy is a private school that follows a Christian curriculum—Abeka—the Belize National Curriculum. It runs from preschool through elementary school. The Stann Creek Ecumenical College is a secondary school in Dangriga. It was established in 1974 during the amalgamation of an Anglican and a Catholic High School. The school has a population of 631 students and 40 staff members. Christ the King School in Dangriga is Anglican and has 220 children and 12 teachers, and is located by the sea in the center of town. Other schools include Seventh Day Adventist Elementary School and Epworth Methodist Elementary School in Dangriga. Founded in 1987, Delille Academy is a Catholic High School, which has grown to approximately 463 students, preparatory (elementary) through form 4 (high school), and 34 full-time staff members. There is a village elementary school in Hopkins and Sittee River Methodist School in Sittee River.

Where to Live

The most popular areas in Stann Creek are along the coast. What appeals to you depends on several factors: your budget; whether you prefer the beach, the lagoon, or the Sittee River; whether you are buying to live or as an investment. There are many retirees in the area and Maya Beach is quite popular. Placencia is said to have the most expensive real estate in Belize. Many North Americans who buy homes in the area are in the 50–60 age group and some who buy investments are in the 35–45 age bracket. The Belizean government wants to maintain the village feel of Placencia (although many old hands complain it has been ruined and overdeveloped) and as a result will be tightening up on building regulations in the area as part of the National Sustainable Tourism Master Plan of Belize 2030 (NSTMP) (www.sustainabletourismbz.org), which aims to double visitors to Belize. Focus for development will be on the Maya Beach area, with potential plans for a casino, among other things. Work is also ongoing in fits and starts to complete an international airport in the area. The areas from Maya Beach to Riversdale are likely to be good investments due to less building regulations.

HOPKINS AND SITTEE RIVER

Halfway down Stann Creek District, the villages of Hopkins and Sittee River lie on the coast. Both Hopkins and Sittee River are just off the Southern Highway. If you are a keen boater, fisher, or ornithologist then this is a place worth considering. The area is famed for its abundant birdlife and excellent fishing in the river and the sea. Sittee Point offers housing lots along the seashore and the beautiful Sittee River.

seafront lot for sale near the Sittee River

Named after a Catholic priest who drowned in 1923, Hopkins became a settlement in 1942 after a hurricane leveled a village called Newtown, a village slightly north of where Hopkins is now, about eight miles south of Dangriga. Hopkins is home to roughly 1,200 Garifuna, many of whom speak Garifuna as their first language. The village is small, stretching along about two miles of coastline. The sea and beaches are nice, the barrier reef is closer to the coast than anywhere else in Belize, and Hopkins is less than two hours away from the Glover's Reef Atoll, which was deemed a heritage site by the World Heritage Foundation. Hopkins is not far from the inland Maya Mountains and the Cockscomb Range, home to Belize's second highest mountain, Victoria Peak (3,674 ft.). There is also a jaguar reserve. Hopkins offers jungle, mountains, and the sea, each 30 minutes away. It's on the mainland but also "out to sea." Hopkins and Sittee River are cheaper than the Placencia Peninsula, mainly because the area is about five years behind in development.

The north end of Hopkins village is known locally as Byla, and the south is False Sittee Point. The south end is more popular with expats. Being only a small village, there is a small clinic, a police station, a few supermarkets, no banks, one main paved road through the village, and a variety of small cafés, bars, and restaurants. There are a variety of accommodations, and many places cater to an assortment of water sports. For any additional needs, your first stop would be Dangriga.

Between False Sittee Point and Sittee Point is a stretch of road that follows the coastline. Boom Creek and Sittee River join together at Sittee Point and from there flow into the Caribbean Sea. You don't have to choose between the Sittee River and the sea because the two are very close. There are developed and undeveloped lots on both sides of the road, on the seafront and along the river. On the seafront people tend to build piers to admire the view and tie up their boats. Along the river people moor their boats or use the Sittee River Marina (www.sitteerivermarina.com) for more shelter. The river is wide and deep enough to sail your boat up into the sea.

Prices

Sittee Point and Hopkins are slightly cheaper than the Placencia Peninsula due to less development and lack of exposure to buyers. The area has had a low profile, and it has attracted a mixture of North American and European retirees and younger couples with small families. The area is very pretty and lots are rapidly being bought up. All listed prices are based on ballpark figures at the time this book went to print. A 60 x 120 feet empty lot without waterfront access in Hopkins sells for around US$40,000. A lot of the same size on the coast sells for around US$120,000. The exact cost may vary on the quality of the beach. A rough guideline to go by is US$2,000 a foot for beachfront land.

house in Sittee River area

FROM ALASKA TO HOPKINS: TWO HOSPITALITY PROFESSIONALS MAKE THE MOVE TO PARADISE

It was a dark, -40°F day in Fairbanks, Alaska, and I had just finished thawing a frozen well head at home and fixing a flat tire on the truck when I said to my wife, "I think it's about time we found a place to do our thing in a warmer climate, preferably a beach!" I'm not sure if I was joking or not, but she agreed.

Internet being what it is, it was a matter of about two hours before I had made contact with a gentleman selling property in Belize who asked about my parameters: price, location, expectations, and a little background on us. He had just the perfect thing: a four-room place with room for a small restaurant and living quarters above. The place was in a bit of deferred maintenance, which can happen quickly on the seafront, but the location and beach were great and the seller, who had a run of personal family tragedies since building in Hopkins and wanted to return to Canada, was motivated to sell.

This was much too soon. The three years I expected to look around while trying to sell our restaurant became three hours, but the more we looked, the more we knew that this was the right place for us. Now we had to change our exit plan and figure out how to get the money to purchase Beaches and Dreams in Hopkins, Belize. After months of corresponding with the current owner, we knew we could make a go of it and made arrangements to go look at it, while figuring out a way to raise the money until our restaurant sold. We ended up re-financing the restaurant and carrying paper for the new buyers, a former employee of mine.

The short version of this is that we purchased the place and have now been operating for more than seven years. We have remodeled the entire property, including our living quarters, using operating revenues, and are now looking at a great year ahead. We have managed the size of our place; we could easily have double rooms, but we have "been there and done that" in Alaska. We are in a beautiful place on the Caribbean Sea. By design our place requires us to actually "work" the resort in the early morning, providing breakfast and getting our guests ready for trips or to spend the day relaxing around Hopkins. Then our day is free until 3 P.M. when we begin preparing fresh menus for the evening, usually with fish bought from the local fisherman, lobsters, and vegetables delivered by farmers in their trucks. As for being a chef, it's as close to the food as you can get. We bought a great lifestyle and a good living for ourselves in Belize, and when people ask me about regrets, my only answer is that I hadn't done it sooner! The benefits of a more active lifestyle, healthier diet, and mild climate are another bonus factor. From Alaska to Belize, at least I won't freeze.

– Contributed by Tony Marsico, who owns and operates Beaches and Dreams Resort in Hopkins Belize, www.beachesanddreams.com, www.chefinbelize.blogspot.com

Half an acre to an acre of riverfront land on the Sittee River costs around US$40,000–60,000. Riverfront land is roughly US$1,000 per foot. Half an acre of land with a citrus orchard can be around US$18,000, while an acre or more will cost about US$36,000. One to three acres on the river costs US$60,000–90,000. A three-bedroom house with two bathrooms of roughly 2,500 square feet on five acres, surrounded by orange trees, costs in the vicinity of US$250,000. Most Sittee River lots have power and good quality water. A 5–10-acre plot on a road with no water or power costs around US$45,000.

Housing Developments

Note that many housing developments are not yet complete. Not everything described on the websites has been constructed yet. In some cases there is controversy regarding protection of the environment in areas where housing developments are planned.

SANCTUARY BELIZE

Sanctuary Belize (http://sanctuarybelize.com) is an ambitious 14,000-acre beachfront development in progress on Sittee Point. It will be a gated community with 24-hour security. The developers claim fewer than 3,000 acres will be developed. The rest—jungle and rainforest—will be held aside as a preserve. Sanctuary Belize will offer 1–10-acre home sites, villas, and bungalows, a marina, yacht club, resort, private island caye, equestrian center, and private beach and beach club.

SITTEE RIVER ORCHARD ESTATES

Sittee River Orchard Estates (www.mlsinbelize.info) is located on the Sittee River in Sittee River Village. The housing lots have good roads along an active citrus orchard. All lots have public utilities, water, and electricity. Water comes from the Cockscomb Basin Jaguar Reserve, making it clean and safe. Placencia and Dangriga are both only a 30-minute drive. Each of these towns has an airport. The beaches of Hopkins Village and Sittee Point are only 10 minutes away. Lots range in price, about US$19,000–90,000.

ROYAL PALM HARBOUR

This 434-acre oceanfront residential and marina development is in the early development stages. The proposed residential development will include a network of canals that will be dug to 14 feet with a navigational depth of 8 feet that will offer canal frontage for each lot. The target market of this residential marina community is foreign retirees, second-home and vacation-home owners, and boating enthusiasts.

PLACENCIA VILLAGE

Placencia is a small warm place with a big heart. The inhabitants are friendly and the vibe is relaxed. If you aren't on the beach or the lagoon, it's a five-minute walk away; you are always close to the water in Placencia. Palm trees are plentiful, most places are sandy, and there is little tarmac, with the exception of the main road through the village and the paved sidewalk, which is listed by the Guinness World Records as the narrowest main street in the world. The sidewalk, originally laid down in the 1940s then paved in the 1960s, is 4,071 feet long and 4 feet wide. It acts as the main artery through the village, leading north from the harbor past shops, guesthouses, and beach bars.

The Maya originally established at least 14 bases around the Placencia Lagoon where they made salt and traded along the coast. English buccaneers are said to have settled here in the early 1600s. In the 1700s English Puritans from Nova Scotia and Providencia settled in Placencia. The settlement died out during the 1820s during the Central American wars of independence.

Placencia got its name from the Spaniards who traveled the southern coast of Belize. They referred to it as Placentia, with the point being called Punta Placentia or Pleasant Point. The Placencia Peninsula was resettled in the late 1800s by the Garbutt family, the Westby family from Scotland, and the Cabral family, originally from Lisbon, Portugal. In the early 1900s the Leslies, originally

PRIME LIVING LOCATIONS

© VICTORIA DAY-WILSON

a Placencia beach house

from Rotan, also came to Placencia. The settlement grew and became a fishing village. In the early 1970s Placencia was provided with electricity from generators, and in 1993 Belize Electricity Limited provided electricity due to the increasing demand. Locals claim Placencia Village to be one of the oldest continually inhabited communities in Belize. When tourists discovered Placencia, many fishermen swapped their lines and nets for binoculars and dive gear, reapplying their local knowledge of the coast. Placencia's international roots continue with a mish mash of Belizeans, foreigners who have made it their home, and tourists from all over the world. Hurricane Iris did considerable damage to the village in October 2001 but has since been repaired.

Expat homes are often small, wooden clapboard or cement and tin houses. Some expats live in Placencia fulltime and run small businesses, such as restaurants, B&Bs, bars, shops, and water sports companies. They often live close to their businesses. Houses come in all shapes, sizes, and colors; some are on the beach, some on the lagoon side, and some in between. Holiday homes, small hotels, and B&Bs lie alongside people's homes.

MAYA BEACH

A small collection of houses and hotels on various developments, Maya Beach is not a village or town, but rather a two-mile stretch of land eight miles north of the village of Placencia. Maya Beach was a Canadian development founded in 1964. A network of canals was dug so that if you're in between the sea and lagoon, chances are you're close to water anyway. Expats, mainly from North America, live here along with Mayans, Spanish, and Creoles. Some people live here all year round, others use it as a vacation home or investment. The view over the lagoon stretches towards the Cockscomb Range and Victoria Peak.

RIVERSDALE

Riversdale is a small, quiet, fishing village on the north end of the Placencia Peninsula. It is just beginning to see commercial development with a few little resorts, restaurant, bar, and store. This area is sure to continue to develop as the new, paved Placencia highway comes to within a half mile of the village and the new international airport is under construction just down the road.

Prices

Properties on the lagoon side of the peninsula tend to be slightly cheaper than on the ocean front. Prices vary greatly depending on location, amount of land,

SPECTARTE ART AND GARDEN GALLERY, MAYA BEACH

People come to the Placencia Peninsula and fall in love. There's just one road in, snaking 23 miles from the Southern Highway along a tree-lined pavement, passing mansions and tropical seaside homes. Here, it is all about the water: the Caribbean dotted with tiny islands and, to the west, the peaceful lagoon with a backdrop of the Maya Mountains, the Cockscomb Range, and the occasional sighting of Victoria Peak.

Half way along the route to Placencia Village, you arrive at the rather laid-back community of Maya Beach, with its small hotels, bars, and a smattering of other businesses. Here there are several places to find good food in settings full of character and atmosphere. One such find is Delite Cafe at Spectarte Art and Garden Gallery. The rooms offer differing venues from the story of food to gentle waterfalls and flowering orchids. The food is fabulously fresh and tasty at highly affordable prices, with plating an artistic display of tropical edibles.

The gallery, which has been here for some years, exhibits and sells the work of many talented Belizean artists and one can find a veritable cornucopia of regional items for gifts and home decor: carvings, lamps, fabrics, furniture, paintings, soaps, jewelry, plants, and patio accessories. Special events such as movie night and live music are offered and rooms are available for bed and breakfast (short or long stay). If you are in search of information, this is the place to come. The owner is a longtime resident of the area and can point you in the right direction. Heading farther down the road you will pass through the Garifuna village of Seine Bight and then, finally, the road comes to an abrupt end in Placencia Village, where there is plenty to see and do.

access, and availability of water and power. Roughly speaking, vacant lots range US$1,000–5,000 per square foot. Plots with homes cost US$350,000–1 million. Far more awareness and interest has been generated over the last 10 years among investors, developers, and tourists.

Housing Developments

Many developments are not complete and not everything described on housing development websites has been constructed. In some cases construction is held up due to controversy regarding protection of the environment. The best thing is to have a look at the websites, make any inquiries, and go and see for yourself!

SUNSET POINTE

Sunset Pointe condominiums (www.sunsetpointebelize.com) sit at the southernmost tip of the peninsula, surrounded by water on three sides. Properties

PRIME LIVING LOCATIONS

have been built ranging from 7,000–8,000 square feet on the peninsula. Condos offer a large open floor plan with West Indies–style architecture and every room opens onto an outside porch. There are four units per building. Each upstairs two-bedroom, two-bathroom unit has 1,674 square feet, including the covered private porches, plus an optional loft area. Private docking and a swimming pool are included.

SURFSIDE

Just beyond Placencia Village lies the development of Surfside (www.mattdee.com/bayshore/surfside.htm). There are mature trees, a beachfront park, and inner roads leading to lagoon lots and parkland. The sandy beaches are beautiful and there are water, electricity, and telephone services. Many North Americans buy homes in this area.

COCOPLUM

Just south of Maya Beach and north of Surfside, Cocoplum (www.cocoplumbelize.net) is a 254-acre gated community which stretches from the Caribbean Sea to the lagoon. It has lots from the seafront to the lagoon. The average home site at Cocoplum measures in excess of one-half acre. The majority of Cocoplum's acreage is set aside as nature reserve. All roads at Cocoplum are paved. Utilities, including electricity, water, and cable television, are underground. There is cellular service and wireless Internet. Cocoplum is a 10-minute drive from Placencia airport and a three-hour drive from Belize City. Most people buy properties here as investments or holiday homes. Prices for waterfront parcels range from US$109,000 to over US$400,000.

WILD ORCHID PROPERTIES

Founded in 2005, Wild Orchid (www.wildorchidproperties.com) consists of first-class lots for sale on premium lagoon-front property stretching across 29 acres of beach to lagoon property. The developers claim lot owners will benefit from a lagoon-front marina, a 12-acre private island, beachfront access, a swimming pool, fitness center, yacht club, and restaurant and bar. The development is five minutes from the Placencia airstrip.

THE INN AT ROBERT'S GROVE

This award-winning beachfront resort (www.robertsgrove.com/html/condos.html) has luxury villas in two oceanfront stucco haciendas. The lower floor consists of two, 1,500-square-foot, two-bedroom units, while the second floor comprises two, 2,000-square-foot, three-bedroom duplex units, which include a penthouse bedroom. Condominium owners have access to all the resort amenities of The Inn at Robert's Grove. Two-bedroom to three-bedroom condos cost US$385,000–485,000.

COPAL BEACH, THE PLACENCIA, AND THE PLACENCIA RESIDENCES

The Placencia (www.theplacencia.com) is an ambitious hotel, condominium, and residential development north on the peninsula. Located north of The Placencia Hotel and Residences (www.theplacenciaresidences.com) on the northern end of the Placencia Peninsula, the Copal Beach development plan includes proposed six 5-story buildings, a swimming pool, 300-foot pier, and office and staff quarters. A casino for Copal Beach was approved by the Belize Department of the Environment in the Environmental Compliance Plan (ECP) for the Placencia Marina. Residences range from 2,200 square feet, with two or three bedrooms and two or three baths to penthouses with over 7,000 square feet, featuring four bedrooms and four baths. Each residence boasts ample outdoor terraces. All residences are waterfront and come with their own private bulkhead boat docks and their own private boat dockage and optional boatlift, allowing owners to sail out directly into the Caribbean Sea through the blue Placencia Lagoon. Owners may access a private beach, gourmet restaurant, wine cellar, rooftop massage area, private pier lounge and bar, swimming pool, plus recreational activities and services.

BLAIR ATHOLL

Just north of Maya Beach are nine development tracts (www.mattdee.com/bayshore/blair.htm) of 5–10 acres in size running from the sea to the lagoon. An average seafront is 425 feet of deep, white-sand beaches and lagoon with views of the Maya mountains. Prices run US$365,000–515,000 for home, resort, or further residential subdivision development.

PLANTATION

Properties at Plantation (www.mattdee.com/bayshore/plantation.htm) are situated just a short stroll up the beach from hotels such as The Placencia Hotel, Maya Beach Hotel, and the Bella Maya resorts, located approximately 10 miles south of where the new International Airport is under construction and about 6 miles north of the existing Municipal Airport. The heart of the Placencia Village is approximately eight miles to the south.

The Hummingbird Highway leads into Stann Creek.

Getting Around

You don't need a car in Placencia Village unless you want to travel farther afield. If you're driving down from the airport, you can rent a car, drive along the Western Highway to Belmopan and turn onto the scenic Hummingbird Highway into Stann Creek. Just before Dangriga, turn onto the Southern Highway and turn off at Riversdale, continue past Seine Bight and you'll arrive in Placencia.

There are regular bus connections from Belmopan to Independence/Mango Creek, a small village on the mainland across the lagoon from Placencia. Catch a taxi from the bus stop or walk (it isn't far) to MnM Hardware/Fuel Dock where you can catch a Hokey Pokey water taxi to Kingfisher Landing in Placencia Village for BZ$10. It's a 10-minute ride. The fastest way to get to Placencia is to fly from Belize City's Philip S. W. Goldson International Airport or municipal airport (usually cheaper) to Placencia. The journey takes 35 minutes.

TOLEDO

Toledo is probably the least visited part of Belize and is virtually untouched, but it has been rapidly rising in popularity among expats since the Southern Highway was paved in 2008. Covered in pristine jungle with lagoons to the east along the coastline and bordered by the end of the Belize Barrier Reef, the district is mainly populated with Mopan and Kekchi Mayas. It is a rugged area, but if you enjoy a bit of a pioneering spirit and adventure, then this is the place for you. In May 2011, with funding from Kuwait, the Belizean government started work on a 28-mile road to Guatemala, which should open up the district. The proposed date of completion is 2015. The existing road is a dirt road and seasonal.

Before the Southern Highway was paved it was known as the worst road in Belize. A trip to Belmopan could take eight hours. It was very bad and some parts were impossible to navigate during the wet season when bridges washed away and Toledo could be inaccessible except by boat. The area was very remote and isolated. At the time, Punta Gorda, the region's largest town, was an

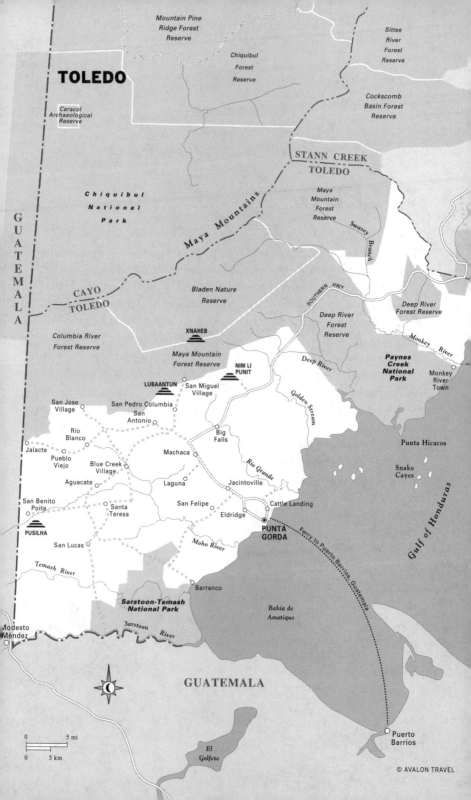

isolated village. Many old-timers speak of those days with nostalgia. There was no cable TV or Internet, and the main source of news was *Newsweek* magazine, which arrived once a week. During the last several years things have changed. Toledo is more popular, and there are more lodges and NGOs. In the old days there were quite a few missionaries and Peace Corps Volunteers, and now there is more of a Mexican, Guatemalan, and North American influence.

The Lay of the Land

The southern-most district in Belize, Toledo is surrounded by the rugged Maya Mountains, to the north on the border with Cayo District; part of the Cockscomb Range along the border with Stann Creek District, which thins out to pine trees and savannah reminiscent of Africa as you approach the coastline; and neat rows of citrus trees. To the west and south, the district borders Guatemala, both by land and sea with the Gulf of Honduras stretching out before Punta Gorda. To the east lie the gleaming waters of the Caribbean with a string of small cayes just offshore and bordered by the end of the barrier reef farther out. Toledo is a beautiful district with a variety of stunning and diverse nature ranging from lush broadleaf tropical forest, high peaks, wide rivers, creeks and streams which flow down from the Maya Mountains snaking through the jungle, Mayan ruins, caves, lagoons, waterfalls, and numerous national parks, forest reserves, and marine reserves.

Families enjoy a refreshing swim and kids play on one of the many piers that juts out into the sea from Punta Gorda.

CLIMATE

Toledo is the wettest part of Belize with rainfall varying from year to year from 12 to 36 inches a month during the wet season. It has the most rainy days a year with an average of 200 days, compared with 125 in Cayo. The climate is still warm and humid, similar to the rest of Belize, and rain often falls at night. It can be a nightmare drying things, so bring rainproof gear and perhaps a spare pair of hiking shoes and socks if you're trekking through the jungle.

CULTURE

Toledo consists of many cultures, including Maya, Garifuna, Creoles, East Indians, Chinese, North Americans, and Europeans. Most of these communities live in Punta Gorda and along the coastline. The Mopan and Kekchi Mayas make up 64 percent of the population in the district and live in over 30 different villages. Tourists come to experience a touch of their rich heritage through cultural exchanges. The ancient Maya were the earliest known inhabitants of southern Belize. They built great cities and ceremonial centers that flourished, including Uxbenka (The Old Place), one of the oldest known settlements on a hill outside Santa Cruz village. Lubaantun (Place of the Fallen Stones) may have been the regional capital, acting as the religious, administrative, political, and commercial center of the region. There are several unexcavated Maya sites across Belize to this day. Nim Li Punit (Big Hat), for example, wasn't discovered until the 1970s. The architects of Maya cities in southern Belize are thought to be the Manche Chol Maya. Successfully resisting attempts by

the main square in Punta Gorda

the Spanish to rule and tax them throughout the 16th and 17th centuries, the Chol remained unconquered, though many were converted to Catholicism. Eventually, diseases such as smallpox decimated the Indian population and, during the 18th and 19th centuries, the entire population of Chols was transported to the highlands of Guatemala by the British.

Following this forced migration, Toledo was more or less unpopulated until the mid 1800s when the Garifuna settlements of Punta Gorda, Punta Negra, and Barranco were founded. In 1868 Confederate soldiers settled in Cattle Landing, just north of Punta Gorda. In the late 19th and early 20th centuries, the Mopan and Kekchi groups of Maya Indians began migrating into southern Belize from Guatemala, fleeing from, among other things, heavy taxation. The Mopan Maya settled in the uplands of Toledo, around the present-day village of San Antonio. The Kekchi Maya spread out into the isolated lowlands and along the many rivers of Toledo.

Daily Life

EXPAT SOCIAL SCENE

There is a fairly large expat community in and around Punta Gorda. It's a small town and everyone knows each other. There are a few gatherings a year and there are groups who socialize more frequently. A favorite haunt is the Snack Shack. Twenty years ago, Toledo was a very laid-back place that was completely cut off during the rains and could only be reached by boat. Since the arrival of phones, the paving of the road, and the building of bridges, more foreigners have arrived. Much as in Cayo District, expats in Toledo live fairly remotely across the district. With all the attractions of the area drawing in tourists, several expats run lodges and resorts. There are also quite a few retirees, missionaries, Peace Corps Volunteers (PCVs), and NGO workers. Most expats know of each other or have heard of others. People socialize on an ad hoc basis, with the occasional dinner party, but many are busy with a variety of projects or businesses.

VOLUNTEERING

There are numerous options to volunteer at the local library, at schools, at clinics, and in organizing fundraising for community projects, such as improving the city park. If you're interested in conservation, contact the Toledo Institute for Development and Environment (TIDE). There is also the Rotary Club of Punta Gorda, founded in 2008.

JULI'S STORY: COTTON TREE CHOCOLATE

Juli first came to Belize in 2003 on vacation and fell in love with the place. She came for a week and stayed for four months! She was taking a year off traveling and continued to Hawaii, where she spent six months. Juli kept her ties with Belize, and one day she received an email that the only cyber café in Punta Gorda was for sale. Without thinking twice, she bought it. She liked Punta Gorda because of the friendly people and nice climate.

By 2006 a few other cyber cafés had opened and Juli decided to try something new: She opened the Reef Bar and Restaurant. That venture didn't work out because she found she didn't like running a restaurant. A friend from California started running a chocolate business and asked Juli to take over in April 2008. She accepted the offer and has been playing Wilma Wonka ever since— and her chocolate is delicious!

Cotton Tree Chocolate is one of only four companies in Belize that make and sell chocolate. Cotton Tree Chocolate originally started at Cotton Tree Lodge and rapidly grew in just six months. The business is entirely Belizean. Juli employs a few local women. She buys the beans from the Toledo Cacao Growers Association, a cooperative that buys beans from local farmers and sells them on to companies like Juli's, as well as internationally to big names like Green & Black's. Juli and the local women process the beans, experiment with different flavors, and sell chocolate in stores across Belize. Juli says the business is successful because it covers the whole country, but she adds that it is hard to run a successful business in Toledo. However, the company has grown a little bit every year. Cotton Tree Chocolate (www.cottontreelodge.com) offers tours of the cacao plantations and their shop.

Cotton Tree Chocolate

© VICTORIA DAY-WILSON

HEALTH

There are 19 medical centers with a total of 37 health workers and 5 satellite clinics in Big Falls, Santa Ana, Pueblo Viejo, Santa Teresa, and San Pedro Colombia. There are two polyclinics, one in San Antonio and one in Punta Gorda; two mobile health units; and one private clinic, Hillside Health Care Center, which operates one mobile unit and is often staffed by North American volunteers. Founded in 2000, Hillside was officially dedicated at its current location on Poppyshow Road in Eldridgeville, outside of Punta Gorda Town. It is a faith-based, health facility supported by the Jericho Road Foundation International (JFRI). There are two private British doctors and the Forest Home Medical/Dental Clinic. North American dentists come down three or four times a year to Forest Home, a modern dental clinic about four miles outside town. There are two part-time vets.

Located centrally in town, Punta Gorda Polyclinic is your first stop for primary healthcare. It is a 30-bed facility that provides services in general medicine, pediatrics, and maternity and delivery to the entire Toledo District. Visiting specialists from the Southern Regional Hospital carry out specialist clinics. The Punta Gorda Polyclinic manages common illnesses, obstetrics and gynecology cases, and levels of trauma that do not require specialist intervention, and prepares patients for referral and ensures that all necessary information (diagnostic results) accompanies the patient. The polyclinic is mainly run by Cuban and East Indian doctors who are good, but the facilities are somewhat wanting. In more serious cases, go to the Southern Regional Hospital in Dangriga, Stann Creek. Other options include going to Belize City, Guatemala, Mexico, or North America for secondary or tertiary care.

EDUCATION

State schools in Toledo are often underfunded, but expats do use them. St. Peter Claver Roman Catholic Primary School in Punta Gorda had 1,100 students enrolled in 2011.

St. Stephen's is located in the beautiful and remote Creole fishing community of Monkey River Village. There are 65 children in school, ages 3–14 years old. The school was built in 2002 after Hurricane Iris, so the building is much more spacious than most Belizean schools. The school has five teachers, including a preschool teacher and a teaching principal.

St. Joseph's Preschool is behind the tiny St. Joseph's Church in the main street of Punta Gorda, and serves over 20 children. Punta Gorda is very much a multiethnic town, and students come from the Maya, Mestizo, and

Garifuna communities. The school has two teachers, and is well supported by parents.

Toledo Community College is the largest and only high school in the Toledo District. Located in the western part of Punta Gorda Town, the school had around 700 students in 2011 with a staff of around 43 including the principal. There are 19 classrooms that consist of five major departments: business, the arts, vocational, science, and general studies. Toledo Community College is a 9–12 grade school (called forms 1–4 under the Belize education system).

Julian Cho Technical High School, a government co-educational institution, with about 400 students and 30 staff, emphasizes vocational, technical education that is relevant to the development of the Toledo District and its people.

Where to Live

Where you live in Toledo really depends on what you want to do. You can be close to the sea or inland in the jungle. You can live remotely on a large tract of land or more centrally in or just outside Punta Gorda. People generally prefer to be on the outskirts of Punta Gorda or far away from town. As awareness increases about Toledo and people are finding out that there is so much to do here, interest is increasing and more foreigners are coming to look at property. Some expats own farms or lodges in rural areas, others run small businesses in or around Punta Gorda and live along the coastline, which is rocky in some places and sandy in others. There are fewer expats in Toledo compared with Stann Creek, Cayo, Corozal, Ambergris Caye, and Caye Caulker. Most people in rural areas are fairly dispersed. Popular expat areas include Eldridge, which lies inland from Punta Gorda, Hopeville, San Pedro, Colombia Village, and Cattle Landing, just north of Punta Gorda on the coastline.

PUNTA GORDA

With a population of almost 6,000, Punta Gorda—known locally as PG—is Belize's largest, southern town and the capital of the Toledo District. It was a small fishing village before being settled by a number of Garifuna emigrants from Honduras in 1823. The population is a mixture of Mopan and Kekchi Maya, Garifuna, Creoles, Lebanese, East Indian, and Chinese. It lies about

a house in Eldridge

210 miles by road from Belize City, along the shoreline. It's a small town with five main streets that run parallel inland. The town has one hospital, a police station, a courthouse, a fire station, an airstrip, two banks, a bus station, a post office, a gas station, a civic center, a number of churches and schools, and various grocery stores, hotels, restaurants, and bars. Punta Gorda is a gateway to and from Puerto Barrios and Livingston in Guatemala with an immigration and customs office near the town dock. The seafront of the town is popular with expats; quite a few rent homes.

CATTLE LANDING

In the 1700s, a group of Koreans came to Cattle Landing and had cattle, which were soon wiped out by insects and disease. In 1868, Confederate soldiers seeking asylum at the end of the American Civil War settled here. They grew sugar and by 1870 operated 12 sugar mills. By the turn of the century, the sugar industry collapsed due to a labor shortage and a drop in sugar prices.

PRICES

Rent for a three-bedroom house on the seafront in Punta Gorda can be as low as BZ$300 a month, but that is very rare. To rent a furnished, one-bedroom apartment or house costs about BZ$150–300 a month. Two bedrooms will cost about BZ$150 more. For a bigger North American–style house rent will be around BZ$2,000, but these are few and far between. Depending on location,

pier in Punta Gorda

access, and utilities, large tracts of land in Toledo can fetch US$800–2,000 an acre. Oceanfront property runs US$5,000–20,000 an acre, depending on the quality of the waterfront, and riverfront property can fetch US$2,000–5,000 an acre. An 18-acre cacao farm with fruit trees costs about US$65,000.

Getting Around

There are several flights a day on Maya Island Air and Tropic Air from Belize City to Punta Gorda. By car from Belize City, take the Western Highway and turn off onto the scenic Hummingbird Highway at Belmopan. Just before reaching Dangriga turn onto the Southern Highway, which culminates in Punta Gorda. There aren't that many gas stations along the way, so fuel up when you can and consider bringing a spare container of gas to be on the safe side. All the highways are good, paved roads. There are several dirt roads leading out of Punta Gorda around Toledo. Some of these are quite rough and can become difficult, if not impossible, to navigate during the wet season. The best thing to do is to rent a four-wheel drive vehicle. There are buses from Belmopan and Belize City to Punta Gorda, as well as a few local buses, but the best way to travel around the district is with your own car, as local buses only travel on selected routes.

RESOURCES

© VICTORIA DAY-WILSON

Consulates and Embassies

BELIZE EMBASSIES IN FOREIGN COUNTRIES

BELIZE HIGH COMMISSION
Third Floor, 45 Crawford Place
W1H 4LP
London
United Kingdom
tel. (+44) 207/723-3603
fax (+44) 207/723-9637
bzhc-lon@btconnect.com
www.belizehighcommission.com

CONSULATE OF BELIZE IN VANCOUVER, CANADA
2321 Trafalgar Street
Vancouver, British Columbia V6K 3T1
tel. (+1) 604/730-1224
fax (+1) 604/648-9095
david@smilingassociates.com
dwsmiling@hotmail.com

CONSULATE GENERAL OF BELIZE
4801 Wilshire Boulevard, Suite 250
Los Angeles, California 90010
tel. 323/634-9900
fax 323/634-9903

EMBASSY OF BELIZE
2535 Massachusetts Avenue, NW,
Washington DC 20008
tel. 202/332-9636
fax 202/332-6888
ebwreception@aol.com
www.embassyofbelize.org

HONORARY CONSULATE OF BELIZE IN CALGARY, CANADA
305 - 10th Avenue SE
Calgary, Alberta T2G 0W2
tel. (+1) 403/215-6072
fax (+1) 403/264-8870
bdhillon@mainst.biz

PERMANENT MISSION OF BELIZE
201 East 42nd Street
New York, NY 10017-5704
tel. 212/986-1240
fax 212/593-0932

FOREIGN EMBASSIES IN BELIZE

BELIZE EMBASSIES AND CONSULATES AND FOREIGN EMBASSIES IN BELIZE
http://bz.embassyinformation.com

BRITISH HIGH COMMISSION
P.O. Box 91
Embassy Square
Belmopan
tel. 822-2981, 877-2717, or 877-2146
Consular Direct tel. 822-3146
fax 822-2761
brithicom@btl.net
http://ukinbelize.fco.gov.uk/en

CONSULATE OF CANADA
80 Princess Margaret Drive
P.O. Box 610, Belize City
tel. 223-1060
fax 223-0060
cdncon.bze@btl.net

U.S. EMBASSY BELMOPAN
4 Floral Park Road
Belmopan
tel. 822-4011
Emergency after-hours tel. 610-5030
fax 822-4050
embbelize@state.gov
http://belize.usembassy.gov

Government Organizations and Initiatives

BELIZE TOURISM BOARD (BTB)
tel. 223-1913 or 800/624-0686
fax 501/223-1943
www.belizetourism.org
www.travelbelize.org
Informative and useful resource on traveling and staying in Belize.

BELIZE TOURISM INDUSTRY ASSOCIATION
www.btia.org

GOVERNMENT OF BELIZE
www.belize.gov.bz

NATIONAL EMERGENCY MANAGEMENT ORGANIZATION OF BELIZE (NEMO)
Belmopan
tel. 822-2054 or 0995
emergency tel. 822-0153
fax 822-2861 or 822-0874
nemohqbmp@nemo.org.bz
www.nemo.org.bz

SOLICITOR GENERAL'S MINISTRY – LAWS OF BELIZE
www.belizelaw.org

STATISTICAL INSTITUTE OF BELIZE
www.cso.gov.bz

Environmental Organizations

AMERICAN CROCODILE EDUCATION SANCTUARY (ACES)
Cherie & Vince Rose
General Delivery, San Pedro Town
Ambergris Caye
tel. 631-6366
acesnpo@hughes.net
www.americancrocodilesanctuary.org

BELIZE AUDUBON SOCIETY
12 Fort Street
tel. 223-5004
www.belizeaudubon.org

BELIZE WILDLIFE CONSERVATION NETWORK
www.wildlifebelize.com

BELIZE ZOO
Mile 29, Western Highway
General Delivery, Ladyville GPO, Belize
tel. 220-8004
fax 220-8010
info@belizezoo.org
www.belizezoo.org

DR. ISABELLE PAQUET-DURAND
Institute for Sustainable International
Studies (ISIS)
San Ignacio
tel. 668-3251
www.isisbelize.com
Wildlife veterinarian and professor.

Emergency Contacts

CRIME STOPPERS
P.O. Box 1960, Belize City
tel. 607-1484
Coordinator@crimestoppersbelize.org
www.crimestoppersbelize.org

POLICE, AMBULANCE, AND FIRE
tel. 911 or 90

PRIVATE AMBULANCE: BELIZE EMERGENCY RESPONSE TEAM (BERT)
tel. 223-3292

RESOURCES

General Travel

BELIZE
www.belize.com
General, useful, and informative site about coming to Belize and traveling around.

BTL 2011 BELIZE TELEPHONE DIRECTORY
www.belizetelemediaedirectory.net

DRIVE ME LOCO
http://drivemeloco.com
Gringo's travel guide and e-book for driving to and through Central America.

DUPLOOY TRAVEL
www.belize-vacation.com
Useful and informative site about traveling around Belize.

ELECTRONIC SYSTEM FOR TRAVEL AUTHORIZATION (ESTA)
www.esta.org.uk
Apply online: https://esta.cbp.dhs.gov/esta.

ESCAPE ARTIST
www.escapeartist.com/Live_In_Belize
Articles on moving to and living in Belize.

FOREIGN COMMONWEALTH OFFICE (FCO)
www.fco.gov.uk

GETTING TO BELIZE
www.gettingtobelize.com
Regularly updated flights from North American cities via Cancún and direct to Belize.

GUIDE TO BELIZE
www.guidetobelize.info
A useful site with air, sea, and land travel information and schedules to and around Belize.

PARADISE HUNTER
www.paradisehunter.com
Excellent information resource on Belize.

U.S. CUSTOMS AND BORDER PROTECTION (CBP)
www.cbp.gov

U.S. DEPARTMENT OF STATE TRAVEL ADVICE
http://travel.state.gov

Expat Resources

AMERICAN AND CANADIAN EXPAT LIVING FORUM
http://sollifestyles.com/forum

BELIZE FIRST
www.belizefirst.com
Magazine and blog on travel and life in Belize.

BELIZE FORUM
www.belizeforum.com/belize

BELIZE SPECIALISTS
www.belizespecialists.com

BELIZE TOTAL
http://board.belizetotal.com
Forum on Belize.

A COUNTRY STUDY
http://countrystudies.us/belize
A good in-depth historical, social, and economical resource.

EXPAT BELIZE
www.expatbelize.com
Life and expat resources in Belize.

EXPAT EXCHANGE
www.expatexchange.com/belize/liveinbelize.
html
Forum and good source for information
and a chance to ask questions.

EXPAT FOCUS
www.expatfocus.com/expatriate-belize
Expat guide for Belize.

GUIDE TO BELIZE
www.guidetobelize.info
Excellent guide and resource on Belize.

INTERNATIONAL LIVING
http://internationalliving.com
Good information source on Belize
with articles. Some information requires
payment.

**SHELTER OFFSHORE:
LIVING IN BELIZE**
www.shelteroffshore.com

BLOGS

This is a modest and by no means comprehensive list of blogs written by expats living in Belize. Some include great
general information, and all write about
day-to-day life here. They provide great
insight as well as personal thoughts and
experiences.

BELIZEAN TRAVEL
http://belizeantravel.com
All about Belize and available activities.

BELIZE BIRD RESCUE
http://belizebirdrescue.blogspot.com
A day-to-day account of life with the
parrots at Belize Bird Rescue in Cayo—
a non-profit rescue, rehabilitation, and
release center for indigenous birds of
Belize.

BELIZEBRITT'S BLOG
http://belizebritts.wordpress.com
After spending most of their lives in the

U.S. Navy, Jim and Jacquelyn moved to
Belize in 2004 from Florida with their
three children, who are now growing up
in the jungle at Barton Creek Outpost,
Cayo.

BELIZE BUS
http://belizebus.wordpress.com
Excellent Belize transport travel blog.

BELIZE DRAGONFLY
http://belizedragonfly.com
Excellent news and information from a
woman who made the move from Oregon to Corozal and opened Scotty's Bar
and Grill.

BELIZE ISLAND LIFE
www.investinbelize.com/blog1
Timothy and Tina Callanan's blog on San
Pedro life and real estate includes useful
information on Belize.

**BELIZE IT OR NOT:
A BELIZE CHEF'S STORY
ON THE CARIBBEAN SEA**
www.chefinbelize.blogspot.com
A real time documentation of Tony Mar-
sico and his family starting Beaches and
Dreams Seafront Inn, cooking, and liv-
ing on the Caribbean Sea in Hopkins.

**BELIZE IT OR NOT...BEAR & EM
IN BELIZE!**
http://bebelize.weebly.com
Emily and Barry retired to Ambergris
Caye in 2011 after several trips to Belize.
The blog is about their life in Belize and
experiences after moving.

BELIZE 101
http://belize-for-sale.blogspot.com
Life in and information on Belize by Ma-
carena Rose, who moved to Cayo with
kids and 10 animals.

THE BELIZE POST
http://bzpost.blogspot.com
Lorenzo writes about Belize, personal
experiences, vacation guides, and culture
and politics.

RESOURCES

BELIZE SNOWBIRD

www.belizesnowbird.com
Everyday life with Chunky and Ruth, who retired and live in Belize during the winter and Minnesota during the summer.

CARIBBEAN COLORS – BACK TO LIVING IN PARADISE

www.caribbean-colors.blogspot.com
Artist Lee Vanderwalker writes from Caye Caulker.

DON'T STOP BELIZE'IN!

http://belizedays.blogspot.com
Tommy, Sara, baby Egan, and dog Jesse share their experiences on Caye Caulker.

EXPAT BLOG

www.expat-blog.com
Summary of blogs written by expats in Belize from Expat Blog.

FILMBELIZE

http://filmbelize.blogspot.com
Musings of the film commissioner of Belize.

FRIENDFEED FOR BELIZE

http://friendfeed.com/belizefeed
Best of the week from Belize: It includes blogs and news sites on Belize and all Flickr pictures and YouTube videos tagged with Belize.

GO TO BELIZE

http://goto-belize.blogspot.com
Musings from a German author on starting a new life in Cayo since moving there in 2010.

IMAGES OF BELIZE

http://blog.tonyrath.com
Photos from Belize by Tony Roth, who lives in Dangriga.

ISLAND TIME – ENJOYING LIFE IN A SAN PEDRO BELIZE BEACHFRONT HOTEL

http://islandtimebelize.blogspot.com
Julie moved from Vermont to San Pedro in 1998 and runs a hotel there.

LIFE AND ADVENTURES LIVING IN BELIZE

http://traversbelize.blogspot.com
Drew and Karen's commentaries on life on the Placencia Peninsula.

MOONRACERFARM BELIZE

http://moonracerfarmbelize.blogspot.com
Photos and commentary on daily life in Cayo from Marge and Tom Gallagher, who left New York in 2006 and run their own business, Moonracer Farm Lodging and Tours.

PICTURE BELIZE

http://picturebelize.blogspot.com
A photo blog featuring the nature and landscape photography of AJ Baxter in Belize.

PICTURING LIFE IN PLACENCIA

http://picturinglifeinplacencia.wordpress.com
Fiona's photo blog from Placencia.

SAN PEDRO SCOOP!

www.sanpedroscoop.com
The author traded Manhattan for San Pedro and runs a bar and a varied and interesting blog.

TACOGIRL

http://tacogirl.com
Useful and interesting expat travel blog from San Pedro.

TAKING BELIZE

www.takingbelize.blogspot.com
Useful and informative blog about travel and living in Belize by Bill and Debra.

WEALTHSHIPS

www.wealthships.com
Sharon Hiebing put everything she owned in three suitcases and moved to Belize in 2010. Her useful and informative blog covers daily expat reflections in Belize.

She also provides an Expat Relocation Consulting service.

WESTERN BELIZE HAPPENINGS!
http://westernbelizehappenings.blogspot.com
News and information from western Belize.

WILDLIFE CONSERVATION AND MEDICINE IN BELIZE
http://wildlife-conservation-belize.blogspot.com
Tropical wildlife rescue and rehabilitation

stories and more from the perspective of a wildlife veterinarian dedicated to conservation and animal welfare.

WINJAMA
http://winjama.blogspot.com
Dave and Dianna Rider's "Adventures in Belize" from Corozal since 2007.

YOBUBBA'S JOURNAL
http://yobubba.livejournal.com
Beautiful photos from Belize with a focus on birds.

People and Culture

THE ARTISTS OF BELIZE
http://ambergriscaye.com/artists

BLISS CENTRE FOR THE PERFORMING ARTS
tel. 227-2110
www.nichbelize.org

HOUSE OF CULTURE
Regent Street
tel. 227-3050
www.nichbelize.org

THE IMAGE FACTORY
91 N Front Street
tel. 610-5072
www.imagefactory.bz

M. OLSEN FARRIER SERVICES
Light Rein Farm
5 Mile, Mountain Pine Ridge Road
Cayo

tel. 663-4609
shotzy08@live.com
Twenty years of shoeing experience and 36 years professional horse trainer available for farrier, training, lessons, and clinics. Specializes in therapeutic shoeing and a light-handed approach to training and teaching. Western, huntseat, showmanship, trail, and speed events. Organizes the Triple Crown Endurance Race, http://tcerbelize.com.

MUSEUM OF BELIZE
Queen Street
tel. 223-4524
www.nichbelize.org

SPECTARTE ART AND GARDEN GALLERY
Maya Beach
tel. 533-8019
www.spectarte.com

Making the Move

ANGELUS PRESS
10 Queen Street
Belize City
tel. 223-5777
Constitution Drive
Belmopan
tel. 822-3861

THE ASSOCIATION OF REAL ESTATE BROKERS OF BELIZE (AREBB)
P.O. Box 2217
Belize City
tel. 223-5616
office@arebb.com
www.arebb.com

BELIZE AGRICULTURAL HEALTH AUTHORITY (BAHA): BELMOPAN
Belmopan Showgrounds
Belmopan City
tel. 822-0197 or 822-0818
fax 822-3084
baha@btl.net
http://baha.bz

BELIZE AGRICULTURAL HEALTH AUTHORITY (BAHA): CAYO DISTRICT
Dr. Victor Gongora
Technical Director
Central Farm
tel. 824-4872
fax 824-4889
animalhealth@baha.bz
http://bahia.bz
Belize City tel. 224-4794
Belize City fax 224-5230

BELIZE CUSTOMS AND EXCISE DEPARTMENT
www.customs.gob.bz

BELIZE NATIONAL ASSOCIATION OF REALTORS (BNAR)
7 Craig Street
Belize City
tel. 804-0195
fax 804-0195
info@belizenar.org
http://belizenational.point2agent.com

BELIZETOURISM BOARD (BTB) RETIREMENT INCENTIVES (QRP)
www.belizeretirement.org

BELTRAIDE LIST OF CUSTOM BROKERS
www.belizeinvest.org.bz

CUSTOMS BROKERS ASSOCIATION OF BELIZE
www.customsbrokers.bz

DEPARTMENT OF CIVIL AVIATION
Phillip S. W. Goldson Airport
Ladyville
tel. 225-2014 or 225-2052
fax 225-2533
dcabelize@btl.net
www.civilaviation.gov.bz

DEPARTMENT OF IMMIGRATION
Market Square, Belmopan City
tel. 822-3860 or 822-0284
fax 822-2662
insbze@btl.net
www.belize.gov.bz

LINK FROM BELTRAIDE TO A LIST OF LAW AND ACCOUNTING FIRMS AND CONTACTS
Law firms: www.belizeinvest.org.bz/PDF/law-firms.pdf
Accountants: www.belizeinvest.org.bz/pdf/accounting-firms.pdf
Insurance Agents: www.belizeinvest.org.bz/PDF/insuranceagents.pdf
Custom Brokers: www.belizeinvest.org.bz/PDF/custombrokers.pdf

LIST OF ATTORNEYS FROM BELIZE.COM
http://belize.com/belize-law.html

LIST OF ATTORNEYS FROM THE U.S. EMBASSY IN BELIZE
http://belize.usembassy.gov

MINISTRY OF THE ATTORNEY GENERAL
General Office Belmopan
tel. 822-2504 or 0519

fax 822-3390
Belize City tel. 227-4114

VITAL STATISTICS UNIT
Belize City
tel. 223-5625

vitalstatsbz@yahoo.com
The Vital Statistics Unit in the Registrar General Department is responsible for issuing birth certificates.

Housing Considerations

THE ASSOCIATION OF PROFESSIONAL ARCHITECTS OF BELIZE
www.architectsofbelize.com

THE ASSOCIATION OF PROFESSIONAL ENGINEERS OF BELIZE
http://apebbelize.com

BELIZE DEPARTMENT OF ARCHAEOLOGY
East Block
Belmopan
tel. 822-2106
fax 822-3345
celbelize@btl.net
www.belize.gov.bz

BRODIES
P.O. Box 365
16 Regent Street, Belize City
tel. 227-7070
fax 227-5593
brodies@btl.net
www.brodiesbelize.com
Brodies is also in Belmopan.

BUILDERS' HARDWARE
160 Constitution Drive
P.O. Box 427
Belmopan
tel. 822-0501 or 1071
fax 822-1458
Info@Buildershardwarebelize.com
www.buildershardwarebelize.com

CARIBBEAN TIRES
tel. 823-0107
fax:823-0097
www.caribbeantire.com
Located in several towns.

CENTRAL BUILDING AUTHORITY
3rd. Fl. - Coastal Zone Management Bldg.
Princess Margaret Drive
Belize City
tel. 223-2616 or 223-1878
fax 223-5738
centralbuildingauthority@yahoo.com
http://cbabelize.com

COURTS – UTILITIES AND FURNITURE
Northern Highway
Belize City
tel. 223-5178
slockefaux@courts.com.bz
www.courts.com.bz
Courts has shops in all main towns.

DAVE'S FURNITURE
53 corner of Basra and Tigris Streets
Belize City
tel. 227-6474
info@davesfurnitureworld.com
http://davesfurnitureworldbelize.com

FARMERS TRADING CENTER
Center Road
545 Spanish Lookout
tel. 823-0111
fax 823-0272
info@farmerstrading.com
www.farmerstrading.com

HUMMINGBIRD FURNISHINGS
54 Hummingbird Highway
P.O. Box 268
Belmopan
tel. 822-3164
fax 822-3993
info@hummingbirdfurnishings.com
www.hummingbirdfurnishings.com
Also in San Pedro.

LANDS DEPARTMENT BELMOPAN
tel. 822-2249
fax 822-2333
www.belize.gov.bz

LINDA VISTA LUMBER AND HOMES
Route 40 West
Spanish Lookout
Cayo
tel. 823-0257 or 823-8052
fax 823-0372
www.lindavista.webpageplusx2.com

MIDWEST STEEL
Center Road
Spanish Lookout
tel. 823-0131 or 0332
fax 823-0270
www.midweststeel.bz

MINISTRY OF NATURAL RESOURCES AND THE ENVIRONMENT
General Office: Belmopan
tel. 822-2249, 822-2711, 822-2232, 822-2226, 822-2307 or 822-2626
fax: 822-2333 or 822-2083
info@mnrei.gov.bz
www.mnrei.gov.bz

MIRAB FURNITURE GALLERY
1½ Miles Western Highway
tel. 222-4333

gallery@mirabsbelize.com
http://mirabsbelize.com

PAPIS HOME CENTER
1902 Constitution Drive
Belmopan
tel. 822-0958 or 822-0976

O'DONOGHUE LANDSCAPES
Mile 71
Western Highway
tel. 823-3052
odonoghue@btl.net

RICHARD BRINCKMANN
Landscape Design
tel. 722-0052
marty@sirmoorhillfarm.com

UNIVERSAL HARDWARE
Center Road, Spanish Lookout
tel. 823-0254
sales@universalhardware.bz
www.universalhardware.bz

WESTRAC AUTOMOTIVE, TRACTOR PARTS AND ACCESSORIES
Box 587, Center Road
Spanish Lookout
tel. 823-0101
mail@westracbelize.com
www.westracbelize.com

Education

MINISTRY OF EDUCATION
www.moes.gov.bz

PRIVATE SCHOOLS

Ambergris Caye
AMBERGRIS CAYE ELEMENTARY SCHOOL (ACES)
P.O. Box 1, San Pedro
tel. 501/226-2226
acesprincipald@gmail.com
http://ambergriscayeelementaryschool.com

THE ISLAND ACADEMY
Lady Dixie Bowen, Director
Coconut Drive, San Pedro
tel./fax 226-3642
www.theislandacademy.com

LA ISLA BONITA ELEMENTARY SCHOOL
San Pedro, Ambergris Caye
Cormorant Street in the San Juan Area
tel. 226-3754
islabonitasch@btl.net
http://islabonitaelementaryschool.com

Cayo
BELIZE CHRISTIAN ACADEMY (BAC)
P.O. Box 267, Belmopan
tel. 822-3048
fax 822-3351
infor@belizechristianacademy.com
www.belizechristainacademy.com

QUALITY SCHOOL INTERNATIONAL (QSI)
Mrs. Valerie Nathanson
Mile 49.5, Western Highway
Camalote Village
tel. 832-2666
belize@qsi.org
www.qsi.org

PRIMARY AND SECONDARY SCHOOLS
This is not an exhaustive list, please refer to the links that follow for a full list.

MINISTRY OF EDUCATION AND YOUTH
www.moe.gov.bz

Ambergris Caye
HOLY CROSS ANGLICAN PRIMARY SCHOOL
Lydia Brown – Coordinator
www.holycrossbelize.org

SAN PEDRO HIGH SCHOOL
http://ambergriscaye.com

SAN PEDRO RC SCHOOL
http://ambergriscaye.com

ST. PETER'S ELEMENTARY AND ST. PETER'S COLLEGE
San Pedro, Ambergris Caye
tel. 206-2123 or 226-3167
frank_nunez39@yahoo.com

Belize City
BELIZE ELEMENTARY SCHOOL
Princess Margaret Drive
tel. 203-0905 or 223-5765
fax 223-5959
www.bes.edu.bz

BELIZE HIGH SCHOOL AT THE UNIVERSITY OF THE WEST INDIES OPEN CAMPUS
P.O. Box 714
Princess Margaret Drive
tel./fax 223-1177
www.belizehighschool.edu.bz

ST. CATHERINE'S ACADEMY FOR GIRLS
6 Hutson Street
P.O. Box 1891
tel. 223-4908 or 223-1758
fax 223-0057
www.sca.edu.bz

ST. JOHN'S COLLEGE
Landivar Campus
Princess Margaret Drive
tel. 223-3732
www.sjc.edu.bz

Cayo
EDEN SEVENTH DAY ADVENTIST (SDA) HIGH SCHOOL
Eden Drive
Santa Elena
tel. 824-2966
fax 824-4479
principal@eden.edu.bz
www.eden.edu.bz

FAITH NAZERINE
San Ignacio
tel. 804-3320

SACRED HEART COLLEGE
P.O. Box 163
Joseph Andrews Drive
San Ignacio
tel. 824-2758 or 824-2102
fax 824-3759
President: president@shc.edu.bz
High School: Mrs. Eufemia Usher: eufemia@shc.edu.bz
www.shc.edu.bz

SAINT IGNATIUS HIGH SCHOOL
7 George Price Avenue
Santa Elena
tel. 824-3294

Corozal

COROZAL COMMUNITY COLLEGE
San Andres Road
tel. 422-3280

COROZAL METHODIST SCHOOL
57 First Avenue
tel. 422-2839

MARY HILL PRIMARY SCHOOL
San Andres Road
tel. 422-2567

ST. FRANCIS PRIMARY SCHOOL
4th Avenue and 1st Street, North Corozal
tel. 422-2520 or 422-2521

ST. FRANCIS XAVIER INFANTS PRESCHOOL
4th Avenue and 1st Street North
tel. 422-3145

ST. PAUL'S SCHOOL
5th Street South
Corozal Town
tel. 422-2480

Stann Creek

DELILLE ACADEMY
tel. 522-3917
delilleacademy@yahoo.com
www.bcapss.com/delille-academy

ECUMENICAL HIGH SCHOOL, DANGRIGA
P.O. Box 84, Dangriga Town
tel. 522-2114
scec@btl.net
www.scecumenicalhighschool.edu.bz

SOLID ROCK CHRISTIAN ACADEMY
Rivas Estate Dangriga
P.O. Box 40 Dangriga
tel. 522-0776
www.srca.edu.bz

Toledo

TOLEDO COMMUNITY COLLEGE
P.O. Box 41, Punta Gorda Town
tel. 722-2334
fax 722-2107
tccpg@btl.net
http://tccpg.org

HIGHER EDUCATION

THE CENTRAL AMERICA HEALTH SCIENCES UNIVERSITY (CAHSU)
U.S. Information Office
P.O. Box 55996
Washington, DC 20040
Toll-free tel. 877/523-9687
cahsu@cahsu.edu
www.cahsu.edu

GALEN UNIVERSITY
62.5 Western Highway
Office of Admissions
P.O. Box 94
San Ignacio
tel. 824-3226
fax 824-3723
admissions@galen.edu.bz
www.galen.edu.bz

UNIVERSITY OF BELIZE
Belmopan Central Campus
University Drive, P.O. Box 340
Belmopan
tel. 822-3680 or 822-1000
fax 822-1107
Registrar: Dr Roy Young: ryoung@ub.edu.bz
www.ub.edu.bz

UNIVERSITY OF THE WEST INDIES
Open Campus Belize
P.O. Box 229
Princess Margaret Drive
Belize City
tel. 223-5320
fax 223-2038
belize@open.uwi.edu
www.open.uwi.edu/belize

OTHER OPTIONS

CALVERT SCHOOL
www.homeschool.calvertschool.org

HOMESCHOOL.COM – THE HOMESCHOOLING COMMUNITY
www.homeschool.com

MICHELLE LEONARDS – HOMESCHOOLING
Georgeville, A.C.E. Homeschool
tel. 629-2179
leonardsnbelize@gmail.com
www.aceministries.com/homeschool

Health

GENERAL INFORMATION

CENTERS FOR DISEASE CONTROL AND PREVENTION (CDC)
1600 Clifton Road
Atlanta, GA 30333
tel. 800/232-4636
cdcinfo@cdc.gov
www.nc.cdc.gov

HOSPITAL NUMBERS AND NAMES
www.belmopancityonline.com

MINISTRY OF HEALTH
http://health.gov.bz

HOSPITALS AND CLINICS

Belize City

BELIZE CITY HOSPITAL
Eyre Street
tel. 227-7251

BELIZE DIAGNOSTIC CENTER
Leslie Street
tel. 224-5778
belizerad@btl.net
www.belizediagnostic.com

BELIZE HEALTHCARE PARTNERS, LTD.
corner of Chancellor Avenue and Blue Marlin Boulevard
tel. 223-7866, 223-7867, 224-5537, 224-5538, or 223-3440
fax 223-7876
bhp@belizehealthcare.com
www.belizehealthcare.com

BELIZE MEDICAL ARTS AND AMBULATORY SURGI CENTER
Chancellor Avenue
tel. 224-5537 or 224-5538

BELIZE MEDICAL ASSOCIATES
P.O. Box 1008
5791 St. Thomas Street
Kings Park

tel. 223-0302, 223-0303, 223-0304, 223-3835, or 223-3836
fax 223-1261 or 223-3837
bzemedasso@btl.net
www.belizemedical.com
Emergency Services: 24 Hours

CLEOPATRA WHITE POLYCLINIC II
tel. 223-5213 or 223-0131

HEALTH CENTER
Hattieville
tel. 225-6106

HEALTH CENTER
Ladyville
tel. 225-2764

INTEGRAL HEALTH CARE SOUTHSIDE HEALTH CENTER
Gibnut/Curassow Street
tel. 227-6722

KARL HEUSNER MEMORIAL HOSPITAL
Princess Margaret Drive
tel. 223-1548 or 223-1671
fax 223-3081
pro@khmh.bz
www.khmh.bz

MATRON ROBERTS POLYCLINIC II
tel. 227-7170

MYO'ON CLINICS LTD
40 Eve Street
tel. 224-5616 or 223-1537

ZUNIGA HAROLD PHYSICAL THERAPY
85 Amara Avenue
tel. 227-1638

The Cayes

HEALTH CENTER
Caye Caulker
tel. 226-0166

SAN PEDRO ANIMAL HOSPITAL
Sea Grape Drive
Ambergris Caye

tel. 610-3647
laurie@sanpedroanimalhospital.com
http://sanpedroanimalhospital.com

SAN PEDRO POLYCLINIC II
Ambergris Caye
tel. 226-2536

Cayo
BELMOPAN HOSPITAL
Florina Drive
Belmopan
tel. 822-2263 or 822-2264

CAYO FAMILY CLINIC & PHARMACY
3226 Bullet Tree Avenue
San Ignacio
tel. 804-3487
cayofamilyclinic@yahoo.com
A dermatologist, Dr. Peter Craig, comes
every Saturday from Belize City.

DR. MEGAN RYAN DENTAL CLINIC
55 Bullet Tree Road
San Ignacio
tel. 631-7400
mryan@ddsbelize.com
www.ddsbelize.com

**IX CHEL WELLNESS CENTER
(NATURAL MEDICINE)**
1458 Eve Street
Santa Elena
tel. 804-0264
www.arvigomassage.com

LA LOMA LUZ HOSPITAL
67 Western Highway
Santa Elena
tel. 824-2087 or 804-2985
fax 824-2674
lalomaluzsdahosp@yahoo.com
http://lalomaluz.org
This is an Adventist hospital, not fully
operational on Saturdays.

MOPAN CLINIC
Benque Viejo
tel. 823-2079

SAN IGNACIO HOSPITAL
Bullet Tree Road
San Ignacio

tel. 824-2066 or 824-2761
fax 824-4894

SPANISH LOOKOUT CLINIC
Route 35 West
Spanish Lookout
tel. 823-0149

**SUNSHINE PHARMACY
AND DENTAL PRACTISE**
Joelyn Flowers and Hans Dyck
Box #222
Route 20 West
Spanish Lookout
tel. 823-0014 or 624-1617

Corozal
BETHESDA MEDICAL CENTER
Santa Rita Road
tel. 422-3000
fax 422-3198

COROZAL HOSPITAL
tel. 422-2076

**COROZAL HOSPITAL OUTPATIENT
CLINIC**
tel. 422-2080 or 422-2081

DR. GLENDA MAJOR
1st Street South
tel. 422-2837

**GABRIEL G. GARCIA DENTAL
CLINIC**
12 4th Street South
tel. 422-2355

NORTHERN MEDICAL GROUP
Paraiso
tel. 422-2589

NORTHERN VETERINARY CLINIC
Corozal Clinic
12 Park St. North
tel. 322-3764 or 322-0330 (Emergencies)

Orange Walk
FAMILY DENTAL CENTER
27 Bakers Street
tel. 322-0732

**NORTHERN MEDICAL
SPECIALTY PLAZA**
Orchid Street, BSI Area
Orange Walk Town
tel. 302-3708
fax 322-2320
medicalplaza@hotmail.com
Emergencies: 24-hour services.

ORANGE WALK HOSPITAL
Orange Walk Town
tel. 322-2143

Stann Creek
DANGRIGA HOSPITAL
tel. 522-2084

DANGRIGA POLYCLINIC
tel. 522-3831

INDEPENDENCE POLYCLINIC
tel. 523-2167

PLACENCIA HEALTH CENTER
tel. 523-3326

PLACENCIA PHARMACY
tel. 523-3346

**SOUTHERN REGIONAL
HOSPITAL DANGRIGA**
Mile 1½ of the Stann Creek Valley Road
tel. 522-3832 or 3833

Toledo
**DR. MANDY TSANG (MBCHB
GLASGOW) & DR. ALESSANDRO
MASCIA (BMBS FLINDERS)**
Private Medical Clinic
Middle Main Street
Punta Gorda
tel. 660-6431
dra.tsang@gmail.com

FOREST HOME DENTAL
James (Jim) Nolan Flach, D.D.S.
P.O. Box 173
Mount Dora
Florida 32756
jim@totcon.com

tel. 702-0065 or international 1-352/383-8112
cell tel. 352/516-6700
fax 1-352/383-8750
Dentist comes a few times a year from
the U.S.

HILLSIDE HEALTH CARE CENTER
P.O. Box 27
Poppyshow Road
Eldridgeville
Punta Gorda
tel. 722-2312
HillsideClinic@gmail.com
www.hillsidebelize.net

PUNTA GORDA HOSPITAL
Punta Gorda
tel. 722-2026

INTERNATIONAL
HEALTH INSURANCE
ATLANTIC INSURANCE CO.
tel. 223-2657 or 223-0502
fax 223-2658
atlainco@btl.net
www.atlanticinsurancebz.com

BELIZE INSURANCE CENTER
212 North Front Street
Belize City
tel. 227-7310
www.belizeinsurance.com
This group offers a variety of insurance
products.

BUPA
7001 Southwest 97th Avenue
Miami, Florida 33173
tel. 305/398-7400
www.bupalatinamerica.com

RF&G INSURANCE
81 N. Front Street
Belize City
tel. 227-3744
fax 501/227-2202
www.rfginsurancebelize.com
RF&G covers most forms of insurance
and has other branches in main towns
around the country.

Employment

WORK PERMITS
LABOUR DEPARTMENT
Labour Commissioner – Mr. Ivan Williams
tel. 822-2297
fax 822-0156
labour.comm@labour.gov.bz
www.belize.gov.bz

STARTING A BUSINESS
BELIZE COMPANIES AND CORPORATE AFFAIRS REGISTRY
Ground Floor Garden City Hotel
Mountain View Boulevard
Belmopan City
tel. 822-0421 or 822-0531
fax 822-0422
www.belizecompaniesregistry.gov.bz

VOLUNTEER WORK AND NETWORKING
BELIZE NATIONAL YOUTH CHESS FOUNDATION
www.belizechess.org

The Cayes
MAMA VILMA'S FAMILY HOME
San Pedro
tel. 651-3533
eves@telus.net

SAGA HUMANE SOCIETY
San Pedro, Ambergris Caye
tel. 226-3266
saga@btl.net
http://sagahumanesociety.org

SAN PEDRO LIONS CLUB
www.sanpedrobelizelions.org

Cayo
BELIZE HUMANE SOCIETY
8 Trio Street
Belmopan
P.O. Box 338
Belmopan
tel. 822-0176 or 602-7947
belmopanhumane@yahoo.com
www.belmopanhumanesociety.com

BELMOPAN INTERNATIONAL WOMEN'S GROUP (BIWG)
P.O. Box 219
Belmopan
tel. Nikki Buxton 602-4291
belmopaniwg@yahoo.com
www.belmopaninternationalwomensgroup.org

THE CORNERSTONE FOUNDATION
P.O. Box 242
43 Church Street
San Ignacio
tel. 824-2373
volunteer@cornerstonefoundationbelize.org
www.cornerstonefoundationbelize.org/contact

THE GEORGE PRICE CENTRE FOR PEACE AND DEVELOPMENT
Price Centre Road
Belmopan
tel. 822-1054
info@gpcbelize.com
www.gpcbelize.com

MARLA'S HOUSE OF HOPE
P.O. Box 148
Belmopan
tel. 011-501-822-3982
General: home@marlashouseofhope.org
Donations/volunteering: donate@marlashouseofhope.org
www.marlashouseofhope.org

OCTAVIA WAIGHT CENTRE
P.O. Box 167
San Ignacio
tel. 824-2214
fax 824-2627
www.octaviawaightcentre.org

ROTARY BELMOPAN
Emile Mena
tel. 610-3591
president@rotarybelmopan.org
www.rotarybelmopan.org

ROTARY SAN IGNACIO
www.rotarysanignacio.org

Stann Creek
PLACENCIA CITIZENS FOR SUSTAINABLE DEVELOPMENT (PCSD)
tel. 523-4018
info@saveourpeninsula.org
www.pcsdbelize.org

PLACENCIA HUMANE SOCIETY
info@placencia-pets.org
www.placencia-pets.org

ROTARY CLUB OF PLACENCIA
www.rotaryclubofplacencia.org

Finance

THE AMERICAN CHAMBER OF COMMERCE OF BELIZE
www.amchambelize.org

THE BELIZE CHAMBER OF COMMERCE AND INDUSTRY
www.belize.org

BELIZE MINISTRY OF FINANCE
www.mof.gov.bz

DOING BUSINESS IN BELIZE
www.doingbusiness.org
World Bank 2011 report and data on doing business in Belize.

THE INSTITUTE OF CHARTERED ACCOUNTANTS OF BELIZE
www.icab.bz

INTERNATIONAL BUSINESS COMPANIES REGISTRY
www.ibcbelize.com

BANKING SERVICES
All main banks in Belize have offices in most towns.

ALLIANCE BANK OF BELIZE
Princess Margaret Drive
Belize City
tel. 223-6111
alliance@btl.net
www.alliancebank.bz

ATLANTIC BANK LIMITED
Cor. Freetown Road/Cleghorn Street
Belize City
tel. 223-4123
atlantic@btl.net

www.atlabank.com

BANK OF NOVA SCOTIA
Albert Street
Belize City
tel. 227-7027
belize.scotia@scotiabank.com
www.belize.scotiabank.com

THE BELIZE BANK, LIMITED
Market Square
Belize City
tel. 227-7132
bzbnk@btl.net
www.belizebank.com

CENTRAL BANK OF BELIZE
www.centralbank.org.bz

FIRST CARIBBEAN BANK
Albert Street
Belize City
tel. 227-7211
barclaysbz@btl.net
www.firstcaribbean.com

INVESTMENT
BELIZE INVESTMENT GUIDE
http://ambergriscaye.com

BELTRAIDE: BELIZE TRADE AND INVESTMENT DEVELOPMENT SERVICE
www.belizeinvest.org.bz

BELTRAIDE INVESTMENT MANUAL AND COUNTRY GUIDE 2007
www.belizeinvest.org.bz
A good all around country and finance guide.

DOING BUSINESS IN BELIZE: 2010 COUNTRY COMMERCIAL GUIDE FOR U.S. COMPANIES
http://belize.usembassy.gov
In-depth information source on finance, commerce, and economy in Belize produced by the U.S. Embassy in Belize, of equal interest to individuals.

TAX INFORMATION
DEPARTMENT OF GENERAL SERVICE TAX
www.gst.gov.bz
There are branches in the main towns.

INCOME TAX DEPARTMENT
incometax@itx.gov.bz
www.incometaxbelize.gov.bz
The Income Tax Department has offices in most towns.

SOCIAL SECURITY BOARD HEADQUARTERS
P.O. Box 18
Bliss Parade
Belmopan
tel. 822-2163 or 2471
fax 822-3331
Customer Service Line: 822-0084
info@socialsecurity.org.bz
www.socialsecurity.org.bz

UTILITIES
BELIZE ELECTRICITY LIMITED (BEL)
2½ Miles Northern Highway
P.O. Box 327
Belize City
tel. 227-0954
info@bel.com.bz
www.bel.com.bz
BEL has offices in all main towns.

BELIZE WATER SERVICES LTD.
7 Central American Boulevard
P.O. Box 150
Belize City
tel. 222-4757
fax 222-4759
www.bws.bz

Communications

MEDIA
AMANDALA
www.amandala.bz

AMBERGRIS TODAY
tel. 226-3462
www.ambergristoday.com

BELIZE AG REPORT
www.belizeagreport.com

BELIZEAN
www.belizean.com

BELIZE FIRST
www.belizefirst.com

BELIZE MAGAZINE
www.belizemagazine.com

BELIZE NEWS
http://belizenews.com

THE BELIZE TIMES
www.belizetimes.bz

CAYE CAULKER CHRONICLES
www.cayecaulkerchronicles.com

CHANNEL 5 TV
www.channel5belize.com

CHANNEL 7 TV
www.7newsbelize.com

CTV3
www.ctv3belizenews.com

ESTEREO AMOR
www.estereoamor.bz

THE GUARDIAN
www.guardian.bz

KREM-FM
www.krembz.com

LOVE FM
www.lovefm.com

MORE FM
www.morefmbelize.com

PLACENCIA BREEZE
www.placenciabreeze.com

PLUS TV
www.plustvbelize.com

THE SAN PEDRO SUN
tel. 226-2070
www.sanpedrosun.net

THE REPORTER
www.reporter.bz

POSTAL SERVICES
DHL and FedEx have agents in most towns in Belize.

DHL
38 New Road
Belize City
tel. 231-0700
www.dhl.org.bz/en

FEDEX
Gutierrez Logistics Ltd.
6 Fort Street

Malcolm House
Ground Floor
Belize City
tel. 223-1577
www.fedex.com/bz

U.S. POSTAL SERVICE (USPS) INTERNATIONAL TO BELIZE
http://pe.usps.com

VIRTUAL MAILBOXES
www.mailboxforwarding.com

SATELLITE TV DEALERS IN BELIZE
COMPUTER RANCH
Spanish Lookout
tel. 823-0373
compranch@hughes.net

TENCHTRONICS COMMUNICATIONS – BELIZE CITY
tel. 227 2175
www.techtronics.com

TELEPHONE AND INTERNET
BELIZE TELEMEDIA LIMITED (BTL)
www.belizetelemedia.net

DIGICELL
www.digicell.bz

SMART
www.smart-bz.com

RESOURCES

Travel and Transportation

BELIZE HOTEL ASSOCIATION
www.belizehotels.org

BELIZE TOURIST BOARD
www.travelbelize.org

BELIZE WEATHER BUREAU
www.hydromet.gov.bz

AIR
ASTRUM HELICOPTERS
Cisco Base
Mile 3.5 Western Highway
Belize City
tel. 222-5100 or 610-4381
info@astrumhelicopters.com
www.astrumhelicopters.com

MAYA ISLAND AIR REGIONAL
Municipal Airstrip
Building #1, 2nd floor
Belize City
tel. 223-1140 or 223-1362
fax 223-1722
www.mayaregional.com

TROPIC AIR
P.O. Box 20
San Pedro
Ambergris Caye
tel. 226-2012
fax 226-2338
reservations@tropicair.com
www.tropicair.com

LAND
DRIVING AND INSURANCE IN MEXICO
www.mexconnect.com

MEXICAN ADO BUS
www.ado.com.mx

MEXICAN INSURANCE
825 Imperial Avenue
Calexico, California 92231
tel. 760/357-4883 or 800/466-7227
fax 760/357-6114
customerservice@mexicaninsurance.com
www.mexicanInsurance.com

SANBORN'S INSURANCE
tel. 800/222-0158
skype: Sanborns.Headquarters
info@sanbornsinsurance.com
www.sanbornsinsurance.com
A good source of information and insurance for travel through Mexico.

Car Rental
BUDGET RENT A CAR
2½ Miles Northern Highway
P.O. Box 2034
Belize City
tel. 223-2435 or 3986
fax 223-2368
reservations@budget-belize.com
www.budget-belize.com

CRYSTAL AUTO RENTAL
5 Miles Northern Highway
Belize City
tel. 223-1600
fax 223-1900
reservations@crystal-belize.com
www.crystal-belize.com

HERTZ BELIZE
tel. 223-5395 or 225-3300
reservations@carsbelize.com
info@carsbelize.com
http://carsbelize.com

THRIFTY CAR RENTAL
tel. 610-27815
www.thrifty.com

OVERLAND FREIGHT
ELBERT FLOWERS
Cayo Adventure Tours
Santa Elena
tel. 824-3426
cattours@btl.net
For moving goods to Belize overland, usually from Houston, Texas.

SEA
CAYE CAULKER
Front Street and Pier (across from basketball court)
tel. 501/226-0225

CAYE CAULKER WATER TAXI
Belize City tel. 223-5752
Caye Caulker tel. 226-0992
San Pedro tel. 226-4646
info@cayecaulkerwatertaxi.com
www.cayecaulkerwatertaxi.com

CHETUMAL, MEXICO
Located on Municipal Pier
tel. +983 119-1431
http://belizewatertaxi.com

HOKEY POKEY WATER TAXI
Independence/Mango Creek – Placencia
Village
tel. 523-2376, 606-1501, or 601-8897
www.aguallos.com/hokeypokey

SAN PEDRO
Black Coral Street (at the San Pedro Belize
Express pier)
tel. 226-3535

SAN PEDRO BELIZE EXPRESS
WATER TAXI
Inside the Brown Sugar Terminal
111 North Front Street
Belize City
tel. 501/223-2225

SHIPPING
AIMAR LTD
Corner of Hutson and Eyre Street
Blake Building, Suite 302
Belize City
tel. 223-3101
aimar@btl.net

BELIZE ESTATE CO. LTD.
P.O. Box 151
Slaughter House Road
Belize City
tel. 223-1783
fax 223-1367
bec@btl.net

BELIZE LOGISTICS
tel. 732-2324
shipping@BelizeLogistics.com
www.BelizeLogistics.com

BELIZE LOGISTICS SERVICES
LTD. (BLS)
34 Albert St.
Belize City

tel. 227-1710
fax 227-3754
jose@belizetransportation.com
www.belizetransportation.com

CARIBBEAN QUEEN
San Pedro
tel. 226-2619

CARIBBEAN SHIPPING
AGENCIES LTD.
P.O. Box 352
115 Albert Street
Belize City
tel. 227-7396 or 227-3015
fax 227-7681
stanlong@btl.net

EASY SHIPPING TO BELIZE
tel. 941/255-1031
easyshippingtobelize@hotmail.com

EUROCARIBE SHIPPING SERVICES
P.O. Box 281
14 Fort Street
Belize City
tel. 224-5286 or 227-8855
fax 223-1657
eurocaribe@btl.net

FRANK EHMAN
belizeae@gmail.com
Frank will drive your car through Mexico for you or assist with a convoy and other services. He provides a trained, experienced, bonded driver who is familiar with the regulations for transporting/importing household goods through U.S., Mexico, and Belize.

HYDE SHIPPING
Universal Customs Brokers
tel. 223-3582 or 223-2310
unibrokers@btl.net
www.hydeshipping.com

KESTREL LINER AGENCIES LLC
Belize City
tel. 227-8855

MARAGE SHIPPING AND TRUCKING
SERVICE
Los Angeles tel. 323/419-1778 or 323/304-8774

RESOURCES

tel. 422-2259, 422-0171, 624-2654, or 621-1917
marage@corozal.com

SEABOARD MARINE
Belize City
tel. 223-0069

SPEED CARGO IN MIAMI
9950 NW 17 St.
Miami, Florida 33172

tel. 305/463-4800

STERLING FREIGHT
Mile 63 Western Highway
Cayo Air Center
Central Farm Airstrip
Cayo
tel. 824-2496
fax 824-2325
info@sterlingfreight.com
www.sterlingfreight.com

Prime Living Locations

GENERAL
BELIZE DISTRICT
www.belizedistrict.com

BELIZE NORTH
www.belizenorth.com

SOUTHERN BELIZE
www.southernbelize.com

THE CAYES
AMBERGRIS CAYE
http://ambergriscaye.com
Excellent resource not just on Ambergris Caye; the site has a wealth of information about everything in Belize.

BELIZE BUSINESS E-MAIL AND WEBSITE DIRECTORY
http://ambergriscaye.com

CAYE CAULKER BELIZE
www.cayecaulkerbelize.net

CAYE CAULKER CASITA
P.O. Box 48
Caye Caulker
tel. 226-0547 or 622-3608
amandabadger@gmail.com
www.cayecaulkercasita.com

CAYE CAULKER RENTALS
Front Street
tel. 226-0029
www.cayecaulkerrentals.com

CRAZY CANUCKS
tel. 206-2031
crazycanucksbelize@yahoo.com
http://crazycanucksbelize.webs.com

GO AMBERGRIS CAYE
www.goambergriscaye.com

GO CAYE CAULKER
www.gocayecaulker.com
The official site of the Caye Caulker Belize Tourism Industry Association.

WINE DE VINE
Coconut Drive
San Pedro
tel. 226-3430 or 223-2444
info@winedevine.com
www.winedevine.com

CAYO
RED ROOF PROPERTY MANAGEMENT
Nigel Tzib & Sharon Hiebing, Owners
San Ignacio Town, General Delivery
tel. 834-4015
manager@redroofpropertymanagement.com
www.redroofpropertymanagement.com

SPANISH LOOKOUT BUSINESS DIRECTORY
www.spanishlookout.bz

COROZAL
ALL ABOUT COROZAL
http://corozal.com

STANN CREEK
HOPKINS VILLAGE
www.hopkinsbelize.com

PLACENCIA
www.placencia.com

Spanish Phrasebook

Although English is the official language in Belize and the majority of people speak it, Spanish is widely and commonly spoken. It is useful to know some basic Spanish phrases and to have an understanding of what is being said around you.

Spanish commonly uses 30 letters the familiar English 26, plus 4 straightforward additions: ch, ll, ñ, and rr, which are explained in "Consonants," below.

PRONUNCIATION

Once you learn them, Spanish pronunciation rules in contrast to English don't change. Spanish vowels generally sound softer than in English. (*Note:* The capitalized syllables below receive stronger accents.)

Vowels

a like ah, as in "hah": *agua* AH-gooah (water), *pan* PAHN (bread), and *casa* CAH-sah (house)

e like ay, as in "may:" *mesa* MAY-sah (table), *tela* TAY-lah (cloth), and *de* DAY (of, from)

i like ee, as in "need": *diez* dee-AYZ (ten), *comida* ko-MEE-dah (meal), and *fin* FEEN (end)

o like oh, as in "go": *peso* PAY-soh (weight), *ocho* OH-choh (eight), and *poco* POH-koh (a bit)

u like oo, as in "cool": *uno* OO-noh (one), *cuarto* KOOAHR-toh (room), and *usted* oos-TAYD (you); when it follows a "q" the **u** is silent; when it follows an "h" or has an umlaut, it's pronounced like "w"

Consonants

b, d, f, k, l, m, n, p, q, s, t, v, w, x, y, z, and ch pronounced almost as in English; **h** occurs, but is silent not pronounced at all.

c like k as in "keep": *cuarto* KOOAR-toh (room), Tepic tay-PEEK (capital of Nayarit state); when it precedes "e" or "i," pronounce **c** like s, as in "sit": *cerveza* sayr-VAY-sah (beer), *encima* ayn-SEE-mah (atop).

g like g as in "gift" when it precedes "a," "o," "u," or a consonant: *gato* GAH-toh (cat), *hago* AH-goh (I do, make); otherwise, pronounce **g** like h as in "hat": *giro* HEE-roh (money order), *gente* HAYN-tay (people)

j like h, as in "has": *jueves* HOOAY-vays (Thursday), *mejor* may-HOR (better)

ll like y, as in "yes": *toalla* toh-AH-yah (towel), *ellos* AY-yohs (they, them)

ñ like ny, as in "canyon": *año* AH-nyo (year), *señor* SAY-nyor (Mr., sir)

r is lightly trilled, with tongue at the roof of your mouth like a very light English d, as in "ready": *pero* PAY-doh (but), *tres* TDAYS (three), *cuatro* KOOAH-tdoh (four).

rr like a Spanish r, but with much more emphasis and trill. Let your tongue flap. Practice with *burro* (donkey), *carretera* (highway), and Carrillo (proper name), then really let go with *ferrocarril* (railroad).

Note: The single small but common exception to all of the above is the pronunciation of Spanish **y** when it's being used as the Spanish word for "and," as in "Ron y Kathy." In such case, pronounce it like the English ee, as in "keep": Ron "ee" Kathy (Ron and Kathy).

Accent

The rule for accent, the relative stress given to syllables within a given word, is straightforward. If a word ends in a vowel, an n, or an s, accent the next-to-last syllable; if not, accent the last syllable.

Pronounce *gracias* GRAH-seeahs (thank you), *orden* OHR-dayn (order), and *carretera* kah-ray-TAY-rah (highway) with stress on the next-to-last syllable.

Otherwise, accent the last syllable: *venir* vay-NEER (to come), *ferrocarril* fay-roh-cah-REEL (railroad), and *edad* ay-DAHD (age).

Exceptions to the accent rule are always marked with an accent sign: (á, é, í, ó, or ú), such as *teléfono* tay-LAY-foh-noh (telephone), *jabón* hah-BON (soap), and *rápido* RAH-pee-doh (rapid).

BASIC AND COURTEOUS EXPRESSIONS

Most Spanish-speaking people consider formalities important. Whenever approaching anyone for information or some other reason, do not forget the appropriate salutation good morning, good evening, etc. Standing alone, the greeting *hola* (hello) can sound brusque.

Hello. *Hola.*
Good morning. *Buenos días.*
Good afternoon. *Buenas tardes.*
Good evening. *Buenas noches.*
How are you? *¿Cómo está usted?*
Very well, thank you. *Muy bien, gracias.*
Okay; good. *Bien.*
Not okay; bad. *Mal or feo.*
So-so. *Más o menos.*
And you? *¿Y usted?*
Thank you. *Gracias.*
Thank you very much. *Muchas gracias.*
You're very kind. *Muy amable.*
You're welcome. *De nada.*

Goodbye. *Adios.*
See you later. *Hasta luego.*
please *por favor*
yes *sí*
no *no*
I don't know. *No sé.*
Just a moment, please. *Momentito, por favor.*
Excuse me, please (when you're trying to get attention). *Disculpe* or *Con permiso.*
Excuse me (when you've made a boo-boo). *Lo siento.*
Pleased to meet you. *Mucho gusto.*
What is your name? *¿Cómo se llama usted?*
My name is... *Me llamo...*
Do you speak English? *¿Habla usted inglés?*
Is English spoken here? (Does anyone here speak English?) *¿Se habla inglés?*
I don't speak Spanish well. *No hablo bien el español.*
I don't understand. *No entiendo.*
How do you say... in Spanish? *¿Cómo se dice...en español?*
Would you like... *¿Quisiera usted...*
Let's go to... *Vamos a...*

TERMS OF ADDRESS

When in doubt, use the formal *usted* (you) as a form of address.

I *yo*
you (formal) *usted*
you (familiar) *tú*
he/him *él*
she/her *ella*
we/us *nosotros*
you (plural) *ustedes*
they/them *ellos (all males or mixed gender); ellas (all females)*
Mr., sir *señor*
Mrs., madam *señora*
miss, young lady *señorita*
wife *esposa*
husband *esposo*
friend *amigo (male); amiga (female)*

sweetheart *novio (male); novia (female)*
son; daughter *hijo; hija*
brother; sister *hermano; hermana*
father; mother *padre; madre*
grandfather; grandmother *abuelo; abuela*

TRANSPORTATION

Where is...? *¿Dónde está...?*
How far is it to...? *¿A cuánto está...?*
from...to... *de...a...*
How many blocks? *¿Cuántas cuadras?*
Where (Which) is the way to...? *¿Dónde está el camino a...?*
the bus station *la terminal de autobuses*
the bus stop *la parada de autobuses*
Where is this bus going? *¿Adónde va este autobús?*
the taxi stand *la parada de taxis*
the train station *la estación de ferrocarril*
the boat *el barco*
the launch *lancha; tiburonera*
the dock *el muelle*
the airport *el aeropuerto*
I'd like a ticket to... *Quisiera un boleto a...*
first (second) class *primera (segunda) clase*
roundtrip *ida y vuelta*
reservation *reservación*
baggage *equipaje*
Stop here, please. *Pare aquí, por favor.*
the entrance *la entrada*
the exit *la salida*
the ticket office *la oficina de boletos*
(very) near; far *(muy) cerca; lejos*
to; toward *a*
by; through *por*
from *de*
the right *la derecha*
the left *la izquierda*
straight ahead *derecho; directo*
in front *en frente*

beside *al lado*
behind *atrás*
the corner *la esquina*
the stoplight *la semáforo*
a turn *una vuelta*
right here *aquí*
somewhere around here *por acá*
right there *allí*
somewhere around there *por allá*
road *el camino*
street; boulevard *calle; bulevar*
block *la cuadra*
highway *carretera*
kilometer *kilómetro*
bridge; toll *puente; cuota*
address *dirección*
north; south *norte; sur*
east; west *oriente (este); poniente (oeste)*

ACCOMMODATIONS

hotel *hotel*
Is there a room? *¿Hay cuarto?*
May I (may we) see it? *¿Puedo (podemos) verlo?*
What is the rate? *¿Cuál es el precio?*
Is that your best rate? *¿Es su mejor precio?*
Is there something cheaper? *¿Hay algo más económico?*
a single room *un cuarto sencillo*
a double room *un cuarto doble*
double bed *cama matrimonial*
twin beds *camas gemelas*
with private bath *con baño*
hot water *agua caliente*
shower *ducha*
towels *toallas*
soap *jabón*
toilet paper *papel higiénico*
blanket *frazada; manta*
sheets *sábanas*
air-conditioned *aire acondicionado*
fan *abanico; ventilador*
key *llave*
manager *gerente*

FOOD

I'm hungry. *Tengo hambre.*
I'm thirsty. *Tengo sed.*
menu *carta; menú*
order *orden*
glass *vaso*
fork *tenedor*
knife *cuchillo*
spoon *cuchara*
napkin *servilleta*
soft drink *refresco*
coffee *café*
tea *té*
drinking water *agua pura; agua potable*
bottled carbonated water *agua mineral*
bottled uncarbonated water *agua sin gas*
beer *cerveza*
wine *vino*
milk *leche*
juice *jugo*
cream *crema*
sugar *azúcar*
cheese *queso*
snack *antojo; botana*
breakfast *desayuno*
lunch *almuerzo*
daily lunch special *comida corrida* **(or** *el menú del día* **depending on region)**
dinner *comida* **(often eaten in late afternoon);** *cena* **(a late-night snack)**
the check *la cuenta*
eggs *huevos*
bread *pan*
salad *ensalada*
fruit *fruta*
mango *mango*
watermelon *sandía*
papaya *papaya*
banana *plátano*
apple *manzana*
orange *naranja*
lime *limón*
fish *pescado*
shellfish *mariscos*
shrimp *camarones*

meat (without) *(sin) carne*
chicken *pollo*
pork *puerco*
beef; steak *res; bistec*
bacon; ham *tocino; jamón*
fried *frito*
roasted *asada*
barbecue; barbecued *barbacoa; al carbón*

SHOPPING

money *dinero*
money-exchange bureau *casa de cambio*
I would like to exchange traveler's checks. *Quisiera cambiar cheques de viajero.*
What is the exchange rate? *¿Cuál es el tipo de cambio?*
How much is the commission? *¿Cuánto cuesta la comisión?*
Do you accept credit cards? *¿Aceptan tarjetas de crédito?*
money order *giro*
How much does it cost? *¿Cuánto cuesta?*
What is your final price? *¿Cuál es su último precio?*
expensive *caro*
cheap *barato; económico*
more *más*
less *menos*
a little *un poco*
too much *demasiado*

HEALTH

Help me please. *Ayúdeme por favor.*
I am ill. *Estoy enfermo.*
Call a doctor. *Llame un doctor.*
Take me to... *Lléveme a...*
hospital *hospital; sanatorio*
drugstore *farmacia*
pain *dolor*
fever *fiebre*
headache *dolor de cabeza*
stomach ache *dolor de estómago*
burn *quemadura*
cramp *calambre*
nausea *náusea*
vomiting *vomitar*

medicine *medicina*
antibiotic *antibiótico*
pill; tablet *pastilla*
aspirin *aspirina*
ointment; cream *pomada; crema*
bandage *venda*
cotton *algodón*
sanitary napkins use brand name, e.g., Kotex
birth control pills *pastillas anticonceptivas*
contraceptive foam *espuma anticonceptiva*
condoms *preservativos; condones*
toothbrush *cepilla dental*
dental floss *hilo dental*
toothpaste *crema dental*
dentist *dentista*
toothache *dolor de muelas*

POST OFFICE AND COMMUNICATIONS

long-distance telephone *teléfono larga distancia*
I would like to call... *Quisiera llamar a...*
collect *por cobrar*
station to station *a quien contesta*
person to person *persona a persona*
credit card *tarjeta de crédito*
post office *correo*
general delivery *lista de correo*
letter *carta*
stamp *estampilla, timbre*
postcard *tarjeta*
aerogram *aerograma*
air mail *correo aereo*
registered *registrado*
money order *giro*
package; box *paquete; caja*
string; tape *cuerda; cinta*

AT THE BORDER

border *frontera*
customs *aduana*
immigration *migración*
tourist card *tarjeta de turista*
inspection *inspección; revisión*
passport *pasaporte*
profession *profesión*

marital status *estado civil*
single *soltero*
married; divorced *casado; divorciado*
widowed *viudado*
insurance *seguros*
title *título*
driver's license *licencia de manejar*

AT THE GAS STATION

gas station *gasolinera*
gasoline *gasolina*
unleaded *sin plomo*
full, please *lleno, por favor*
tire *llanta*
tire repair shop *vulcanizadora*
air *aire*
water *agua*
oil (change) *aceite (cambio)*
grease *grasa*
My...doesn't work. *Mi...no sirve.*
battery *batería*
radiator *radiador*
alternator *alternador*
generator *generador*
tow truck *grúa*
repair shop *taller mecánico*
tune-up *afinación*
auto parts store *refaccionería*

VERBS

Verbs are the key to getting along in Spanish. They employ mostly predictable forms and come in three classes, which end in *ar*, *er*, and *ir*, respectively:

to buy *comprar*
I buy, you (he, she, it) buys *compro, compra*
we buy, you (they) buy *compramos, compran*
to eat *comer*
I eat, you (he, she, it) eats *como, come*
we eat, you (they) eat *comemos, comen*
to climb *subir*
I climb, you (he, she, it) climbs *subo, sube*
we climb, you (they) climb *subimos, suben*

Here are more (with irregularities indicated):

to do or make hacer *(regular except for hago, I do or make)*

to go ir *(very irregular: voy, va, vamos, van)*

to go (walk) andar

to love amar

to work trabajar

to want desear, querer

to need necesitar

to read leer

to write escribir

to repair reparar

to stop parar

to get off (the bus) bajar

to arrive llegar

to stay (remain) quedar

to stay (lodge) hospedar

to leave salir *(regular except for salgo, I leave)*

to look at mirar

to look for buscar

to give dar *(regular except for doy, I give)*

to carry llevar

to have tener *(irregular but important: tengo, tiene, tenemos, tienen)*

to come venir *(similarly irregular: vengo, viene, venimos, vienen)*

Spanish has two forms of "to be":

to be estar *(regular except for estoy, I am)*

to be ser *(very irregular: soy, es, somos, son)*

Use *estar* when speaking of location or a temporary state of being: "I am at home." *"Estoy en casa."* "I'm sick." *"Estoy enfermo."* Use *ser* for a permanent state of being: "I am a doctor." *"Soy doctora."*

NUMBERS

zero cero
one uno
two dos
three tres
four cuatro
five cinco
six seis
seven siete
eight ocho
nine nueve
10 diez
11 once
12 doce
13 trece
14 catorce
15 quince
16 dieciseis
17 diecisiete
18 dieciocho
19 diecinueve
20 veinte
21 veinte y uno **or** veintiuno
30 treinta
40 cuarenta
50 cincuenta
60 sesenta
70 setenta
80 ochenta
90 noventa
100 ciento
101 ciento y uno **or** cientiuno
200 doscientos
500 quinientos
1,000 mil
10,000 diez mil
100,000 cien mil
1,000,000 millón
one half medio
one third un tercio
one fourth un cuarto

TIME

What time is it? ¿Qué hora es?
It's one o'clock. Es la una.
It's three in the afternoon. Son las tres de la tarde.
It's 4 A.M. Son las cuatro de la mañana.
six-thirty seis y media
a quarter till eleven un cuarto para las once
a quarter past five las cinco y cuarto
an hour una hora

DAYS AND MONTHS

Monday lunes
Tuesday martes

Wednesday *miércoles*
Thursday *jueves*
Friday *viernes*
Saturday *sábado*
Sunday *domingo*
today *hoy*
tomorrow *mañana*
yesterday *ayer*
January *enero*
February *febrero*
March *marzo*
April *abril*
May *mayo*
June *junio*
July *julio*

August *agosto*
September *septiembre*
October *octubre*
November *noviembre*
December *diciembre*
a week *una semana*
a month *un mes*
after *después*
before *antes*

Courtesy of Bruce Whipperman, author of Moon Pacific Mexico.

Suggested Reading

This is by no means a comprehensive list of books on Belize; there are plenty more out there! There is a mixture of old and new titles, as some of the older books contain invaluable information that people still rely on, and others are constantly being updated, like travel guidebooks, and books on the Maya as new research emerges.

MAPS

Belize 1:250,000 Travel Map. ITMB Canada Publishing Ltd, 2005.

Belize 1:500,000 Travel Map. Cubola Productions, 2006.

Mexico, Guatemala, Belize, El Salvador Marco Polo Map. Marco Polo Travel Publishing, 2011.

TRAVEL

Berman, Joshua. *Moon Belize.* Berkeley, CA: Avalon Travel, 2011.

Berman, Joshua. *Moon Maya 2012: A Guide to Celebrations in Mexico, Guatemala, Belize & Honduras.* Berkeley, CA: Avalon Travel, 2011.

Berman, Joshua. *Moon Spotlight Belize Cayes: Including Belize City.* Berkeley, CA: Avalon Travel, 2011.

Joynes-Burgess, Kate. *Explorer's Guide Belize: A Great Destination.* Countryman Press, 2010.

Lougheed, Vivien. *Adventure Guide to Belize.* Hunter Publishing, 2006.

Morris, Charlie. *Open Road's Best of Belize.* Open Road, 2009.

Perdue, L. *San Pedro, Belize: Belize It or Not!* CreateSpace, 2011.

Sluder, Lan. *Belize Islands Guide: Guide to Ambergris Caye, Caye Caulker and the Offshore Cayes and Atolls of Belize.* Equator Publications, 2010.

Sluder, Lan. *Belize's Best Hotels & Restaurants.* Equator, 2008.

Sluder, Lan. *Rambles Around Belize.* Kindle Edition, Equator, 2011.

Sluder, Lan. *San Pedro Cool, Guide to Ambergris Caye, Belize.* Equator, 2002; eBook, 2009.

RESOURCES

DRIVING

King, Emory. *Driver's Guide to Beautiful Belize*. Tropical Books, 2007.

Johnson, Rochelle. *The Essential Guide to Driving North, Central and South America*. www.lulu.com, 2010.

RELOCATING

Dhillon, Bob. *Business and Retirement Guide to Belize: The Last Virgin Paradise*. Dundurn, 2011.

Gray, Bill and Claire. *Belize Retirement Guide: How to Live in a Tropical Paradise on $450 a Month*. Preview Pub, 1999.

King, Emory. *How to Visit, Invest, or Retire in Belize*. Tropical Books, 1996.

Peham, Helga. *Escaping the Rat Race—Freedom in Paradise*. World Audience, Inc., 2010.

Sluder, Lan. *How to Find Your Dream Home in Belize: Buying or Building on the Caribbean Coast*. Kindle Edition, Equator, 2011.

Sluder, Lan. *Island Living in Belize*. Equator, 2010.

Sluder, Lan, and Lambert-Sluder, Rose Emory. *Easy Belize: How to Live, Retire, Work and Buy Property in Belize, the English Speaking Frost Free Paradise on the Caribbean Coast*. CreateSpace, 2010.

DIVING

Middleton, Ned. *Diving Belize*. Aqua Quest Diving, 1994.

Rinaldi, Roberto. *Honduras And Belize: White Star Guides Diving*. White Star, 2005.

Rock, Tim. *Lonely Planet Diving & Snorkeling Belize*. Lonely Planet Publications, 2007.

SAILING

Calder, Nigel. *The Cruising Guide to the Northwest Caribbean*. McGraw-Hill, 1991.

Rauscher, Freya. *Cruising Guide to Belize and Mexico's Caribbean Coast*. Windmill Hill Books, 2007.

FLORA

Ames, Oakes, and Correll, Donovan Stewart. *Orchids of Guatemala and Belize*. Dover Publications, 2012.

Balick, Michael J., et al. *Checklist of the Vascular Plants of Belize: With Common Names and Uses*. The New York Botanical Garden Press, 2001.

Bannochie, Iris, and Light, Marilyn. *Gardening in the Caribbean*. Macmillan Education Ltd., 1993.

Belize Botanic Gardens. *Grow Native Belize, A Gardener's Guide to using Native Plants*. BRC Printings, 2007.

Bol, Petronila, and Fidencio. *A Book of Mayan Herbs*. Flatrock Press, 1994.

Courtright, Gordon. *Tropicals*. Timber Press, 1988.

Harris, Kate. *Trees of Belize*. Self-published, 2009.

Horwich, Robert H. *A Belizean Rain Forest*. Orang-utan Press, 1990.

Keesmaat, Irene. *A Rainbow of Colours, A Guide to the Flowers of Belize*. Cubola Productions, 2011.

Light, Marilyn. *Growing Orchids in the Caribbean*. Macmillan Education Ltd., 1995.

Lutz, Dick. *Belize: Reefs, Rain Forests, and Mayan Ruins*. DIMI Press, 2005.

McLeish, I., et al. *Native Orchids of Belize*. A A Balkema Publishers, 1995.

Morton, Julia F. *Fruits of Warm Climates.* Florida Flair Books, 1987.

Rietsema, Jacob and Beveridge, Dorothy. *The Plants of Caye Caulker.* Produccicones de la Hamaca, 2009.

Sayers, Brendan, and Adams, Brett. *Guide to the Orchids of Belize.* Cubola Publications, 2009.

Rauch, Fred D., and Weissish, Paul R. *Plants for Tropical Landscapes, A Gardener's Guide.* University of Hawaii Press, 2000.

Whistler, Arthur W. *Tropical Ornamentals, A Guide.* Timber Press Inc, 2000.

FAUNA

Beletsky, Les. *Belize and Northern Guatemala: The Ecotravellers' Wildlife Guide.* Natural World Academic Press, 2004.

Beletsky, Les, et al. *Travellers' Wildlife Guides Belize & Northern Guatemala.* Interlink Pub Group Inc., 2004.

Campbell, Jonathan A. *Amphibians and Reptiles of Northern Guatemala, the Yucatan, and Belize.* University of Oklahoma Press, 1999.

Chalif, Edward L. *A Field Guide to Mexican Birds: Mexico, Guatemala, Belize, El Salvador.* Houghton Mifflin Harcourt, 1999.

Edwards, Ernest Preston, and Butler, E.M. *A Field Guide to the Birds of Mexico and Adjacent Areas: Belize, Guatemala, and El Salvador.* University of Texas Press, 1998.

Garel, Tony, and Matola, Sharon. *Field Guide to the Snakes of Belize.* Belize Zoo & Tropical Education Centre, 1995.

Greenfield, David W., and Thomerson, Jamie E. *Fishes of the Continental Waters of Belize.* University Press of Florida, 1997.

Howell, Steve N.G., and Webb, Sophie. *A Guide to the Birds of Mexico and North ern Central America.* Oxford University Press, 1995.

Humann, Paul, and DeLoach, Ned. *Reef Fish Identification: Florida, Caribbean, Bahamas.* New World Publications, 2002.

Jones, H. Lee, and Gardner. *Birds of Belize.* University of Texas Press, 2004.

Lee, Julian C. *A Field Guide to the Amphibians and Reptiles of the Maya World: The Lowlands of Mexico, Northern Guatemala, and Belize.* Comstock Pub Assoc., 2000.

Lieske, Ewald, and Myers, Robert. *Coral Reef Fishes: Indo-Pacific and Caribbean.* Princeton University Press, 2001.

Meyer, John R. and Foster, Carol Farneti. *A Guide to the Frogs and Toads of Belize.* Krieger Publishing, 1996.

Miller, Carolyn M., et al. *101 Birds of Belize.* Produccicones de la Hamaca, 2009.

Reichling, Steven B. *Tarantulas of Belize.* Krieger Publishing Co., 2003.

Reid, Fiona A. *A Field Guide to the Mammals of Central America and Southeast Mexico.* Oxford University Press, 2009.

Van Perlo, Ber. *Birds of Mexico and Central America.* Princeton University Press, 2006.

CULTURE

Cayetano, E. Roy. *The People's Garifuna Dictionary.* Angelus Press, 1993.

Crosbie, Cynthia, and Decker, Ken. *Kriol-Inglish Dikshineri English-Kriol Dictionary.* Belize Kriol Project, 2007

Durán, Víctor Manuel. *An Anthology of Belizean Literature: English, Creole, Spanish, Garifuna.* University Press of America, 2007.

Ellis, Zoila. *On Heroes, Lizards and Passion, Seven Belizean Short Stories.* Cubola Productions, 1994.

Foster, Byron. *Heart Drum* Cubola Productions, 1994.

Gabb, George; Galvez, Carol Fonseca; Hyde, Evan X.; Stuart, Glady; Warde, Shirley; and Young, Colville. *Ping Wing Juk Me, Six Belizean Plays.* Cubola Productions, 2004.

Hagerthy, Tim, and Parham, Mary Gomoz. *If Di Pin Neva Bin, Folktales and Legends of Belize.* Cubola Productions, 2000.

Hernandez, Felicia. *Those Ridiculous Years.* Self-published, 1996.

Jermyn, Leslie, and Yong Jui Lin. *Belize (Cultures of the World, Third).* Marshall Cavendish Children's Books, 2011.

Lindo, Louis. *Tales of the Belizean Woods.* Cubola Productions, 1995.

Mwakikagile, Godfrey. *Belize and Its People: Life in A Multicultural Society.* Continental Press, 2010.

Phillips, Michael. *Of Words, an Anthology of Belizean Poetry.* Cubola Productions, 1997.

Young, Colville. *Creole Proverbs of Belize.* Cubola Productions, 1980.

COOKING

Arvigo, Rosita. *Food of the Gods, Vegetarian Cooking in Belize.* Cubola Productions, 2010.

Belize Hospital Auxiliary Cookbook. Angelus Press.

Belize Cookbook Committee. *A Guide to Belizean Cooking.* Self-published.

Belizeous Cuisine, Delicious Belizean Recipes. Los Angeles Belizean Educational Network (LABEN), 1997.

Burns, E. L. *What's Cooking in the Belizean Kitchen.* Angelus Press.

Crooked Tree Village Creative Women's Group. *Silly Bug & Bittle Recipes.* Self-published.

De Langan, Tracey Brown. *Mmmm...A Taste of Belizean Cooking.* Cubola Productions, 2003.

Minerva Aponte-Jolly, ed. *Aaaah—Belizean Rum Recipes.* Cubola Productions, 2007.

Nord, Alice; Martinez, Myrna; and Shrine, Kaaren. *Cooking Belize.* Self-published, 1995.

Nord, Alice; Martinez, Myrna; and Shrine, Kaaren. *U Toucan Cook Belize Cookbook.* Self-published, 1995.

South Ambergris Caye Neighborhood Watch. *To Catch a Cook.* Self-published, 2009.

Wilk, Richard. *Home Cooking in the Global Village: Caribbean Food from Buccaneers to Ecotourists.* Berg Publishers, 2006.

HISTORY

Ávila, Tomás Alberto. *Black Caribs— Garifuna Saint Vincent' Exiled People: The Roots of the Garifuna.* Milenio Publishing, 2008.

Awe, Jaime J., et al. *Taking Stock: Belize at 25 Years of Independence.* Cubola Productions, 2007.

Bolland, Nigel O. *Colonialism and Resistance in Belize.* Cubola Productions, 2003.

Campbell, Mavis Christine *Becoming Belize: A History of an Outpost of Empire Searching for Identity, 1528–1823.* University of the West Indies Press, 2011.

Cayetano, Sebastian. *Garifuna History, Language & Culture of Belize, Central America & the Caribbean.* BRC Publishing, 1990.

Dobson, Narda. *A History of Belize.* Longman Caribbean, 1973.

Foster, Byron. *The Baymen's Legacy.* Cubola Productions, 1992.

Frankson, A. S. *A Caribbean Identity: Memoirs of the Colonial Service*. Radcliffe Press, 2008.

Grant, C. H. *The Making of Modern Belize: Politics, Society and British Colonialism in Central America*. Cambridge University Press, 2008.

Gudmundson, Lowell and Wolfe, Justin. *Blacks and Blackness in Central America: Between Race and Place*. Duke University Press Books, 2010.

Hartman Strom, Sharon and Weaver, Frederick Stirton. *Confederates in the Tropics: Charles Swett's Travelogue*. University Press of Mississippi, 2011.

Heusner, Karla. *Food for Thought, Chronicles of Belize*. Cubola Productions, 2004.

King, Emory. *Hey, Dad, This is Belize*. Tropical Press, 1994.

King, Emory. *The Road to Glory*. Tropical Books, 1991.

Koop, Gerhard S. *Pioneer Years In Belize*. Angelus Press, 1991.

Macpherson, Anne S. *From Colony to Nation: Women Activists and the Gendering of Politics in Belize, 1912-1982*. University of Nebraska Press, 2009.

Murray, Roy. *Family and People All Well…*. Cubola Publications, 2006.

Palacio, Joseph O. *The Garifuna. A Nation across Borders*. Cubola Productions, 2005.

Penner, Heinrich R. *Spanish Lookout since 1958, Progress in Action*. Self-published, 2008.

Roessingh, Carel and Plasil, Tanja. *Between Horse & Buggy and Four-Wheel Drive: Change and Diversity among Mennonite Settlements in Belize, Central America*. Vu University Press, 2009.

Shoman, Assad. *Thirteen Chapters of a History of Belize*. Angelus Press, 2000.

Silva, Hector David Sr. *Brief History of Cayo District, Vol. I*. Self-published, 2010.

Simmons, Donald C. Jr. *Confederate Settlements in British Honduras*. McFarland & Co., 2001.

Thomson, P. A. B. *Belize, A Concise History*. MacMillan Caribbean, 2005.

Twigg, Alan. *Understanding Belize: A Historical Guide*. Harbour Publishing, 2006.

ANCIENT MAYA

Awe, Jaime. *101 Questions and Answers about the Ancient Maya of Belize*. Factory Books, 2005.

Belli, Francisco Estrada. *The First Maya Civilization: Ritual and Power Before the Classic Period*. Routledge, 2010.

Chladek, Stanislav. *Exploring Maya Ritual Caves: Dark Secrets from the Maya Underworld*. Altamira Press, 2011.

Coe, Michael D. *The Maya*. Thames and Hudson, 2005.

Demarest, Arthur. *Ancient Maya: The Rise and Fall of a Rainforest Civilization*. Cambridge University Press, 2005.

Ferguson, William M. and Adams, R.E.W. *Mesoamerica's Ancient Cities: Aerial Views of Precolumbian Ruins in Mexico, Guatemala, Belize and Honduras*. University Press of Colorado, 2000.

Freidel, David, and Schele, Linda. *A Forest of Kings: The Untold Story of the Ancient Maya*. Harper Perennial, 1992.

Ford, Anabel. *The Ancient Maya of Belize: Their Society and Sites*. CORI/Meso American Research Center, University of California Santa Barbara.

Garber, James F. *The Ancient Maya of the Belize Valley: Half a Century of Archaeological Research (Maya Studies)*. University Press of Florida, 2011.

RESOURCES

Graham, Elizabeth. *Maya Christians and Their Churches in Sixteenth-Century Belize (Maya Studies).* University Press of Florida, 2011.

Grube, Nikolai. *Maya: Divine Kings of the Rainforest.* H. F. Ullmann, 2008.

Guderjan, Thomas H. *Ancient Maya Traders of Ambergris Caye.* Cubola Productions, 1993

Guderjan, Thomas H. *The Nature of an Ancient Maya City: Resources, Interaction, and Power at Blue Creek, Belize.* University Alabama Press, 2007.

Hammond, Norman. *Cuello: An Early Maya Community in Belize.* Cambridge University Press, 1991.

Harrison, Peter D. *Pulltrouser Swamp: Ancient Maya Habitat, Agriculture and Settlement.* University of Utah Press, 2000.

Harrison, Peter D., et al. *The Lords of Tikal: Rulers of an Ancient Maya City* Thames & Hudson, 2000.

Henderson, John S. *The World of the Ancient Maya.* Cornell University Press, 1981.

Huff, Sandy. *The Mayan Calendar Made Easy.* Self-published, 1984.

LeCount, Lisa J., and Yaeger, Jason. *Classic Maya Provincial Politics: Xunantunich and Its Hinterlands.* University of Arizona Press, 2010.

Martin, Simon, and Grube, Nicolai. *Chronicle of the Maya Kings and Queens.* Thames and Hudson, 2005.

Miller, Mary Ellen. *Maya Art and Architecture* Thames and Hudson, 1999.

McKillop, Heather Irene. *The Ancient Maya: New Perspectives.* W. W. Norton & Company, 2006.

Montgomery, John. *Cycles in Time: The Maya Calendar.* Editorial Laura Lee, 2007.

Montgomery, John. *Dictionary of Maya Hieroglyphs.* Hippocrene Books, 2002.

Montgomery, John. *Tikal: An Illustrated History of the Ancient Maya Capital.* Hippocrene Books, 2001.

Rugeley, Terry. *Rebellion Now and Forever: Mayas, Hispanics, and Caste War Violence in Yucatan.* Stanford University Press, 2009.

Sharer, Robert, and Traxler, Loa. *The Ancient Maya.* Stanford University Press, 2005.

Thompson, J. Eric S. *The Maya of Belize: Historical Chapters Since Columbus.* Cubola Productions, 1988.

MAYA RUINS

Awe, Jaime. *Maya Cities and Sacred Caves.* Cubola Productions, 2005.

Bogard, Dr. Eva A. *Altun Ha Visitors' Guide: The Most Comprehensive Full-Color Guide to the Altun Ha Mayan Temples Located in Belize.* CreateSpace, 2011.

Coe, William R. *Tikal, A Handbook of the Ancient Maya Ruins.* University Museum at the University of Pennsylvania, 1967.

Foster, Byron. *Warlords and Maize Men, A Guide to the Maya Sites of Belize.* Cubola Productions, 1992.

Kelly, Joyce. *An Archaeological Guide to Northern Central America: Belize, Guatemala, Honduras, and El Salvador.* University of Oklahoma Press, 1996.

ENVIRONMENT AND NATURE

Barcott, Bruce. *The Last Flight of the Scarlet Macaw.* Random House, 2008.

Bridgewater, Samuel. *A Natural History of Belize: Insights from the Chiquibul Forest and Las Cuevas Research Station.* University of Texas Press, 2012.

Freed, Paul. *Of Golden Toads and Serpents' Roads* TAMU Press, 2003.

Lumb, Judy, and Waight, Lydia. *Belize Audubon Society: 40 Years of Conservation*. Produccicones de la Hamaca, 2011.

Rabinowitz, Alan. *Jaguar: One Man's Struggle to Establish the World's First Jaguar Preserve*. Island Press, 2000.

NATURAL MEDICINE

Arvigo, Rosita. *Sastun: My Apprenticeship with a Maya Healer*. HarperOne, 1995.

Arvigo, Rosita, and Balick, Michael. *Rainforest Remedies: One Hundred Healing Herbs of Belize*. Lotus Press, 1993.

Arvigo, Rosita and Epstein, Nadine. *Rainforest Home Remedies: The Maya Way to Heal Your Body and Replenish Your Soul*. HarperOne, 2001.

Taylor, Leslie. *The Healing Power of Rainforest Herbs: A Guide to Understanding and Using Herbal Medicinals*. Square One Publishers, 2004.

MEMOIRS, AUTOBIOGRAPHIES, BIOGRAPHIES

Burnworth, Joe. *No Safe Harbor: The Tragedy of the Dive Ship Wave Dancer*. Clerisy Press, Emmis Books, 2005.

Conroy, Richard Timothy. *Our Man in Belize*. St. Martin's, 1997.

DeMarks, Dean Fortune. *The Tourist Who's Too Dangerous for Belize*. BookSurge Publishing, 2009.

Dickens, Barbara Gish. *Belize Journal: Peace Corps Experience of a New Widow*. Mill Xlibris, Corp., 2006.

Edelman, Hope. *The Possibility of Everything: A Memoir*. Ballantine Books, 2010.

Faber, Carol, and Perlow, Paula. *2 Jamericans Travel to San Pedro, Belize*. Trafford Publishing, 2006.

Fry, Joan. *How to Cook a Tapir: A Memoir of Belize*. University of Nebraska Press, 2009.

King, Emory. *I Spent It All In Belize*. Tropical Books, 1986.

King, Emory. *The Little World of Danny Vasquez*. Tropical Books, 1989.

LeBard, George. *A School for Others*. Xlibris Corporation, 2010.

Koerner, Nancy R. *Belize Survivor: Darker Side of Paradise* NK Marketing, 2007. A young woman's story of betrayal, courage, and survival after a move to the jungle in Belize.

Koop, Gerhard S. *Pioneer Years in Belize*. Self-published, 1991.

Miller, Carlos Ledson. *Belize*. Xlibris Corporation, 2000.

Molanphy, Tom. *Following Mateo*. Trafford Publishing, 2006.

Musa, Said W. *With Malice Toward None—Notes on a Political Life*. The Image Factory Art Foundation, 2009.

Peham, Helga. *Escaping the Rat Race, Freedom in Paradise*. World Audience, 2007.

Salisbury, Christina, and Salisbury, Kirby. *Treehouse Perspectives: Living High on Little*. Mill City Press, 2009.

Straughan, Robert P. *Adventure in Belize*. A.S. Barnes & Co., 1975.

Taylor Shaw, Whitney. *A Taste for Belize*. Tate Publishing, 2010.

PHOTOGRAPHIC BOOKS

Crandell, Rachel. *Hands of the Maya: Villagers at Work and Play*. Henry Holt & Company, 2002. Photos of daily Maya life.

RESOURCES

Janson, Thor. *Belize: Land of the Free by the Carib Sea*. Bowen and Bowen Ltd., 2000. A beautiful coffee-table book with photos of all aspects of Belize.

Janson, Thor. *In the Land of Green Lightning: The World of The Maya*. Pomegranate Communications, 1994. Beautiful photos across Central America of ancient Maya areas.

Jovaiša, Marius. *Heavenly Belize*. Unseen Pictures, Ltd., 2011. Beautiful aerial photos of Belize.

Turner, Maggie. *Made in Belize*. Factory Books, 2007. Photos and information about 33 Belizean contemporary artists and their work.

CHILDREN AND TEENS

Casanova, Mary. *Jess (American Girl Today)*. Amer Girl, 2005.

Coley, Liz. *Out of Xibalba*. CreateSpace, 2011.

Coulter, Laurie. *Secrets in Stone: All About Maya Hieroglyphics*. Little, Brown Young Readers, 2001.

Crouch, Jane. *Maya Moon Colouring Book*. Cubola Productions, 2010.

Curling, Debbie. *Pancho's Great Adventures: Belize* Xlibris, Corp., 2009.

Gibson, Ian. *Booby Trap*. Image Factory Art Foundation, 2007.

Hatkoff, Craig. *Scholastic Reader Level 2: Junior Buddy*. Scholastic Paperbacks, 2010.

Leslie, Robert, ed. *A History of Belize, Nation in the Making* Cubola Publications, 2002.

Matola, Sharon. *Story of Hoodwink the Owl*. Macmillan Caribbean, 1988.

Maynard, Caitlin et al. *Rain Forests & Reefs: A Kid's-Eye View of the Tropics (Cincinnati Zoo Books)*. Franklin Watts, 1997.

Mora, Pat. *The Night the Moon Fell: A Maya Myth*. Groundwood Books, 2000.

Pearce, Jayne E. *Creature Quests: Belize and The Jaguar Sun King*. CreateSpace, 2011.

Ruiz, Carmita, and Rempel, Byron. *The Geography of Belize, The Land and Its People*. Cubola Publications, 2011.

Shields, Charles J. *Belize (Central America Today)*. Mason Crest Publishers, 2007.

Stray, P.J. *The Danger on Lighthouse Reef*. Silver Burdett Press, 1997.

Torres, Vania, and Van Pelt, Katy. *I Decide, One Day, To Make Some Tamalitos: A Cultural Recipe Story For Children—Belize!* Blanket Press, 2011.

FICTION

Andrews, Sylvia. *Black Jaguar, Green Jade*. Kindle Edition, SylvanArts Press, 2011. An adventure about a young woman realizing her dream of joining an archaeological dig in Belize.

Auxillou, Ray. *Blue Hole*. Self-published. Stories about adventure, drug runners, and mercenaries.

Edgell, Zee. *Beka Lamb*. Heinemann, 1986. A story about coming of age for old and young alike.

Edgell, Zee. *The Festival of San Joaquin*. Macmillan Caribbean, 2008. A tale set in the Mestizo Spanish community in rural Belize portraying peasant life.

Edgell, Zee. *Time and the River*. Heinemann, 2007. Historical novel about freedom, slavery, hope, and betrayal.

Kalla, Dick. *Belize Blues (Volume 1)*. CreateSpace, 2011. A thriller about an ex-State Security Officer who foils a plot by Jihadists to attack the U.S. from Belize.

Neilson, Ray. *Eyes of the Jaguar*. lulu.com, 2011. A teenager grows up in the jungles of Belize and stumbles upon an ancient secret which leads to an adventure.

Phillips, Michael. *Snapshots of Belize, An Anthology of Belizean Short Fiction.* Cubola Productions, 2004.

Price, David W. *The First Annual Tikal to Caye Caulker Mud Bog and Hurricane Run.* CreateSpace, 2011. Two men on a road trip to see Tikal when everything goes wrong and they end up caught up in a civil war.

Ruiz Puga, David Nicolas. *Old Benque.* Cubola Productions, 2007. Short stories in Spanish.

Vasquez, Ian. *In the Heat.* St. Martin's Minotaur, 2008. Mystery set in Belize City and Cayo by a prize-winning Belizean writer.

Vasquez, Ian. *Mr. Hooligan.* Minotaur Books, 2010. A crime thriller set in Belize where a freak car accident draws the main character into the drug-running world.

Watler, John Alexander. *The Bomba Codex.* CreateSpace, 2011. A book about stolen Maya antiquities in the jungles of Belize.

Wilentz, Gay, ed. *Memories, Dreams and Nightmares, Vol. 1, a Short Story Anthology by Belizean Women Writers.* Cubola Productions, 2002.

Wilentz Gay, ed. *Memories, Dreams and Nightmares, Vol. 2, a Short Story Anthology by Belizean Women Writers.* Cubola Productions, 2005.

Wouk, Herman. *Don't Stop the Carnival.* HarperCollins, 1994. A New Yorker sets off to the Caribbean to start running a small hotel. The tale highlights the attitudes and difficulties of living and working in the tropics, and the fact that things don't work in the same way or at the same pace as in North America.

Young, Colville. *Pataki Full.* Cubola Productions, 2009. Collection of short stories by a noted Belizean writer and scholar.

GENERAL BELIZE

Feucht, Dennis L. *Your Own Home Electric System.* Self-published, 2007.

Sutherland, Anne. *The Making of Belize: Globalization in the Margins.* Greenwood Press, 1998.

Wright, Ronald. *Time Among the Maya: Travels in Belize, Guatemala and Mexico.* Grove Press, 2000.

Household Costs

GROCERIES

Prices vary enormously between different shops, brands, and locations. Rural areas are cheaper. Many things are 2–3 times more expensive on the Cayes because of the logistics of getting them there, and partly because there is a large expat population, some of whom will pay the price without thinking about it. Variety and availability of products also vary extensively and it's a bit of a hit or miss affair. If you have a favorite product, stock up on it. Many things are imported and therefore quite expensive, but there is quite a lot of local produce, which is worth trying and just as good if not better than the imported variety. Imported pet food is expensive and a personal choice. Many feed their dogs leftovers with rice and eggs, chicken, and stock bones. Prices and availability of fruit and vegetables vary between seasons. If you buy a lot of imported alcohol, your costs will increase substantially. The best thing is to find a middle road between local products and imported ones, and throw in the odd treat of your favorite item from time to time. There are quite a few bakeries and butchers scattered around. This list was compiled in Cayo, thus the frozen fish. All prices are in Belize dollars.

BASIC PANTRY AND SNACKS

- Apple Cider Vinegar – BZBZ$2.85/16 fl. oz.
- Bread – BZ$2.50 (bakeries do a variety of fresh types, BZ$2.50-4.50)
- Campbell's soup – BZ$3.50
- Coffee Mate – BZ$6.75/11 oz.
- Doritos – BZ$8.50
- Eggs – BZ$3.50/dozen
- Golden Crisp garnachas shells – BZ$4.50
- Kellogg's cornflakes – BZ$2.75/200 g.
- La Castaña salsa dip – BZ$1/220 g.
- McVities digestives – BZ$3.95/250 g.
- Olive oil – BZ$6.95/500 ml.
- Pringles – BZ$3.95
- Purity flour – BZ$7.95/5 lb.
- Red beans – BZ$2/1 lb.
- Rice – BZ$2/2 lb.
- Salt – BZ$0.50/500 g.
- Spaghetti – BZ$1/200 g.
- Sugar – BZ$1/2 lb.
- Vegetable cooking oil – BZ$2.50/16 oz.
- Vinegar – BZ$1.95/liter
- Whole wheat flour Hi-Rise – BZ$7.25/5 lb.

DAIRY

- Anchor butter – BZ$5.95
- Blue cheese – BZ$15.95
- Crystal Farms cheese (imported from the U.S.) – BZ$8.65
- Feta cheese – BZ$10/lb.
- Fresh cream – BZ$6
- Mozzarella cheese – BZ$13.44
- Pack of Kraft single cheese slices – BZ$5.95
- Philadelphia cream cheese – BZ$6.95
- Western Dairies Cheddar – BZ$11.65/lb.
- Yogurt – BZ$4/16 oz.

MEAT AND FISH

- Back bacon – BZ$10.75/12 oz.
- Chicken breast, boneless – BZ$5.75/lb.
- Chicken leg and thigh – BZ$5.25/lb.
- Cooked sliced ham – BZ$14.50/lb.
- Cooked sliced roast beef – BZ$12.25/lb.
- Flank steak – BZ$6.25/lb.
- Ground beef – BZ$5/lb.

- Pork chops - BZ$6.75/lb.
- Ribs (traditional) - BZ$10/lb.
- Roast leg of lamb - BZ$15/lb.
- Sardines - BZ$125/tin
- Shrimp (frozen) - BZ$16.80/lb.
- Soup bones (good for dogs) - BZ$1.50/lb.
- Tenderloin beef (aged) - BZ$18/lb.
- Tenderloin pork - BZ$10/lb.
- Tilapia fish fillet (frozen) - BZ$13.30/lb.
- Tuna - BZ$2/can
- Whole chicken (frozen) - BZ$2.50/lb.

FRUIT AND VEGETABLES

- Apple - BZ$1
- Avocado - BZ$1
- Bananas - BZ$1/ten
- Broccoli - BZ$3/lb.
- Cauliflower - BZ$3/lb.
- Cucumber - BZ$1
- Garlic - BZ$2/three
- Grapefruit - BZ$1
- Grapes - BZ$6/lb.
- Green beans - BZ$1/lb.
- Limes - BZ$2/six
- Onions - BZ$1.50/lb
- Orange - BZ$1
- Mango - BZ$1
- Papaya - BZ$2
- Pineapple - BZ$3
- Pitaya - BZ$3/lb.
- Salad - BZ$3
- Spinach, local - BZ$3
- Tomatoes - BZ$3.50/lb.
- Watermelon - BZ$2.50/lb.

BEVERAGES

- Carnation evaporated milk - BZ$2.10/can

- Dilmah loose tea - BZ$3.95/125 g.
- Dilmah tea bags - BZ$8.95/100 bags
- Imported Caribbean Pride fruit juice - BZ$2.95/liter
- Large soda - BZ$3.50/liter
- Local concentrated fruit squash, Citrus Valley - BZ$6.25/liter
- Nescafé - BZ$9.50/200 g.
- Orange juice, 1 gallon - BZ$5.95
- Soda - BZ$1.25 per bottle (BZ$0.25 per return)
- Water - BZ$1.50/liter
- Western Dairies milk (whole or skim), 0.5 gallon - BZ$8

ALCOHOL

- Absolut Vodka - BZ$75
- Barefoot Chardonnay California - BZ$30
- Beefeater Gin - BZ$90
- Belikin beer - BZ$3
- Black Swan Merlot Australia - BZ$37
- Caribbean Rum - BZ$10.95/750 ml.
- Carlo Rossi Rosé California - BZ$30
- Concha y Toro Sunrise Chardonnay Chile - BZ$30
- Concha y Toro Sunrise Cabernet Sauvignon Chile - BZ$30
- Ernest & Julio Gallo Chardonnay California 2007 - BZ$30
- Heineken - BZ$4
- Grants Whiskey - BZ$85/liter
- Guinness - BZ$4
- Johnnie Walker Black Label whiskey - BZ$123
- Jose Cuervo tequila - BZ$95
- Lerskaa Vodka - BZ$19.95
- One Barrel Rum - BZ$29
- Pouilly Fuissé - BZ$60
- Premium beer - BZ$4

CONDIMENTS

- Country Barn peanut butter – BZ$4.95/ 8 oz.
- Country Barn mustard – BZ$1.95/9 oz.
- Del Monté ketchup – BZ$3.35/680 g.
- Del Monté strawberry jam – BZ$2.50/ 270 g.
- Heinz salad dressing – BZ$5.15/285 g.
- Honey – BZ$6.95/350 ml.
- Kraft mayonnaise – BZ$3.95/350 g.
- Marie Sharp's habanero sauce – BZ$4.50/10 oz.
- Marie Sharp's mixed fruit jam – BZ$4.95

FOR INFANTS AND TODDLERS

- Baby jelly (like Vaseline) – BZ$5.75/ 368 g.
- Huggies diapers 5.5kg–9.5, BZ$19.25/18 diapers (local brands are about BZ$10 cheaper but may not be as good)
- Johnson & Johnson baby powder – BZ$6.75/200 g.
- Johnson & Johnson baby oil – BZ$9.50/300 ml.
- Johnson & Johnson baby shampoo – BZ$9.95/400 ml.
- Johnson & Johnson baby soap – BZ$4.95
- Klim formula 1 yr+ – BZ$7.60/360 g.
- Milk bottle – BZ$4
- Nestlé lactogen formula – BZ$12.25/400 g.
- Tylenol for 2–12 year olds – BZ$14.95/ 100 ml.

PETS

- Friskies canned cat food – BZ$1.50
- Pedigree canned dog food – BZ$2.50
- Whiskas cat biscuits – BZ$30/3 kg.

SUNDRIES

- Ariel laundry detergent powder – BZ$5.10/1 kg.
- Axion laundry detergent liquid – BZ$2.40/400 ml.
- Baygon bug spray – BZ$8.95/600 ml.
- Candles – BZ$7.95/16 candles
- Cigarettes "Independence" – BZ$5/ 20 pack
- Diamond aluminium foil – BZ$3.95/ 75 sq. ft
- Duracell D2 batteries – BZ$8.50/two
- Duracell AA batteries – BZ$9.95/four
- Paper towels – BZ$2.20/60 sheets
- Plastic hangers – BZ$2.95/eight hangers

TOILETRIES

- Aspirin – BZ$8.50/100 pills
- Avon roll-on deodorant – BZ$1.25
- Carefree normal feminine pads – BZ$2.15/15 pads
- Colgate toothpaste – BZ$3.25/130 g.
- Dettol – BZ$6.95/250 ml.
- Dove body wash – BZ$10.50/250 ml.
- Dove deodorant – BZ$5.95
- Dove soap – BZ$2.95
- Gillette Mach 3 razor – BZ$7
- Lux soap – BZ$1.25
- Pantene shampoo – BZ$16.95/400 ml.
- Pureflex shaving cream – BZ$4.50/30 g.
- Tampax regular – BZ$8.45/10 tampons
- Toilet paper "Elite" – BZ$2.45/four rolls
- Tresemmé shampoo – BZ$10.95/946 ml.
- Tylenol extra – BZ$0.50/2 pills
- VO5 shampoo – BZ$3.25/443 ml.

PRESCRIPTION MEDICATION

Prescription medication costs vary depending on the brand and the pharmacy. The following is a rough guideline of costs from Codds Pharmacy in San Ignacio. To fill a prescription, sometimes pharmacies require the previous prescription or a letter from a doctor, and sometimes they issue the medication if you explain why you need it. Some pharmacies will order in medication if they don't have it. Do check the brand, place and date of manufacture, and expiration date.

Medication	Quantity	Cost in BZ$
Alprazolam	0.25 and 0.5 mg	2.10 per tablet
Ambian	packet of 28	140
Amiodarone	200mg, pPacket of 28	34.90
Amlodipine	10 mg	45 per box
Amlodipine	10 mg	0.35 per tablet
Amoxicillin	500 mg	0.75 per tablet
Ampicillin	500 mg	0.75 per tablet
Augmentin bid	box of 14	88
Azathioprine	50 mg	1.3 per tablet
Benazepril	40 mg	1.25 per tablet
Carbamazepine	200 mg	0.85 per tablet
Cefixime	400 mg	56 per box
Cinaricine	75mg, packet of 30	77.95
Ciprofloxacin		8.40 per tablet
Cliane	packet of 21	20
Climene	packet of 21	22
Codeine		1.00 per tablet
Co-diovan	packet of 14	89.95
Diazepan	5 mg	1 per tablet
Digoxin	125 mcg	0.75 per tablet
Doxycycline	100 mg	1 per tablet
Femiane contraceptive	packet of 21	18.95
Fluconazole	200 and 150 mg	10 per tablet
Fluoxetine	20 mg	1.25 per tablet
Glyburide	5 mg, box of 28	4.50
Hydralazine	25 mg	0.50 per tablet
Levitra	20 mg	35.00 per tablet
Lexapro	28 tabs	278
Lipitor	20 mg, packet of 20	145
Lisinopril		0.51 per tablet
Lorazepam	2 mg	2.10 per tablet
Losartan	50 mg, packet of 30	28.95

RESOURCES

Lasartan	100 mg, packet of 30	39.95
Medroxyprogesterone		1 per tablet
Metformin	500mg, box of 100	25
Methotrexate		1 per tablet
Metoprolol	100 mg	0.37 per tablet
Metronidazole		0.50 per tablet
Microgynon 21	packet of 21	8.95
Nexium	box of 14	145
Nifedipine	10 mg	0.35 per tablet
Nimodipine	30 mg, box of 30	68.80
Omeprazole	20 mg	1 per tablet
Pravastatin	40 mg	1.25 per tablet
Progyluton	packet of 21	22
Propranolol	40 mg	0.25 per tablet
Rivotril/Clonazepam	2 mg, 30 pills	67.50
Sertraline	50 mg	3.35 per tablet
Sinemett/Carvidopa/Levadopa	packet of 30	94.15
Spirolactone	25 mg	0.55 per tablet
Tetracycline	500 mg	0.75 per tablet
Tramacet		3.90 per tablet
Verapamil	80 mg	0.45 per tablet
Viagra	100 mg	45.00 per tablet
Warfarin	5 mg	0.75 per tablet
Yasmine contraceptive	packet of 21	25.50
Zolpidem	packet of 30	36

Index

www.moon.com

DESTINATIONS | ACTIVITIES | BLOGS | MAPS | BOOKS

MOON.COM is ready to help plan your next trip! Filled with fresh trip ideas and strategies, author interviews, informative travel blogs, a detailed map library, and descriptions of all the Moon guidebooks, Moon.com is all you need to get out and explore the world—or even places in your own backyard. While at Moon.com, sign up for our monthly e-newsletter for updates on new releases, travel tips, and expert advice from our on-the-go Moon authors. As always, when you travel with Moon, expect an experience that is uncommon and truly unique.

KEEP UP WITH MOON ON FACEBOOK AND TWITTER
JOIN THE MOON PHOTO GROUP ON FLICKR

MAP SYMBOLS

▦▦▦ Expressway	○ City/Town	✈ Airport	▱ Archaeological Site
▬▬ Primary Road	◉ State Capital	✗ Airfield	⚲ Church
▬ Secondary Road	⊛ National Capital	▲ Mountain	⛽ Gas Station
▪▪▪▪ Unpaved Road		✦ Unique Natural Feature	▨ Mangrove
------ Trail	★ Point of Interest		▨ Reef
············· Ferry	▪ Other Location	⩘ Waterfall	▨ Swamp
▪▬▪▬ Railroad		♠♠ Park	

CONVERSION TABLES

$°C = (°F - 32) / 1.8$
$°F = (°C \times 1.8) + 32$
1 inch = 2.54 centimeters (cm)
1 foot = 0.304 meters (m)
1 yard = 0.914 meters
1 mile = 1.6093 kilometers (km)
1 km = 0.6214 miles
1 fathom = 1.8288 m
1 chain = 20.1168 m
1 furlong = 201.168 m
1 acre = 0.4047 hectares
1 sq km = 100 hectares
1 sq mile = 2.59 square km
1 ounce = 28.35 grams
1 pound = 0.4536 kilograms
1 short ton = 0.90718 metric ton
1 short ton = 2,000 pounds
1 long ton = 1.016 metric tons
1 long ton = 2,240 pounds
1 metric ton = 1,000 kilograms
1 quart = 0.94635 liters
1 US gallon = 3.7854 liters
1 Imperial gallon = 4.5459 liters
1 nautical mile = 1.852 km

°FAHRENHEIT   °CELSIUS

230 — — 110
220
210 — — 100 WATER BOILS
200
190 — — 90
180
170 — — 80
160
150 — — 70
140
130 — — 60
120 — — 50
110
100 — — 40
90
80 — — 30
70
60 — — 20
50
40 — — 10
30
20 — — 0 WATER FREEZES
10
0 — — -10
-10
-20 — — -20
-30 — — -30
-40 — — -40

MOON LIVING ABROAD
IN BELIZE

Avalon Travel
a member of the Perseus Books Group
1700 Fourth Street
Berkeley, CA 94710, USA
www.moon.com

Editor and Series Manager: Elizabeth Hansen
Copy Editor: Naomi Adler Dancis
Proofreader: Deana Shields
Graphics and Production Coordinator:
   Lucie Ericksen
Cover Designer: Lucie Ericksen
Map Editor: Kat Bennett
Cartographers: Chris Henrick, Kaitlin Jaffe,
   Kat Bennett
Indexer: Rachel Kuhn

ISBN: 978-1-61238-180-0
ISSN: 1555-9114

Printing History
1st Edition – 2005
2nd Edition – August 2012
5 4 3 2 1

Front cover photo: Fly fishing for bonefish
on a shallow flat in Belize. © 24BY36/Alamy

Title page photo: Sittee River pier © Victoria
Day-Wilson

Interior color photos: pages 4-8 © Victoria
Day-Wilson; pages 6 small and 7 bottom-left:
© Lorenzo Forbes
Back cover photo: Colorful houses on the beach
in Placencia © Lorenzo Forbes

Printed in Canada by Friesens

KEEPING CURRENT

Although we strive to produce the most up-to-date guidebook that we possibly can, change
is unavoidable. Between the time this book goes to print and the time you read it, the
cost of goods and services may have increased, and a handful of the businesses noted
in these pages will undoubtedly move, alter their prices, or close their doors forever.
Exchange rates fluctuate – sometimes dramatically – on a daily basis. Federal and local
legal requirements and restrictions are also subject to change, so be sure to check with
the appropriate authorities before making the move. If you see anything in this book that
needs updating, clarification, or correction, please drop us a line. Send your comments via
email to feedback@moon.com, or use the address above.